the Artillerist
a Civil War novel

Rod Canham

Copyright © 2019 by Rod Canham

All rights reserved. No part of this book may be reproduced in any form or by any electronic or mechanical means, including information storage and retrieval systems, without permission in writing from the author, except by a reviewer, who may quote brief passages in a review.

the Artillerist / Rod Canham. — 1st ed.

ISBN: 978-1-7338423-2-7

United States—History—Civil War—Union—Artillery—Christian—1861-1865—Fiction

This is a work of fiction. Any resemblance to actual persons, living or dead, is purely coincidental.

Cover Design—Todd Shear at www.toddshear.com

Rear Cover photo—courtesy of Bruce Landis of photosbybruceandassociates.com

artillerist - ar·til·ler·ist - *a person who is skilled in the use of artillery;*
a person who serves in the artillery;
a person who serves in support of the artillery

— *for Big Grandpa*

table of contents

dedication	3	change of command	98
table of contents	4	pontoons	103
decision	7	prospect hill	107
jim & will	15	anderson & lew	112
training days	23	mud	119
camp berry	31	another change	125
private will	39	new IDs	129
fever	43	the furnace	135
fifteen thousand	48	battle	139
shipping out	55	wounded	146
camp winfield scott	61	left behind	150
on to richmond	69	field hospital	157
gaines's mill	74	carver hospital	167
changing bases	78	surgery	172
colonel hunt	85	captain turnbull	177
malvern hill	89	mr. president	183
harrison's landing	93	elizabeth & hannah	188

table of contents

furlough	195
the harmers	203
brother	208
goin' to meetin'	213
news from the front	216
the pastor	221
will & clarinda	225
expiring furlough	228
return to carver	233
return to duty	239
ramsey's story	241
in camp	245
unexpected	253
home again	255
surrender	261
grace	266
decision	270
robert & susan	275
first sergeant grover	277
the request	281
sergeant kempf	284
sentry duty	289
mrs. kempf	293
infantry command	299
it's not personal	302
acceptance	309
chevrons	312
the best news	316
the worst news	318
the package	322
celebration	329
celebration day two	333
glossary of terms	337
author's notes	347

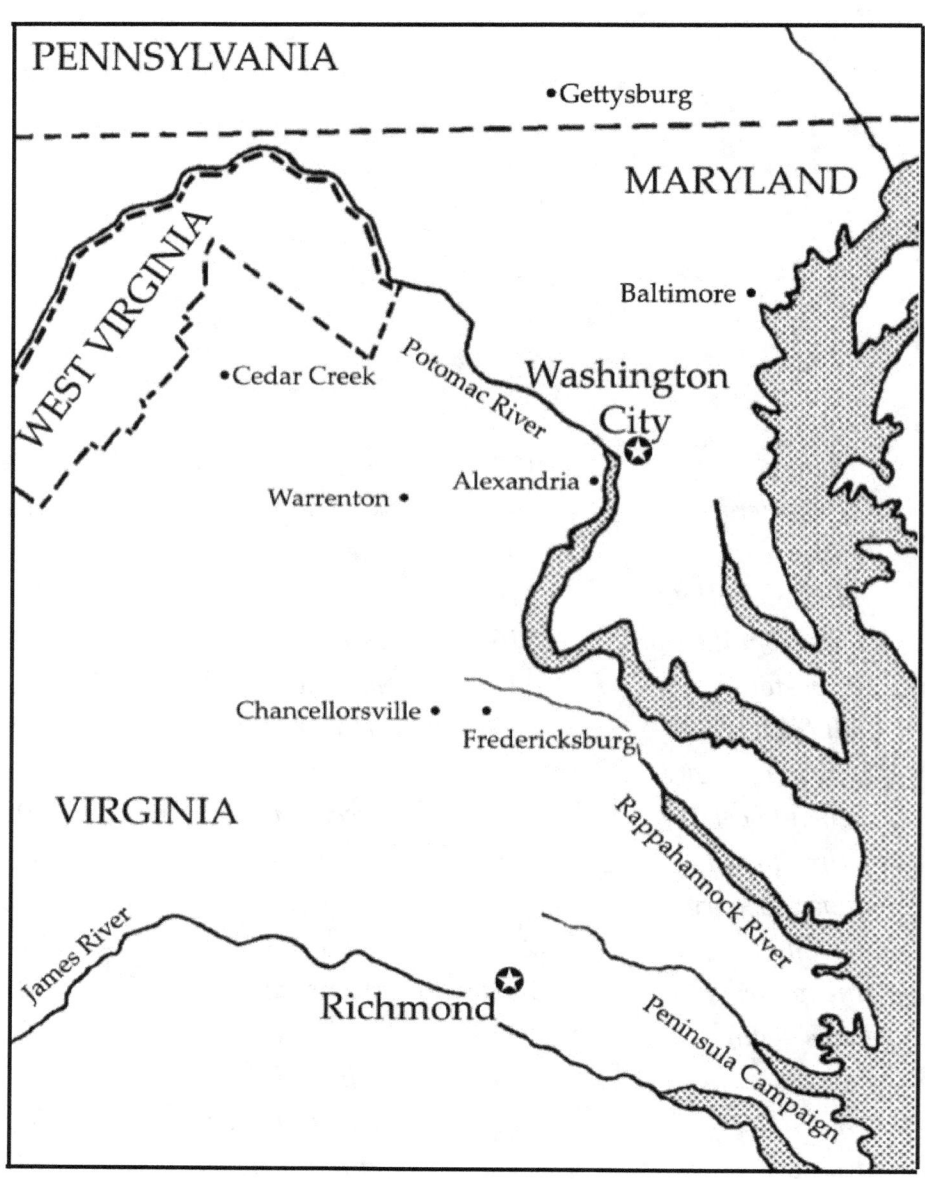

Field of operations, Batteries F & K, Third U.S. Artillery, Army of the Potomac

decision

December 1862
Prospect Hill, Fredericksburg, Virginia

Robert stretches out his gloveless hands to draw warmth from the barrel of his cannon. The men in his gun crew are huddled with him, trying to withstand the harsh chill riding on the easterly breeze. The ground in front of them tenaciously holds onto the snow from an earlier storm——the field soaked with the blood of the fallen. Blues mixed with butternut grays——a panoramic amalgam of death that Robert and his crew played no small part in. It's his first battle as an artillerist, and his only thought, *How did I end up here?*

Tuesday, 19 February 1861
Medina, New York

The winds are light, but the temperature hovers close to zero, otherwise the conditions are ideal for sleighing. Medina is less than six miles away, and it's important the three men get an early start to make it back before losing precious daylight. Flanked by Will and Robert, their father James directs the sleigh away from the barn. They keep their conversation to a minimum in the harsh chill. Will notices the bag Robert tossed in the back, but doesn't make the connection that only two of them are returning.

As the men get down from the wagon, Will is tasked with caring for the horse and sleigh, but he's puzzled. "Why did we stop here? The mercantile is another quarter mile down the road."

James is rustling through his coat pocket for his pipe, and cautiously answers, "Your brother's joining the army."

"The army!" Will bristles. "Why haven't I heard about this?"

Robert stands firm. "Because I needed to tell the folks first."

Will is more impulsive than his younger brother, and his temper gets the best of him. He grabs the front of Robert's jacket. "I can't believe you didn't tell me about this."

Robert pushes him away, "Then come in and join with me."

"You know I can't do that. Dad needs help on the farm, especially now." Robert knows the farm has nothing to do with his objection. Will has a girl, Clara, and it's serious.

Stiff from the ride, James puts his hands on the back of his hips, and stretches out his spine. "I've never needed to separate you two, and don't intend to start now." Neither of his sons move. When he puts his arm between them, Robert takes a step back. "Robert's got his mind made up." He taps Will on the chest with his pipe as he says, "And *you* need to support your brother."

Will continues to glare at Robert, and James starts to lose his patience. "Look, it's cold out here, and the horse still needs to be cared for." James gets a grip on the sleeve of Robert's coat, and leads him to the front door. "We have business to see to inside."

* * *

Small and spartan, the office has two desks on a bare-wood floor that faces the entry with chairs lining each side of the office. The thirty-three-star flag of the United States hangs limp from its staff, secured upright by a bronze stand in the corner behind the empty desk. In the opposite corner, a wood-burning stove keeps the room comfortable. Seated at the front, a uniformed man in his late twenties stands to greet them. He holds himself erect, and represents the army well in appearance and bearing.

He looks at Robert, but directs his question to James. "My name is Corporal Ritter. How may I be of service?"

James leads Robert by the shoulder to the forefront to answer him directly. "I'm here to see about signing up, but I have some questions."

Will walks in, still in a snit, and sits in one of the side chairs. The corporal acknowledges him. "I'll be with you shortly."

"There's no need," Will responds. He points to his brother, "I'm with him."

The corporal keeps his eyes on Will at that point. "Are you both here to enlist?"

Will again points to his brother, and answers peevishly, "No. I'm just here for moral support." James sits down next to Will, and gives him the familiar look when they've done something he disapproves of.

James taps his pipe on the heel of his boot, scrapes out remnants from its bowl, and reloads a fresh wad of tobacco. "Is it okay to light up?" he asks the corporal. The corporal nods, so he breaks out a match and stokes up his pipe.

Corporal Ritter finishes his interchange with Will. "If you change your mind, I can get you two duty together, if that's what you'd like." Will just shakes his head. He turns his attention to Robert, then asks, "What are your questions?"

He reaches into his coat pocket and pulls out a well-worn slip of paper. "First off, can you sign me up for the cavalry?"

He shakes his head as he speaks. "Right now the government has need of animals as well as men. Early applicants, who provide their own horses, are given first priority for those billets. Is that something you can do?"

Robert glances toward his father, then turns back. "No, sir."

"Well, what are some of the *other* questions on your list?"

"I like horses, and I'm good at caring for them. If I can't get into——"

"Hold on. I didn't say you couldn't get into the cavalry, but that's a decision I don't have the power to make." He points to the empty chair behind the desk in back of him. "Captain Burkholder can better help you out with that. He'll be here soon if you can wait."

After a minute, Robert asks, "What's life like in the army?"

"It's kinda exciting, with the Secesh movement, a new President, and the jawin' in Congress the papers are reporting." He measures his words. "Things are not boring, that's for sure."

"Secesh movement? What's that?" asks James.

"It's what we call the states seceding from the Union."

The news of secession has troubled Robert since it gained traction in northern newsprint. He's spent many a night with his father and brother, discussing the possible repercussions of slavery, and Lincoln's election.

Robert looks back at the corporal. "What can I expect once I go in?"

"After you sign up, you'll be put on a train to Rochester. You'll swear an oath of allegiance with other recruits. Where you go from there depends on what branch you get into, most likely Washington City. It will include a lot of drills, learning the rules, and the discipline of army life in camp."

A rush of cold air signals Captain Burkholder's return. He looks to be in his early fifties, with hardened facial features, gray hair, and a thick mustache to match. The wear on his uniform shows he isn't new to the army, maybe came up through the ranks. He has a slight limp, which Robert pretends not to notice. He looks him directly in the eyes, and shakes his hand. "I met you a few weeks ago ... Robert is it?"

"Good memory, sir." He's impressed. "This is my father, James, and next to him my brother, Will." The two men stand to greet the captain.

"You've got a fine son there, sir." He turns his attention to Will. "Here to sign up with your brother?"

"Not today," he sighs.

The captain senses some hostility, so he refocuses on Robert. "Well then, what can I help *you* with?"

"I thought about what you said about signing up." He's distracted by the loud clock on the wall as it chimes in the top of the hour. "I'd like a good posting."

"That's not an unusual request. What do you have in mind?"

Robert looks back down at the paper. "The cavalry ... hopefully," then points to Ritter, "but the corporal——"

The captain holds up his hand to interrupt, then leads him over to his desk, and directs him to a chair. James sits back down next to William and leans to the side to listen.

"Why the cavalry?"

"I'd like to work with horses."

"I take it you have an affinity for them?"

"Yes, sir."

Robert's two months past his twenty-third birthday, fresh-faced, and by any standard, handsome——tall, lean, and farm-strong, with dark brown hair, a pencil-thin mustache, and a tuft of hair from the cleft of his chin to the edge of his lower lip.

The captain reaches into his desk and pulls out a small, but thick book to cite a passage. It's in the first few pages and easy to find. "'... *they should be intelligent, active, muscular, well-developed, and not less than five feet seven inches high: a large portion should be mechanics.*' It sounds like you'd fit this bill. Much experience with mechanics?"

"What kind?"

"Wagons, wheels, rigging ... guns."

"I know my way around."

"That's good," the captain says as he closes the book and lays it on the desk. "These are requirements for artillery candidates. The mobile light artillery sounds like a good fit for you. You wouldn't be stuck in a fort all the time, and you'd work with horses daily. It's a critical position in support of the gunners."

A bit puzzled, Robert asks, "I'd be a gunner?"

"Not at first, but over time everyone in a battery has to learn everyone else's duties. Then, if you're needed, then yes, you'd be considered a gunner ... an artillerist."

Robert likes the sound of that, but it's a lot to digest. "Can I have some time to think about it?"

"Take whatever time you need, Robert. You have a big decision to make."

He rehashes the same internal dialogue he's dealt with the last several months; the life of a farmer versus a world he's read and dreamt about.

He still can't decide, and looks to his father to get a read on his expression for some encouragement. James remains inscrutable. He's sixty-three, and intuits the restlessness in his youngest child. Though he wants, and needs his help to keep the farm going, he raised his children to become independent. His knows that time with his sons is marked, but nobody can make Robert's decision for him. He must make his own choice and live with its aftermath.

Robert turns back to the captain. "You mentioned 'if you're needed'. What exactly does that mean?"

Recruiters make it a point to not talk about the potential consequences of battle. The unwritten rule is never discuss death, injuries, and the horrors of war. As uncomfortable as he is with Robert's question, he knows there's no easy way around it. He senses Robert wants an honest answer and feels obligated to give it to him. "If a man goes down, for whatever reason, anyone in the battery has to be ready to assume his position, without hesitation."

Robert understands, as does his father. Will doesn't like the direction any of this is headed, but he's resigned to watch and listen.

Burkholder knows he might as well lay it on the table. "Robert, this a position in the Regular Army, not state, not militia. These are serious-minded men doing perilous work, with the best equipment, experienced leadership, and a battle-tested knowledge base to draw from." The captain gives it a minute to sink in then adds, "And Robert, it requires a five-year commitment from you."

"Five years!" Will exclaims, as he jumps up from his seat.

His father looks at William with shock and disgust.

"Get your things on and go wait for me in the sleigh! Right now!"

"But father, five years!"

James stands, takes a step toward Will, and points to the door. "Out, now!"

Will grabs his coat and storms out of the office muttering to himself, "Five years."

James looks over to the captain, red-faced. "My apologies, sir. My son has always been impulsive."

"I understand. It's a big commitment that we ask for. How say you, Robert?"

James sits back down. Robert thinks for a long time, *five years seems like an eternity, but what do I have here——a hard-scrabble existence trying to eke out a living on a farm? It's a life I've never loved, much less liked. I feel trapped by my obligations to the farm, the boredom of relative idleness, and the restrictions the weather imposes on travel. There are no other prospects, no girl I'm interested in, and now the government can take care of me. I can do five years.*

It won't affect his decision, but Robert feels the need to ask. "What's the pay, sir?"

"Thirteen dollars a month plus a modest allowance for uniforms."

Robert takes a few more minutes to digest the information. "Yes, sir." He looks at his father, then back to the captain. "Yes, sir, I'll do it."

Captain Burkholder smiles, shakes Robert's hand, and looks to Ritter, "Please draw up the paperwork, Corporal." He turns back to Robert, and says, "You will take an oath of allegiance to the Union, then we'll board you on a train for Rochester. Once there, you'll receive further instructions." He gestures toward the door. "I think you better go patch things up with your brother before he leaves."

Robert nods and buttons his coat back up. He's excited at the prospect of unknown adventures and knowing the uncertainty of the decision is over. He goes out to the sleigh while his father stays inside.

"What's next for him, Captain?"

He looks at his pocket watch and says, "There's a train that leaves town at 11:00 a.m. Your boy will be well-looked after, sir."

James shakes his hand. "Thank you. Again, my apologies for the outburst." With that he takes his leave and joins the two outside.

Will climbs down from the sleigh when Robert approaches. "Well, are you a *soldier* now?"

Robert nods.

"A soldier for the next *five* years?" This is the first time Robert has ever taken the initiative without Will's knowledge or approval, and for the first time in their lives they will be apart. "Good luck, brother. You'll need it." Will stares at Robert with a look of betrayal.

"I'll miss you too, Will." He holds out his hand, and as Will shakes it, he pulls him close and gives him a bear hug.

"Take care of yourself, Robert." He climbs back aboard.

He gives his father a hug then grabs his bag. "Please tell mother I love her and will write soon."

"Be good, boy. Keep your nose clean and do what they tell you."

His father directs the sleigh back onto the road.

He holds his bag and watches until it disappears over the knoll.

Robert is now property of the United States government.

Bird's eye view of Sixth Street wharf, Washington City, 1863

Charles Magnus publisher
Library of Congress
Prints and Photographs Division
LC-DIG-pga-07412

jim & will

Wednesday, 27 February 1861
Washington City

The ticket agent verifies Robert's orders, and hands him a boarding pass for the ship tied up at the pier. Their destination, Fort Monroe, a massive structure at the southeastern tip of the Peninsula, between the York and James rivers. It's a hundred and ninety miles down the Potomac into the Chesapeake Bay and on to the fort, a sailing time of about twenty-seven hours.

A building runs the length of the wharf where scores of passengers are lined up to do the same. Robert hates being hemmed in by people, and has to jostle his way through the crowds to access the very end of the pier, where he feels more comfortable. When he finds a spot to set his bag down, he catches the attention of two men having an animated conversation about ten feet from him.

The older, and shorter of the two, keeps his back to Robert. The younger one smiles, gives him a slight wave, then asks, "Whereabouts you headed?"

His companion pokes him in the chest, and mutters, "Remember, this is the big city. You need to be a little more cautious about who you talk to."

The youth ignores his advice and says, "My name is Will." He points to his friend. "And this here is Jim." Jim turns to face Robert with a smile of resignation.

"Hi, Jim, my name is Robert Canham." He holds out his hand, and Will reaches over Jim to shake first.

"Nice to meet you, Robert."

Jim follows suit. "Same here. I'm James Ramsey, but people just call me Jim. Sorry about the intrusion. My young friend is a bit on the impulsive side."

"No need for apologies," says Robert. "I'm looking forward to meeting some new people."

Will swats Jim in the chest lightly. "See, there's nothing to worry about." Jim gives him an irritated look, but doesn't respond. Jim is well-dressed with a hat that covers his curly, but thinning blond hair.

Robert looks at Will. "To answer your question, I've just enlisted, and am on my way to Fort Monroe."

"No kidding, us too." Will puffs out his chest and proclaims, "But we've joined the artillery." Robert smiles at the coincidence, but doesn't offer a response.

Robert asks, "Just how old are you, Will?"

The youth tries to stand as straight as he can and says, "I am twenty-four years old." James coughs and tries to suppress a laugh. Will has an incredulous expression when he looks back to Jim and says, "What, you don't believe me?"

"You are *not* twenty-four. You may have fooled your recruiter, but we're not stupid. How old are you, really?"

"Well," Will hesitates, "I'm going to be, and real soon, too." Will is tall, lean, and has a full head of brown hair. His face has pockmarks after a bout of small pox in his youth, which he's unsuccessfully attempts to cover with a wispy beard.

Jim responds, "Just keep this in mind, Will. You said you wanted to be friends. Real friends don't lie to each other."

Will looks duly chastened, and quick to change the subject. "Where are you from Robert?"

"I'm from a very small community in western New York, between Rochester and Buffalo."

"No kidding. We're both New Yorkers too. I'm from Owego, and

Jim here is from, uh, where you from again, Jim?"

Jim thinks that he needs to have a talk with Will about his listening skills. "I'm from Weedsport, Will."

Robert bashfully smiles. "Sorry, fellas, but I don't know where either of those two places are."

"Weedsport is due east of where you live, a little before you'd get to Syracuse," says Jim.

"Yeah, and Owego is west of Elmira," Will interrupts.

"East of Elmira."

"Oh, yeah. It's east of Elmira, in the Southern Tier."

They are approached by a man in a long blue coat with a hat and a badge. "You men better get aboard. The crew is going through the process of casting off."

* * *

They find the pickings are slim for seating protected from the elements, and the three are left with spots along the passageway. They'll be exposed, but have no other option. Robert prefers being out in the fresh air and claims a spot along the railing to watch the scenery. Jim joins him to take in the view. As the ship passes a series of piers, he points out the dozens of stevedores loading and unloading the cargo vessels. "Must be hard work, day in and day out, heavy loads, exposed to the elements."

"What did you do in Weedsport for work?"

"My folks owned a mercantile, not a very successful one. The town is small, and if it wasn't for the canal, we couldn't have kept it going."

"So, you worked for them."

"I did mostly stock work until my mother took ill. Dad gave me more and more things to take over, and when she died, he just lost interest in it."

"Sorry for your loss."

"Thanks, but it was a long time ago."

"Where's your young friend?"

Jim laughs at the thought. "Probably gone to pester someone else. We met at the train depot at Elmira, and this is the first breather I've had since then."

"He seems to have a good heart though."

"He does at that. I think he had a hard upbringing though. According to him, his family owns one of the largest dairy farms in the Southern Tier, but it's hard to tell what's true with him. He says he's the youngest of eight, and his five older brothers run the place. Said he enlisted as soon as he was old enough to get out on his own."

"He must be what then, eighteen or nineteen?"

"I think so. He certainly is no twenty-four."

"You're a good man for befriending him."

"Maybe, maybe not. I never had any siblings, and he obviously needs some guidance."

"How did your father take to your joining up?"

"I guess you could say it was a parting of convenience. My dad remarried, and my step-mother wanted control of the store, which meant there wasn't room for both of us. When I told them I'd signed up, they were both polite and more than a little relieved. There certainly weren't any tears shed."

"Hey fellas. I did some exploring. I saw the boiler room, then tried to get on the bridge, but the mate threw me out. So, Robert, you never told us what you did before joining up."

"Well, my father is a tenant farmer. We've been working a property since we moved here from England ten years ago."

"You must not have any money then."

"Oh, Will," says Jim. "You need to think before you speak."

"That's okay. I'm not ashamed. We are doing what we can to get by, and we never missed a meal, or had to sleep in the cold."

"I'm sorry. I wasn't thinking."

"Come on Will, time we settle down for the night. Good night, Robert."

"Yeah, good night you two."

* * *

The fortress comes into view early the next afternoon. It's another two plus hours before the passengers are able to step onto steady ground. Robert is struck by the size of the fort's granite walls that reach thirty-five feet high, and a surrounding moat that varies from seventy-

jim & will

five to a hundred and fifty feet wide. The combination of the architectural similarities and the respective waterside locations remind him of New York's Old Fort Niagara, forty miles west of his home. That's where the similarities end.

A man in uniform with a lot of stripes, waits at dockside to greet the recruits as they disembark. He points to an area on the pier out of the flow of regular passenger traffic, and yells out, "I need you new men to line up over here. Let's put some life in those lazy legs of yours. The pleasure cruise is over, boys."

Sergeant Francis P. Sawyer looks up and down the line of the recruits as they disembark. They look the same as every new arrival—tired from their travels, wide-eyed, and full of anticipation. His responsibility is to turn these "fresh fish" into soldiers. He understands the need to strip the men of their individualism and make them think of their role as part of the army.

The recruits are confused about where to go. Eventually lined-up by height, the sergeant counts them off by fours. Segregated into squads, three-stripe sergeants take over to march them into camp. The NCOs find innovative ways to humiliate those in their charge.

They make their way to the North Gate walkway which spans the moat surrounding the fortress. The men are billeted by squad, told to store their packs, and report back to the parade grounds at the center of the compound.

As the men start to learn close-order drills, a too-young-to-be-in-the-army drummer boy marches alongside the company, and taps a cadence to help the recruits keep in step. They are eventually issued rifles which are incorporated into the drills. Everyone is required to stand sentry duty, whether in camp or in the field. They will need to be armed, even though at present their rifles carry no ammunition.

"Hey, Sergeant," says Will. "When are we going to start learning how to fire a cannon instead of these things."

Jim closes his eyes, and shakes his head. Robert grimaces. The sergeant smiles.

"What's your name, young man? Private what?"

"Uh, Private Hickman, Sergeant."

"Corporal Simmons, please give our young Hickman here our

"personal tour" of the fort."

"Private Hickman, fall out." He points to the stairs to the rampart. "We'll get a good view of the bay from up there. So if you'd please join me."

Hickman looks at him and smiles.

"Now MOVE IT!" He's made an example by being chased around the ramparts of the fortress, his rifle held at-arms, until allowed to rejoin the group over half an hour later. It's an effective means to teach the men to keep their mouths shut and listen to their instructors.

* * *

The next phase of training introduces them to live ammunition at the firing range. Save for a few city boys, a large percentage of the men are experienced hunters, but need to learn the capabilities of the weaponry and themselves. The instructors at the range are patient, and coach them through the process. Even the experienced need to be taught the "Load in Nine Times" technique. From there, it's evaluating and improving their marksmanship.

Robert is issued two cartridge packs with ten rounds in each. He shoots high with the first shot, then cuts target with the second. It isn't long before he attracts the attention of his squad sergeant.

"Looks like you're pretty handy with the rifle," says the NCO.

"I've had to hunt for a long time. We needed the food."

"And you're here for *artillery* duty?"

"Yes, Sergeant."

"I think you, and the army, will be better served in an outfit of sharpshooters."

"I'd rather work with horses."

"Then it seems like the cavalry might be more to your advantage? There are plenty of horses to care for, and you'd get to use your skills with a rifle."

Robert smiles at the irony. "That was my first choice, but not an option open to me at the time. Now that I'm here, I think I'd like to stick with the artillery."

"Well, if you ever change your mind …" With that the NCO leaves to oversee the others.

Robert finishes off his supply of cartridges and leaves his station for the next man in line.

That night the men are assigned duty on watch, to guard the fort and patrol specific areas of the perimeter, inside and outside its walls. NCOs, some in civilian garb, approach and challenge the sentries. A few in each squad fail the first time around. Verbal dress-downs ensure they rarely repeat the same mistake.

Despite spring-like conditions, come evening-time campfires are lit, closely maintained, and well-attended. Groups engage in spirited conversations, and laud the lives they led before this latest adventure. Others share stories of drudgery, escapism, or patriotic fervor to justify their enlistment. Politics and religion dominate many of the gabfests, along with commonplace complaints about the inanities of military life. Everyone's story includes the girl back home, and when camps finally grow quiet, the men seek solitude to write those in faraway places.

Fortress Monroe, Old Point Comfort, Virginia, 1861

Charles Magnus painting
Library of Congress
Geography and Map Division
84692454

training days

Wednesday, 27 March 1861
Fort Monroe, Virginia

The men are called to attention, and rise as their instructor, Captain Randolph, enters the makeshift training compound. He is affable, articulate, and intelligent, and a New Englander through-and-through. His superiors and subordinates take to him immediately.

"Take a seat and relax, men. If you wish to smoke, go ahead and light 'em up." Several men take him up on his offer. Captain Randolph takes a drink of water before starting. "First off, welcome to the 'Long Arm of the Army'. I will give you an overview of what we will cover over the next several days. This may overwhelm some and bore others. I'll try my best to minimize both, with the hopes you walk away from this with a better understanding of our mission. If there are any questions, try to save them for the end of each lecture. Those of you who stood sentry duty last night, and find it hard to keep your eyes open, stand at the back of the room."

The organization of the army is the lead topic in the series of lectures——the corps, divisions, brigades, regiments, battalions, and companies——and what kind of manpower makes up each of them. It's followed by specialized divisions such as cavalry and artillery. Randolph explains how complicated it can get as units can be moved around and assume different responsibilities under various commanders. He explains the importance of flexibility and absolute obedience; orders are not to be questioned. Authority and discipline are natural offshoots. He covers the gamut of minor infractions to capital offenses, the process for assessing guilt through court martial, and methods of punishment. The men stand as the captain departs the room.

"Do you think they'd go so far as to shoot any of us?" asks Hickman. "It seems so radical. What does anyone do to deserve punishment that harsh?"

"Desertion may be pretty big on the list," adds Ramsey.

Hickman looks confused.

"When a soldier leaves the field in the face of the enemy," he clarifies.

"Isn't that called a retreat?"

"Not when the rest are left to do his fighting," says Case. "I look at it as serving two purposes, to punish the offender, and deter the rest of the men from committing the same offense."

* * *

Randolph opens the second day with a question. "What are the roles of the artillery?"

"To blast the Secesh back to their maker," yells out one of the attendees.

He nods his head, and points to the man. "I like that ... a lot, but the artillery has several *other* functions. Effective long-range fire can be used to weaken and hopefully destroy enemy fortifications and materials, which includes their artillery. Nothing can be a greater deterrent against massing forces than some well-placed shells to disrupt their plans. Keep in mind this also works in reverse. We are as vulnerable as the enemy."

"A question, sir," says Price.

"Okay, I'll take just this one."

"Who determines where to fire?"

"Field commanders constantly assess enemy emplacements, and look for both weaknesses and strong points. It can be a regiment's colonel, down to your battery's Gunner. When you're in the thick of it, you will see officers as they ride back and forth, with field glasses in hand, communicating with each gun crew. Defense plays a huge role in our duties. The enemy looks for ways to kill, capture, or drive us from our positions. We need to break apart their assaults, and canister fire can have a severe negative impact on their progress. Worse case scenario, a retreat, the artillery might be called upon for rear guard action, to protect the troops from being overrun. We work in tandem with each other, whether on the offense or defense. Concentrated fire from multiple guns is much more effective.

Let's talk about the make-up of an artillery unit. Most of our batteries consist of six cannon. There are between twenty and thirty men per gun, which includes your NCOs. That doesn't mean everyone's on line at the same time; it would be a bit crowded.

Each battery will be commanded by a captain, a lieutenant will be in charge of two guns, and each has a sergeant designated the Gunner. You will answer to him. Besides the men in your gun crew, *he's* the man you want to cultivate a close relationship with. Each cannon and wagon requires a team of six horses. Doing the math, that works out to about seventy-five horses per battery—and that's a lot of horse manure."

Twenty-five year old Ordnance Sergeant Robert Sanger was assigned to the department as a fledgling corporal to assist in the paperwork that comes with managing an armory. With his organizational talents, he quickly mastered the administrative duties, and devised a tracking system for distribution and replacement throughout the entire Third Regiment. When his senior NCO medically retired, his superiors looked no further to fill the billet. But he's difficult to work with. He runs his department as his personal fiefdom, requires procedures followed to the letter, and new trainees better learn to do things his way, or they are quickly shown the door.

Eight new men, along with Jim, Will, and Robert report to Sanger to begin their day of training on ammunition. "Good morning, men," says Sanger. "Move on in as best you can." He stands in back of a large leather covered table, affixed to its top is a foot-square, thick metal plate, stained with black powder burns. "Any of you carry matches?"

"I do." Private Johnson rummages through his pockets. "Here ya' go, Sergeant."

Sanger brings out a small leather satchel and produces a fused roll of tightly wound paper the size of an olive. He places it on the center of the metal plate, directs Johnson to light the fuse, and tells the men to step back a couple of paces. Sanger steps away from the table as soon as it's lit. The explosion startles nearly everyone. The trainees respond with universal yelps, some stumble backwards, and others scatter to the far corners of the room. Their ears still ring as they work their way back, coughing from the lingering smoke. By the time the trainees compose themselves and regroup, Sergeant Sanger stands there with a self-satisfied grin on his face.

"That's only a minuscule measure of propellant we use for the ordnance." He holds up a two and a half pound bag of gunpowder. "This bag holds eighty times the amount of gunpowder in that little demonstration. We use this as a standard propellant to force, among other things, a twelve-pound ball out of the barrel of the cannon up to a mile away. You make a mistake in how you handle this … well, you can imagine the ramifications."

Sanger reaches under the table to pull out the four different types of ammunition. "These are inert demos. Take some time to look them over before I cover them individually."

He holds a solid, round cannon ball with a bag of gunpowder sandwiched between a wooden plate called a *sabot*; the whole assembly is held together with metal straps. "This twelve-pound solid shot is an offensive weapon, its most effective range around fifteen hundred yards. It can be used with devastating results on fortifications, enemy emplacements, artillery, wagons, and troops. It can shatter trees, and demoralize the soldiers who have sought refuge behind them.

Next, a spherical case that explodes over and slightly ahead of troop formations, then shatters into six or more pieces of deadly shrapnel."

Hickman raises his hand.

"Yes, Private?"

"Why slightly ahead, Sergeant?"

"Momentum. Otherwise the projectiles will overshoot the target."

He holds up another cannon ball, different than the solid shot, with a place for a fuse. "Called a case shot, it carries close to eighty balls and a charge designed with timed fuses to explode while airborne to rain down hellfire on the troops"

He then breaks out a tin casing with the familiar attached *sabot* and gunpowder bag. "This will be one of your Gunner's favorite choices. The canister holds twenty-seven iron balls tightly packed in sawdust. Used at close range, it's a defensive weapon, most effective within three hundred yards. It requires no fuse, can be fired two at a time, called a double-load, and will kill ten to twenty men, officers, horses, or anything else unfortunate enough to find itself in its path. It discharges from the muzzle of your cannon in a conical pattern with the greatest concentration of destruction at its center point. Combine that with an entire battery of six guns that work together, each shooting two to three times a minute, you can imagine the results."

The afternoon class moves outdoors to a caisson in back of the building. There are two ammunition cases affixed to the wagon. Sanger lifts up the cover of one of them and points to a chart inside the lid of the case. "You'll see these on the inside of most ammunition cases. The 'Table of Fire' serves as a guide for the ammunition—effective ranges, gun elevations and transit times. There are approximately five hundred pounds of ammunition in each one of these cases when fully loaded. You can see it's precisely packed to facilitate easy access when on the line. No wasted space."

Hickman raises his hand reluctantly. "Yes, Private."

"When do we get to try this out?"

"You will soon receive orders to transfer to a training command outside Washington City. You will drill with the cannon more than you did your rifle. Because you'll be part of a team of eight, you will need to learn each of the seven positions, other than the Gunner's. Successful artillery teams stay alert and remain flexible. In time, you will gain self-confidence, and the trust of your battery mates. The hard truth——there will always be a need for replacements, thus the drills until the war's conclusion." The men thank the sergeant individually before they report back to their encampment.

* * *

In the woods at Chancellorsville, bivouac at night

Edwin Forbes drawing
Library of Congress
Prints and Photographs Division
LC-DIG-ppmsca-20542

That evening the men gather around the campfire. The discussions center on what they were shown and their instructors. Robert slips away from the men and heads over toward the shoreline to be by himself. He finds a dry place to sit, and removes his shoes to let the water gently lap over his feet. He watches the lights flicker from the ships at anchor, and takes in the sights, sounds, and smells of the bay. It reminds him of Lake Ontario. He lets his mind wander to his family, *How are things on the farm? Is Will still angry with me? Does mother still worry about me? Will I make it back home alive, and in one piece?*

Monday, 6 May 1861

"It's time to move back to Washington City for the next phase of your training," announces Randolph. "Your sergeants will accompany you to Camp Barry."

Robert takes a moment to look out over the Chesapeake Bay from the dock. "Whatcha thinkin' there?" Ramsey startles him.

"Oh, hi, Jim. Just home. Remembering Fort Niagara. My family's been to that region a couple of times, first to see the great falls, then north to the coast to view the old fort."

"Are the falls as spectacular as they say?" asks Jim.

"You don't live that far from them. You really need to make the trip. My words can't do them justice. You need to see, hear, and feel them before you can appreciate just how grand they are. The water cascading over the precipice roars. The sound … well … if you get close enough it travels through your very essence. You can get so close that your clothes get wet from the mist, and when the sun catches it just right, the rainbows are spectacular." Both men are snapped from their reverie when ordered to board the ship.

17th New York Battery, Artillery Depot, Camp Berry, Washington City
Alexander Gardner Photograph
Library of Congress
Prints and Photographs Division
LC-DIG-ppmsca-33203

camp berry

Tuesday, 7 May 1861
Washington City

It's a five-mile march through the city to its northeastern border, where Delaware Avenue conjoins with Old Bladensburg Road, and another mile and a half to the newly-minted artillery training grounds at Camp Barry. Spread out over a sizable tract of land, it's bordered by tree-covered rolling hills, with a commanding view of the capital. A quarter mile past the front gate is a field of tents, temporary dwellings until more permanent housing can be erected. The base accommodates training facilities, a firing range, large stables, foraging grounds, and to the south a vast array of supply wagons.

Jim, Will, and Robert settle into their quarters. The three of them retrieve enough straw for their bedding, which they cover with their rubber blankets, then unfurl their bed rolls.

"I intend on spending as much free time as I can in the city," says Will.

"Wonder when we'll get passes," says Jim.

"Just how far do you think your thirteen dollars a month will take you?" asks Robert.

"Far enough to meet my needs," quips Will. "'Sides, stop being a stick in the mud. You'll have a good time."

"I still have that commitment to help out the folks."

Will raises his eyebrows and shakes his head. "Your loss."

Wednesday, 8 May 1861

After morning rations, Robert runs his finger down the posted roster until he finds his name and trainer. He's directed to a battery of cannon facing the hills. They are spaced so that instructions given on one gun does not interfere with groups adjacent to them.

Twenty-eight men gather around the bronze cannon where their orientation begins. The sergeant stands at his usual station in back of the cannon, and seven men stand in line behind him.

He scans the group. "I'm Sergeant Welker, one of the Gunners in Battery F." He points to the men in back of him, and adds, "This is my crew. It's our job to train the lot of you how to be part of a team that can safely and efficiently fire this repeatedly."

Welker earned his stripes in the Mexican War, fifteen years earlier. Ironically, he fought under Thomas Jackson, a brilliant young artillery lieutenant, before he became known as "Stonewall". Welker found the Army to be a means of escape from a dead-end future, and with it a family of men with whom he lives and serves. Now a grizzled veteran in his late thirties, it's rare to find him without a rolled cigarette. His voice is deep and nicotine raspy.

He starts his training with a walk around the specialized support wagons: the traveling forge, battery wagon, caisson, and limber. "The caisson to the left …" After he touches all the highlights of the equipment, he tells the men to have a seat, and smoke 'em if they've got 'em. He leans back against the limber, takes off his hat, and lights up. "Listen fellas, let's take an informal look at what we are trying to accomplish here. I've been in the army since most of you were still mastering the art of walking. And in the Mexican War, I fought under one of the best generals in this country's history. Besides the advances in the weaponry, and better looking uniforms," he smiles, and the men snicker, "not a lot has changed. You need to learn the process 'til it becomes as natural as breathing to you. We will give you all the latitude you need, and frankly some of you won't make it."

"What happens to those who don't?" asks Will.

camp berry

"You'd really rather not know, but in involves a lot of horses, a pair of gloves, and a pretty big dung fork." Laughter circulates around the group.

"It's a matter of applying yourself, you learn the drills——cold——keep me in smokes and bourbon, and you've taken the first big step."

"Tell us a little about yourself, Sergeant," asks Jim.

"Why would you want to know that?"

"We'd like to know who we're fighting for."

"That's an easy one ... each other. As a member of a gun crew, performing your particular duties, you are as important as anyone in the battery."

"Any family?" asks Will.

"Okay, that's enough for now. When we wrap up here, we will divide you into groups of seven. Each group will have a Gunner, and each position will be assigned an experienced crew member as a shadow. You are responsible for learning the duties of each position, and hopefully become as efficient as these men."

The group reconvenes by the cannon. "We will now demonstrate, in slow motion, the steps it takes to fire a gun." Welker gives the orders to his team and they hurry over to their assigned stations around the cannon and limber. "At the ready, load up for shell fire, set the fuse at five seconds." The crew walks through their paces. Welker narrates as they move. Three men are involved with the ammunition, including the one who carries it to the muzzle of the cannon. The rest of the crew completes the load sequence before the number four man pulls the lanyard to fire the gun——*BAH-ROOM!*——a large yellow flame accompanies the explosion from the muzzle. The concussion from the blast travels along the ground buckling some of their knees. The rest crouch low and cover their ears. The cloud of black smoke hovers near the trainees. On the ground, Robert coughs from the harsh sulfurous cloud as it permeates his lungs. He unsuccessfully tries to spit out the acrid taste in his mouth. His eyes water, his ears ring, and he looks away for fresh air.

"Back on your feet!" barks Welker. "That ground won't protect you." His seasoned crew shares a laugh, like they are initiating new pledges into their secret organization.

Robert pulls out a handkerchief and wipes his eyes. "I thought this would be a demonstration only. Where'd the shell land?"

"That was a demonstration, but with a blank charge of gunpowder." He points to unseen forces in the field. "The enemy's still directly ahead of us. Prepare the next round." This time Welker orders his crew to shift stations before they go through the process in real time. They set up and fire three rounds in succession, with a one-minute space between each, and shift to a different station with each round. After the sequence, the trainees know what to expect from the caustic smoke, thunderous noise, and bone-jarring concussions. They marvel at how efficiently the crew operates.

Welker adds, "Over the next several weeks we will train you to the point where you can operate at that level of efficiency. The drills will become monotonous, but you will eventually gain the confidence and skill to operate this cannon the same as you just witnessed."

Robert is assigned to Welker's crew of trainees. Of the other six in his team, he knows Jim, Will, and Price. Johnson, Schroeder, and Case make up the remainder. Welker motions the trainees over to the side of the cannon, out of the way of the seasoned gun crew. "Pick a place around the gun where you'd like to start out."

The men scramble for positions. Most make a beeline for the limber, attracted to its distance from the exposed front, but oblivious to their proximity to a case full of explosive ammunition. Robert likes the look of the number one position——to seat each round of ammunition with the ramrod, and swab out the muzzle after the cannon's discharge. Welker assigns the rest of the stations from the cluster of men around the limber.

The men go through their paces in slow motion, each shadowed by an experienced crew member. They practice the timing, then start to speed up the pace. Their "shadows" eventually back away as the men demonstrate more confidence and efficiency. Robert is shown how to hold the ramrod, to point his thumbs away from the muzzle. It's awkward, but by two full cycles he turns to his mentor and says, "I think I've got this."

On the next walk-through he has his role in the formula down. Welker closely watches the numbers three and four men, Ramsey and

Hickman, who have difficulty with their timing; Welker and his team let them eventually work out their role in the sequence.

"Just to let you know, stable duty starts tomorrow after muster." A groan comes up from many, but not everyone. Robert signed up for this.

Several men from other crews gather around the campfire. Smokes are lit, coffee mugs filled, and the conversations animated. Hickman stands. "How many of you ended up on your ass after the first round let go?" A chorus of laughter rises as a few men admittedly raise their hands. "Get your hand up there, too, Schroeder. I saw your ankles fly up over your elbows."

The embarrassed youth rubs his butt as he answers. "Ah, heck, fellas. I weren't the only one." Everybody laughs along with him.

"I bet most of us'll eat dirt once the real shells start flying," says Ramsey.

Private Case, older than most of the men, joins the conversations. "I think by the time they get done with us, it'll be so ingrained that nothing will distract us. The Gunners will see to that."

Robert breaks away to find a quiet place where he can write home. He tries to remember the lighter stories of the last several days, with hopes his mother will laugh, rather then fret, when his father reads them to her. It's been a couple of months and he misses his family—thoughts which he keeps to himself.

Wednesday, 15 May 1861

The care and well-being of the seventy plus horses assigned to Batteries F & K fall under the experienced eyes of Quartermaster Sergeant James Davenport. His responsibilities ensure the animals are properly fed, groomed, trained for the harness, shod, provided vet services, and their stables refreshed daily. That doesn't mean *he* performs the tasks; he assigns them to the others and oversees their completion.

He has close to thirty men under his charge this morning. He looks over the trainees and asks, "Show of hands. Anyone here ever *not* worked in a stable?" About seven of the men, city-born and raised, lift their hands. "You men pair up with someone who has experience." He gives them a moment to team up with a farm boy for help.

Davenport continues. "You'll need to meet our horses and get to know their personalities." The city boys chuckle. "Okay. Can anyone demonstrate to these skeptics how we *meet* these horses?" After a long pause, Robert reluctantly raises his hand. "You there. Good. What's your name?"

"Private Canham, Sergeant."

"Find the roan and show these men how to introduce yourself."

Robert makes his way through the crowd. He looks around until he finds the horse with a light brown, even-colored torso and jet black mane, legs, and tail. It's quartered in its stall looking over the gate at the activities. Robert slowly lifts the back of his hand from below the mouth of the horse to its nose to ensure the horse picks up his scent and doesn't feel threatened. He gently rubs the top of its nose. The skin feels soft and dry. He speaks softly to the horse, which sticks out its tongue; it is not dry. Robert gently says, "Good boy," pats it on the side of its face, and wipes his hand on his pant leg as he rejoins the group.

"You've obviously worked with horses before. You don't mind one of these city boys under your charge, do you?"

"No problem."

Davenport covers the litany of chores the men will be tasked with. "The horses need time to trust you. Treat them well. Your lives depend on these beasts doing their jobs. On average, they eat ten pounds of hay and about fifteen pounds of grain a day. Their stalls need to be cleaned twice a day. It's called 'mucking'——shoveling the thirty to fifty pounds of manure each horse deposits daily." Groans from the city boys are mixed with the laughter of the experienced farm hands who knowingly nod their heads. The sergeant continues, "You'll share that pleasant task, but as there are a lot of you, it shouldn't be too difficult. Trust me, you'll get used to the smell. Before we continue, don't get attached to these animals. When we're under fire, the largest targets the enemy has to slow down or disable the batteries are these poor souls."

He pauses. "Finally, be constantly aware of your surroundings. You may find yourself in the wrong place around the wrong animal, and you can end up with a serious injury. We try our best to cull out the biters, but the animals can, and do kick, putting you in a world of hurt."

Private Price raises his hand. "How often will we be assigned to this duty?"

"Daily, unless we're in the thick of an extended battle. Your company clerks will handle the duty assignments."

The men are divided into teams of two and set to the tasks that will become ingrained into their daily routines. The sergeant approaches Robert with Private Winston in tow. "The young private here is from Philly, and will work with you for the next several days." He points to Robert, but looks directly at Winston. "What this man says, goes. Understand?" The wide-eyed youth nods and acknowledges him with a weak smile.

* * *

As the weeks progress, and spring takes hold, training outdoors is a pleasure. The men continue to gain proficiency with the cannon, then rotate to new stations. With each position change the seasoned crew resumes shadowing the men, and the cycle of drilling repeats itself.

The crew is assembled when Captain Randolph gallops over to Welker's team. The men comes to attention. "At ease, men. Sergeant, I'm here to assess the progress of each team, and your crew is first. Let's see what they can do."

"Yes, sir," answers Welker. He orders the men to assume their stations. The veteran crew moves out of the way as the trainees take their assigned positions. When Welker gives the order, they go through their paces, and thirty seconds after the initial order, the cannon fires.

"Excellent job, Sergeant, to both you and your men. Training days are over, and you are to be assigned to your operational battery." The men are dismissed to gather their belongings for a march to Fort Duncan, where they will join their regular unit.

Feeding and resting horses

Alfred R. Waud drawing
Library of Congress
Prints and Photographs Division
LC-DIG-ppmsca-21536

private will

Friday, 21 June 1861

Robert gets ready to call it a day in the stables, when he hears his name mentioned. An infantryman, with his back to him, is talking to Sergeant Davenport. As the soldier turns, Robert sees that it's his brother. "Will!" He laughs with joy to see him, and strides over to give him a hug. He backs off a step, and grabs Will by the front of his field jacket. "What's with this? I didn't hear you joined up."

"You didn't think I'd let you have all the fun, did you?" He looks around and takes an exaggerated sniff. "I can see you're finally living your dream." Robert snorts a chuckle.

"How in the world did you ever find me?"

"It doesn't take long if you know who to ask."

"How long are you here for?"

"I've got an overnight pass. Can we get out of here?"

Robert looks up at Davenport. The sergeant pauses. "Let me see what I can do." As they wait, Will fills Robert in on his enlistment. "The Twenty-eighth New York Infantry recruited a unit from Medina. So I signed up for two years, not five." He holds up two fingers to emphasizes the point.

"Yeah, funny. What about the folks?"

"Well, mother wasn't too happy about it, but father seems to understand."

"How will he manage the farm alone?"

Pastor Foye connected him with a couple of local lads who needed the work."

"How can he afford it?"

"He offered them room, board, and a small stipend."

"Room?"

"Yeah, they took over our room."

Sergeant Davenport arrives with Robert's pass. "You two boys try to stay out of trouble."

"Yes, Sergeant," they respond in unison, then walk off laughing.

The two brothers make the hike into the city, and within an hour are at a small restaurant that Robert heard good things about. "Food's good, lots of it, and cheap."

"You come here a lot?"

"It's my first time out of camp since we transferred. Couple of the guys in my gun crew adopted the city as their home away from home, and they recommended it. Catch me up with the news about everyone."

"Well, mother worries about you, and I'm sure with my absence she frets about both of us now. Father seems to take it all in stride. He knew it'd be only a matter of time before I signed up. He's mentioned a number of times how much he appreciates the money you've sent home. I think he's dropping me a bit of a hint."

"Yeah, he's too proud to come right out and ask. How about Hannah?"

"When she's not busy chasing her kids around, she's worried, too, and misses you a lot. Interested in some sightseeing?"

"My friends also recommended a boarding house, but cautioned it fills up fast on the weekend. I guess we best try there first." They settle their tab and walk some thirty minutes closer to city central until they find the boarding house. There's a dorm room available—bunk beds on the second story with a dozen other men. They are cautioned that it gets a little noisy on the weekend, but the price is right. A heavy rain and brisk winds are brewing. They are happy to secure a place for the night out of the elements. They stay up late, and are up and about early the next day. The widow who owns the place has coffee ready for them and recommends a cafe that serves a good breakfast. The weather has eased up, and they head out to catch some of the sights.

The brothers navigate the puddles and muddy streets on their way to the nearby Capitol Building. They find the entire grounds filled with bustling workmen, materials for the expansion wings, the cast iron dome to replace the wood and copper one, and a strong military presence. They sense they are more in the way than anything, and continue down the hill along Pennsylvania Avenue. It takes them about a half hour to reach the Executive Mansion.

As they view the outside of the iconic building from Lafayette Park, Will asks, "You meet Lincoln yet?"

"How do you suppose that might happen?"

"I've heard he likes to talk with the troops. Supposed to be pretty approachable."

"Sorry, but not yet. If I do see him, I'll let him know you asked for him. Have you heard where you're headed yet?"

"Someplace to shoot at Johnny Reb, I guess. Doesn't much matter where or when."

"That'll allay the Rebs' fears especially when they realize you can't hit the ocean from the deck of a ship. Then they'll have the pleasure of shooting back."

Will tilts his head to the side. "What's the serial number on your dung fork?"

Robert laughs hard. "They've trained us to be part of a gun crew, but we've received no movement orders. We're currently 'in defense of our nation's capital', whatever that means. They're adding more equipment and new men to each of the batteries. Other than that, we're sitting tight."

"Consider yourself lucky, I guess."

"I imagine we'll get the call soon enough."

The brothers spend the day around the city, taking breaks for food and coffee. They arrive at the truncated shaft of the Washington Monument. When he points to a large field of grazing cattle, Will asks, "What's with the critters over there?"

"That's the Union's 'Beef Depot'."

The stench is revolting. "I never smelled anything like *that* on our farm."

"Kind of puts you off your feed, doesn't it. That's not from the cattle, it's sewage from the nearby Washington City Canal."

"It's no wonder this place is overrun with flies."

"Welcome to our nation's capital."

It's a short walk to the Smithsonian Institution. The castle-like architecture houses an assortment of artifacts that take up the balance of the brothers' day. Toward late afternoon, and a few more coffees, they realize it's time to return to their respective commands. They make a commitment to try to get together whenever they can, but know it may be a futile promise.

* * *

About mid-July Robert receives a letter from Will; his unit has moved out to western Virginia. Shortly after that, news of the rout at the Battle of Bull Run sweeps through their camp. The men are restricted to the base for now. The Provost is indiscriminate in their attempts to round up the men who fled the field and are loathe to return to their outfits. Many innocents are swept up in the dragnet.

Robert doesn't hear from Will again until late August, when his unit arrives at Ball's Bluff, Virginia, *At least he's getting to see some of the country. I'm bored with staying put at one base, even though it is in 'defense of the capital'. We've been there for three months now, with no end in sight.*

fever

Thursday, 12 September 1861

As Robert wakes up and plants his feet on the ground, he realizes something's not right. He has a throbbing headache and feels weak. He tries some coffee, winces when he takes a sip, and tosses the rest on the ground. He has to sit back down. He's exhausted. *How can this be? My day hasn't even started.*

Ramsey approaches him. "Morning, Robert. Want to get some grub with me?"

"Yeah ... no ... sorry, Jim. I feel pretty shaky today."

"You do look a bit peaked. Better go see the doc."

"I'm okay." But he isn't. Robert has severe cramps and has to make a quick trip to the latrine. Afterward he trudges over to the aid station.

It isn't long before a doctor, a young lieutenant, introduces himself and starts an examination. He begins to work up a diagnosis.

"When did you first notice this?"

"A couple of days now. The headache wasn't bad, but——"

"How's your appetite?"

"I couldn't even choke down the coffee today."

He checks Robert's forehead, and says, "Well, you've got a fever. We need to get you hydrated. Here. Drink this water, even if you don't feel like it. Tell me about your bowel movements."

"Well, uh ... I got hit with the 'runs' shortly after I got up."

"Let me check one more thing." The doctor has Robert unbutton his pants and feels his abdomen. He taps on it and listens. "This been swelled long?"

"I don't know. My head's been demanding most of my attention."

Once he does a visual examination of Robert's chest and back, he says, "You have red lesions, what we call 'rose spots'. You need to be hospitalized."

"What's wrong with me?"

"It looks like we're facing an outbreak of typhoid. You're not our sole patient."

The word "typhoid" rattles Robert. He knows men who did not survive their bout with it. "Typhoid? Am I about to die from this?"

"It is serious, but we caught it pretty early."

"How long will I be here?"

"Not long here," he answers. "We'll transfer you to the camp hospital where you may be for a number of weeks. It depends on how you respond to treatment."

"Weeks! How many weeks?"

"Three to four. Once the infection runs its course it'll take some time for you to get your strength back, but don't worry. You won't be alone."

Several of the crew's Gunners confront Captain Randolph about the command's dwindling numbers. He consolidates the healthy men to make complete crews, then visits the hospital to confer with the doctors. The occupation of the large wards grow as fever sweeps through the artillery encampment. The readiness of the corps is seriously compromised. "Not much we can do about this, Captain," says the doctor. "We need to let the disease runs its course."

* * *

Four weeks after his initial hospitalization, Robert returns to camp to resume his duties. The first bit of news he hears about is the battle at Ball's Bluff. The Rebs routed the Union troops again, and the casualty counts are high. *I wonder how Will made out ... if anything happens to him.* Eventually word reaches him that Will made it through without a scratch. Many of the men he fought with didn't.

Saturday, 8 March 1862

The winter months pass slowly in camp. Reports continue to circulate about battles fought in the west, a new Secretary of War, and the revolving door of generals.

It's a bitterly cold day, and stable duty is especially harsh. Sergeant Davenport hands Robert a two-day pass. "I think you need to take a break and get out of here for a couple of days. Go see some sights, and eat some good food for a change."

Jim and Will are ready to hit the road when Robert returns. "Another weekend close to camp?" asks Jim.

He holds up his pass. "Not this time, mind if I join you fellas?"

"If you feel you're up for it, sure. We're considered regulars at a couple of joints. We'll show you a good time."

"Yeah. Good food, cheap drinks, and females," winks Will.

"I'll go for the food, but that's about it."

"No problem. We'll get our rooms first, and you can stick with us as long as ya' feel up for it. That way you can hit the bunk anytime you want."

* * *

It's close to 10:00 a.m. before Robert wakes up. He sees his companions' bunks are unruffled, and starts out for the restaurant where he ate breakfast with his brother.

The familiar aroma of fried bacon greets Robert as he opens the door. The decor of the eatery matches the prices on the menu, plain and popular with the troops. He spots his two friends in the far corner. Jim sits with his head down as if in a trance by the half-consumed mug of coffee and untouched plate of food in front of him. Robert isn't sure if he's awake. Will leaves no doubt. His head lies on the table, his forage cap is upside down on the plate of pancakes congealed with whatever syrup Will generously poured on them.

"Need I ask how your night went, Jim?"

He fights back nausea as he tries to formulate a coherent sentence. "You should have stuck with us. We met up with a couple of ladies and caroused pret-tee hard."

"Mind if I join you two?"

"No, take a seat. Just push ole Will out of the way."

Robert sits down and rustles Will's shoulder to wake him up. After several attempts, he lifts his head a few inches, opens his eyes, and says, "Robert. Where ya' been?" Then closes his eyes and lays his head back down on the table.

Jim offers Robert his untouched breakfast. He pushes the cold plate back to him, then gets the attention of the cook and orders a fresh plate of hot food and coffee to go around. They serve it with a tab for the three meals and a request to take his friends with him when he leaves. When finished, he settles the bill, with apologies.

"Come on, Jim. Drink some coffee. I think I need a hand with Will." They both work on him until he wakens. He tries to grab his forage cap from the plate of pancakes, but the syrup is reluctant to give it up. He's confused, but eventually pries it up, scrapes off the remnants of pancakes with his fingers, and puts the hat on as if it's all part of his daily routine.

Jim drinks the coffee Robert ordered.

"We'd best get back to base." Will loudly announces to the other patrons. The cook shakes his head and smiles as scattered applause follows them out the door.

* * *

Robert awakens Jim and Will who are still dressed in the uniforms they wore over the weekend. Will takes his hat off, untangles his hair from the mess, but doesn't understand why it's sticky. When he takes a sniff, the pieces of the puzzle fit together.

Welker notes the bloodshot eyes of the two and calls the team to order. He gives the command, "Load." The crew goes through their paces, a little more slowly and shakier than usual, but they are thoroughly ingrained with the routine, and when Welker yells, "Fire," Hickman pulls the lanyard and unceremoniously falls. With the explosion, Ramsey and Hickman both let out a shriek, in fear their heads will burst along with the shell. Welker smiles. At his command, "Load," the process resumes. The two inebriates look to him for mercy.

"Fire." Hickman obeys, pulls the lanyard, and tries to withstand the shock of the explosion. He drops to his knees and retches in front of his station. He stands and sweeps dirt over the mess with his boot. Welker halts the drill an hour and a dozen rounds later. The men are ordered to fall in by the side of the cannon. Ramsey and Hickman stumble into place, while the other five do what they can to suppress their laughter.

Welker walks in front of the line, looks at each man face-to-face, and struggles to maintain his own composure. "I think that you men understand why ammunition, artillery, *and* alcohol do not mix." With that everyone lets go and laughs without restraint. Everyone except poor Jim and Will.

Robert wonders why the extensive live-fire training. "What's the occasion, Sergeant?"

"The officers are in conference with General McClellan. We've been put on alert to be ready to deploy. We're going to war!"

fifteen thousand

∞

Monday, 17 March 1862

Buglers sound reveille, and the NCOs roust the men from their bedrolls for muster. It's a harsh way for them to start their day, and the weather only adds to their woes. It rained the entire day before and today's temperature is near freezing. The troops struggle to formation, and Sergeant Welker impatiently considers sterner measures to get his crew motivated. "Get your butts up, outside, and in line." He yells, "Now!" as he swats the outside walls of their tent.

"Wonder what's special 'bout this day," carps Will, as he stretches and slowly makes his way over to where he dumped his uniform the night before. "Haven't even made our coffee yet."

"I imagine it must be important," says Jim as he suppresses a yawn.

Lieutenant Turnbull has been given the task by the combined batteries' commander to deliver the day's news. The young officer grows impatient; he's stuck in the cold while the men dilly-dally into formation. The Gunners report to Sergeant Major Lawton who relays it to Turnbull, "All present and accounted for, sir."

"Finally," Turnbull mutters to himself. He looks out at the half-awake assembly. "Word has come down that we are to prepare to move out. We are ordered to proceed to Alexandria. Once there, the entire Army will board transport ships for points southeast."

As many questions as rumors immediately float through the ranks.

"Back to Fort Monroe?"

"Yorktown?"

"Richmond!"

Turnbull pauses until the muttering dies down. "We will leave in force with everyone *and* everything. Your Gunners will see to the assignments of their respective troops. Those of you in support positions need to report to your area non-coms for assignment." After a pause, "Sergeants, dismiss your troops." He returns the salutes from the NCOs, steps down from the platform, wet, cold, and angry, and heads back to the command post.

"Looks like we'll finally see some action," Jim says to Robert. They hoped they'd all be assigned together, but with his difficulties in training, Will's been relegated to the stables.

Jim tries to console his friend. "You're still part of *our* gun crew, and as one of our teamsters, we'll be handling the horses and traveling together."

"Yeah, well, good for you guys," says Will as he starts to eat.

When he wipes the last bit of pork grease from his plate, Robert asks, "You two about ready to go?"

The three of them shoulder their packs and head over to the stables. Close to fifty men are already there. The horses need to be fed, then harnessed up. Six hours from the time they received their initial orders, the vehicles assemble to begin the movement. The lieutenant has put together a good plan and Batteries F & K start the nine-mile trek.

Robert's crew is mounted atop the lead horses and the ammo case of the limber. The rain-softened streets slow the pace and force the horses to work a little harder. Sergeant Welker rides alongside his new crew. "You men alright?"

Jim answers him, "No problems, Sergeant. Looks like the new lieutenant has got his part of the movement well-organized." Welker nods.

"Hope he's that reliable when we come under fire," mutters Price.

"I don't think we need to worry about *his* conduct. I think you need to be more concerned about how *you* perform under fire," says Welker.

"No problems here, Sergeant. We're gonna whip them Rebs and send 'em with their tails tucked in back to Richmond," boasts Will.

"I think the Rebs deserve more respect than that, young man. Especially after Bull Run. As I recall, they sent our boys scurrying home in a panic."

"We didn't have Little Mac leading us then," says Jim. "It'll be a different story now we got someone who knows how to run an army."

"I hope you're right, Private." Then he looks to Robert next to Price. "You holding up okay?"

He's preoccupied, but answers, "I'm alright, thanks."

Welker reins his horse to a halt and waits for the next wagon to catch up to him before he resumes his pace. By the time they reach Long Bridge, he has touched base with each wagon in their crew.

Lieutenant Turnbull halts his horse at the entry to the bridge, which spans the Potomac. "Hurry it along, men. The guards pull the planks from the bridge once it gets dark."

"Why's that?" Will asks Jim.

"I imagine it's to discourage any late-night visits from the Rebels."

After they cross the river, they find the road follows a track south, parallel to the river and next to the railroad for about four miles. The road then narrows along an embankment where Four Mile Run empties into the Potomac.

Robert remains quiet throughout the remainder of the trip. He listens intently to the conversations and answers direct questions, but otherwise wanders into his own thoughts when the men don't engage him. *How will I react when the gunfire starts? Will I be reliable, or will I panic? I wonder if any of the other men in the crew harbor the same thoughts?* He doesn't know it, and no one will readily admit to it, but they do share similar insecurities, every one of them.

It's dark by the time they reach Alexandria. Lieutenant Turnbull rides over to the men. "Follow the lead gun crew over to the artillery park, then bed down the animals for the night. Tomorrow may be another long day."

* * *

The stables are a massive complex of long, open-sided sheds at the southwestern corner of the city. As the forces of the entire Army of the Potomac gather for the campaign, there are several thousand horses and mules that need food and shelter.

"You ever see anything like this, Robert?" asks Jim.

"Not by a long shot. Back home, you can count the horses we own on one hand. Will's family are the big-time dairy farmers. He's the one you need to ask."

"How 'bout it, Will?"

"Not even when we'd go to the auction houses in Chicago."

It isn't long before a sergeant, a stranger to the men, walks over with a ledger. "What outfit you men with?"

"Third U.S., Batteries F & K," answers Jim.

He makes a notation in his ledger, then points to a numbered placard just outside the stable. "You're in building number forty-six. Figure out how to get back here early, otherwise you'll be frettin' 'bout who took your animals. Allow yourselves enough time to feed 'em, and clean out their stables before you leave. We'll make a pretty big fuss, if you don't." He points to a huge shed outside. "That's where the fodder and grain are stored. There's plenty for everyone, just take what you think you'll need. There's fresh straw to bed down your critters."

"Just how many animals are quartered here, Sergeant?" asks Jim.

"Right now, close to fifteen thousand. I'll be here early, so let me know if you need anything. Just remember to do what I said about cleaning your stalls; it's not a request."

"Don't worry, we'll take care of 'em. Now can you point us to our campsite?" asks Jim.

He gestures to the east without looking up from his journal. "Just follow that road there up past the tracks and the bakery. You'll be stayin' in that gathering of tents up the hillside." The men look to where he's pointing. Campfires accentuate the silhouettes of the conical Sibley tents in the growing darkness, but no one knows which ones are theirs.

The harness assemblies are removed from the teams and the horses are led in two at a time for feed and water. Sergeant Welker makes an appearance. "You men got everything in hand here?"

"We do, Sergeant, but where are we supposed to stay?" asks Jim.

"That's why I'm here. When you get finished, meet outside stable number forty-four, just a couple of buildings over to the east. We'll go together as a group."

More than thirty of the men are gathered at the assigned rendezvous to wait for the sergeant to show. They all look downhill toward the noise and activity at the docks. They only catch a glimpse of it between the weather-beaten red brick buildings that line the street. A couple of the men urge the others to join them for a closer look. Welker appears within minutes. "Everyone here?" he asks. Nobody responds. "Let me take a head count before we work our way up." He looks at his troops staring down toward the docks. "Don't none of you entertain ideas about slipping out to the bars in town tonight. This place is filled with Secesh sympathizers. Lemme tell you what can happen. A few of you go to a bar. A couple of hours later, you're robbed of your money and get into a fight. They summon the Provost, you're arrested, and end up in the guardhouse, formerly used as a slave pen, to sleep it off. Still sound like fun?" The men look around at each other and decide to pass on town.

They start their hike up the hill, past the government bakery to the encampment where they're greeted by Corporal Wingate, who directs them to their tent area. A Sibley tent holds a dozen men, and their battery has three rows of ten tents to house their unit. "The chow line's open for you right now. There's fresh bread to go with your meal; better get yourselves fed and to bed. Reveille will be at 6 a.m. Mess will be ready by the time you get up."

The men toss their packs into their assigned tents and hurry over to get their plate of beans, a cut of salt pork, and large slabs of fresh bread. Robert and his friends find a place near a roaring campfire, not too far from their tents. They acknowledge the men who set up the fire and get the okay to join them.

"I wonder where we're headed tomorrow?" asks Robert.

"It's gotta be something to do with those huge paddle-wheelers tied up along-side the docks in the city," says Will. "I think that's why Welker warned us not to go into town. He thought we might entertain ideas."

"Of course it does," adds one of the men who was there when the three showed up to the campfire. "This whole army will be boarding those ships to head out to who-knows-where. But we're way too many to make it in one big trip. It's gonna be spread out for a while … a long

fifteen thousand

while. You might be right back here tomorrow, and the next day as well."

Price stands, and looks at the rest of the men. "I'm sorry, fellas, but I'm bushed. I'm gonna call it a night."

"Me, too," says Schroeder. Robert follows the two of them to their tent. The others around the campfire follow suit and leave Jim and Will to themselves.

Will looks side-to-side, then over to Jim. "Guess it's just the two of us." He offers his tobacco pouch to Jim, "Wanna smoke?"

"Thanks," Jim says as he grabs the paper and pouch from his friend.

After they light up and enjoy the quiet for a few minutes, Will says, "I'm not happy about being stuck with the teamsters. Why didn't none of you stick up for me ... especially you? I thought we were friends."

Jim throws his hands out to his side. "What do you mean? It's not our call. We're not back in school anymore, choosing up sides for a game. Besides, you'll get on soon enough. I don't think we'll come out of battle untouched. You belong, sure enough. You'll see. Now we get ready to fight, for real."

Shipping Artillery in Alexandria, Virginia

Alfred R. Waud drawing
Harper's Weekly
April 19, 1862

shipping out

Tuesday, 25 March 1862

Welker spreads the word that their crew has gotten its departure orders.

"It's about time we're getting outta here. I'm sick to death of trying to get some sleep in these cold tents," Ramsey grouses to no one and everyone.

As the group makes their way down the hill, Will comes running up. "Whatdaya think, fellas? I hear the lot of us are going to Fort Monroe."

"Where'd ya' hear that?" asks Price.

"I saw one of the guys on his way back to camp from town, and asked if he heard anything. He said one of the ship's crewmen told him. It seems pretty reliable to me."

"Yeah, I can believe it," says Robert.

"Sounds like a real hullabaloo down by the dock area with bands and everything," says Will.

BAH-ROOM!

He jumps at the round of cannon fire coming from the river——a salute to the departing ships. "What's that? We under attack? Should we seek cover?"

"Probably just shot someone who wasn't supposed to be there," says Robert.

***

Jim, Will, and Robert are initially tasked with feeding the horses, and harnessing them, then on to the artillery park to hitch up their vehicles. To reduce the confusion when reclaiming them, each wagon is clearly identified with large white letters painted on the sides. The rest of the men are split between cleaning the stables and reporting to the docks to assist in loading. As Robert's crew approaches, they are signaled by Welker to hold fast next to the stables.

Will's head moves from one sight to the next. "Kinda exciting, isn't it fellas? Seems like they got a good plan in place. Wonder if they'll be having us load at the dock up ahead, or maybe a different kinda ship? What ship do you think we'll be using? Never worked on a ship before."

"Take a breath," says Jim. "I doubt it'll be long before your questions are answered."

Welker finally signals approval for the crews to take their charges into the city. The train of horse-drawn artillery slowly makes its way down to the wharves. The closer they get to the docks, the louder the noise. It's as festive as Will anticipated. Each pier a bustle of activity, infantry troops march in formation, rifles shouldered, while bands play martial music, and crowds of onlookers jostle to get closer to the activity, but wisely stay out of the way.

Filled with a large assortment of ships, steamers, schooners, and barges, the river sightings are occasionally interrupted by passing gunboats, security escorts for the flotilla's trip down the river.

The leaders of the battery greet the men as they arrive dockside at the foot of King Street. A large paddle wheeler, tied up alongside the pier, waits to be loaded. Long ramps are in position to give crews a smooth-graded transition from the road to the dock, then onboard the ship. The men manning the cranes await their role in the process.

Robert's men hold the horses in place while Will and his crew free them from their harnesses. Once inside the hold, Robert needs a moment to acclimate to the lower light, then marvels at the efficient use of space.

By the time he reports back on deck, the loading process has begun. Will's team stows the tools of the gun crews, then eight men push and pull each cannon up the ramp; four men lift and pull the stock-trail, one at each of the two wheels helps their rotation, and two push the rear.

Once the gun reaches a set spot on the dock, two men grab the looped ropes lowered from the block and tackle assembly. They are laid flat and spread into oblong circles to center under the cannon's wheels. The Loadmaster signals the crew to slowly hoist the lift lines until they are nearly taut on the gun's axle. After the wheels clear the deck, and a final inspection is made, the signal to hoist the twenty-three hundred pound load sends it aloft, then swings around to a gentle landing in the storage hold. The process repeats for each remaining gun.

The men overlap and nestle the cannon into single lines, making the maximum use of the available space. The fifteen hundred pound limbers are next. The caissons are followed by the traveling forge, then the battery wagons filled with forage, and finally the covered wagons.

It's late in the day before the men are ordered aboard. Once the ship casts off, the crowds cheer and wave, the bands continue to play, and naval guns fire a salute. They are officially underway.

Robert realizes the stables aren't the only areas of the ship that smell. He feels the need to clear his head and tries to find an unoccupied vantage along the rail. He's enjoying the relative solitude, but the neighing of the horses grab his attention. He decides to go below and check on them, then call it a night.

* * *

It's mid-afternoon of the next day before Fort Monroe comes into view. Robert stands on the foredeck of the ship, pleased to catch the familiar sight of the massive fortress again. It isn't the only sight that grabs his attention. Scores of ships, transports, and boats are anchored in the surrounding waters. His is only one of nearly four hundred pressed into duty to facilitate the movement. Ships that haven't unloaded are riding low, close to the waterline; the rest steam back for their next load.

Only two of the docks are large enough to off-load ships the size of Robert's, which take much longer. Even though they cast off as soon as they are done, another takes its place. There's a waiting list, and a pecking order. Robert's ship has to wait at anchor, which pleases no one.

Jim takes a place on the rail alongside Robert. "Found you at last. We're wondering where you roam off to. Thought maybe you took an early morning dip."

Robert smiles and shivers at the thought. "I'm glad you're here." He points out the passing gunboats. "It looks like we've got good protection." But an odd sight catches his attention. He points to the low-lying vessel off to their left. "Ever see one of those?"

Jim leans over to look at what's caught his eye. "That's gotta be the *Monitor* we heard about, the Union's armored vessel that recently took on the *Merrimack*. I didn't expect to see that here."

"I'm curious how it stays afloat. It looks so low in the water, like one heavy wave could sink it."

"Guess it's just good naval engineering at work."

Robert and Jim aren't the only two taking notice of the oddity. As word spreads, men fueled with low-grade whiskey, line the side rails to catch a glimpse and shout out derisive comments.

Monday, 31 March 1862

Robert stands at the railing as the ship pulls alongside the dock. The men were warned to stay out of the way until it's their turn to unload. Jim and Will join him there.

"Welker said he'd come get us when the time comes," says Jim.

"Can you believe how slippery these decks are?" Will looks back at the passageways. "There's at least two inches of snow on 'em."

"Best be careful there, Will," laughs Robert. "Wouldn't want to see you take an icy bath too early this morning."

Corporal Wingate joins the group. "What's the word, Corporal?" asks Robert.

"The sergeant sent me up here to let you know as soon as the infantry disembarks, it's our turn to unload." As he speaks, the troops are forming on the dock, then marching along the sandy shoreline to stack arms.

Welker yells at the men from dockside. "Are you four going to just stand there? We've got work to do."

shipping out

Robert's battery assembles their wagons and start the trek along a two hundred and seven-foot long pontoon bridge spanning the mill pond to the shores of the Peninsula.

Welker briefs them before getting underway. "We're headed to that large tract of farmland where the tents are concentrated along the shoreline."

"I don't remember this going through basic," says Will.

"The army "appropriated" it from the Segar family last May, and designated it Camp Hamilton," says Welker. "There are six long stables for the horses, but I doubt there'll be room for ours. Best to let them graze in the fields. We'll be heading out in a few days."

The men lead their horses to the pasture. After driving a sturdy stake into the ground and uncoiling its long line, the horses are individually tethered to keep them from roaming. Training days are over. Richmond awaits.

General headquarters near Yorktown, Virginia, April 1862

William McIlvaine watercolor
U.S. National Archives
559420

camp winfield scott

Friday, 4 April 1862

Lieutenant Turnbull addresses his troops. "General McClellan has issued orders to advance to Yorktown as part of Colonel Hunt's Artillery Reserve. We will pass through Hampton, toward Newport News, then north up the Peninsula. The general's staff will be behind our artillery train. There will be close to a hundred cannon with us, and you should expect delays."

Hickman can't contain his excitement. "Hey, fellas ... the bands are playing music, the flags are unfurled ... it's like we're in a parade, on our way to war." He stands in his saddle as they pass by the commanding general, lifts his hat in homage, and thrilled when the diminutive McClellan smiles at the gesture.

Sunny skies, and unseasonable warmth help dry the rain-soaked roads, but Ramsey finds it difficult to control the wagon. He takes a look at the landscape, and says, "The rains did a number on these roads. I doubt they can stand up to this kind of traffic." He's validated as their column proceeds in fits and starts.

They pass by the burned out remnants of Hampton—made uninhabitable by the Southerners when they got wind of the plans to turn the town into homes for contraband—runaway slaves who seek Union protection at Fort Monroe.

Progress is furthered slowed by inaccurate or incomplete maps, and skirmishes with Rebel pickets at the Warwick river. Halfway into their nineteen mile journey, the movement finally halts for the night—a night inundated with heavy squalls.

* * *

The next day, in heavy rains, they reach the turn just south of the river, and head west toward their immediate destination, Camp Winfield Scott.

"This place is massive," exclaims Will as the encampment comes into view. As they draw closer, they are greeted by a sea of pup tents needed to handle the hundred thousand or more men of McClellan's army. The camps are segregated by regiments, brigades, and companies. The commanders are housed in larger tents, as per their rank, identifiable by their unfurled standards on makeshift flagpoles.

Spaces are designated for the vast quantities of ammunition, food, medical supplies, and the train of wagons needed for transport when on the move. There is plenty of acreage for the livestock to graze, and stables are assembled close by.

"Welcome to Camp Winfield Scott," says Welker. He points toward the west, and continues, "We will set up on the grounds immediately south of the commanding general's. As it's heavily patrolled by Union gunboats, we should be relatively safe."

* * *

McClellan intends to drive the Confederates out of their stronghold at Yorktown, in hopes of opening a clear path to Richmond, but the Rebels successfully use deception and cunning to make him believe they have far greater numbers. Despite a two-to-one advantage in manpower, McClellan is convinced he is left with one recourse, to lay siege to Yorktown. He knows the tactics. He'd been to the Crimea to observe and study the year-long siege of Sevastopol. Considered an expert in the field, he now has a chance to prove it.

That necessitates bringing up the heavy guns, a hundred and eleven from Fortress Monroe. Guns that dwarf his mobile light artillery by tonnage and destructive capability. Guns that require the building of heavy-duty roads to transport, and works to accommodate them. Guns that give him the firepower to drive the Confederates out of what, in reality, is an empty fort.

The Confederates keep the Union men looking over their collective shoulders with occasional well-place shots from snipers, and a new weapon they buried around their works——rudimentary land mines, triggered by stepping on a firing pin, which results in grievous losses. Once the Federals figure out how to root them out, Rebel prisoners are pressed into service to find these "torpedoes".

As a result, the Army of the Potomac languishes south of Yorktown for a month.

Tuesday, 8 April 1862
Camp Winfield Scott

Robert buttons up warmly for his trek to the stables. Heavy downpours of rain and sleet are exacerbated by heavy winds and frigid temperatures, a challenge even for those used to severe winters. Once there, he removes his coat, and lays it over the stall's partition. He gratefully receives Jim's offer of hot coffee, then gets to work shoveling out his area. After spreading fresh straw, Robert draws two buckets of grain for the troughs.

As he nears the the pack mules, one of the new recruits, Hollis, runs in. "You guys hear? We've got orders to move out!" Robert sets the buckets down to listen.

"Say again?" asks Jim. It isn't the first time Hollis has shared a "can't miss" bit of news that didn't pan out.

"I heard the general——"

Robert figures it isn't worth the time and bends down to pick up the buckets. He bumps into the rear of one of the mules curious about the feed. With one quick motion, the mule catches Robert under the sternum. Both buckets of grain spill as he lets out a loud "Oof!" and collapses to the floor. He curls into a fetal position, and desperately gasps to catch his breath. Within seconds he passes out.

Will runs over to Robert. With his background at his family's dairy farm, it's not his first exposure to someone laid out by livestock. He rolls him over to check his breathing, then yells to Hollis to get the sergeant. Hollis runs out of the stables, slips and falls sideways in the mud, but rebounds quickly, and awkwardly continues to the sergeants' tent area. Will unbuttons Robert's shirt and the top part of his pants. By the time Hollis returns with Sergeant Welker, Robert starts to regain his senses. Welker tries to get him to speak, but the most he can elicit is a pained groan. Welker unbuttons the rest of his shirt, then the front of his long johns. His abdomen already shows signs of internal bleeding.

"Hollis, go to the musicians' area and get two of them to hitch up a wagon with blankets and a stretcher. We need to get this man to the hospital," says Welker. A wagon parks outside the stable. Will and Welker load him onto the back then climb aboard.

* * *

Robert opens his eyes to find several men around his cot. He looks around to Lieutenant Turnbull then fixes on Sergeant Major Lawton. "What happened? Where am I?" He starts to sit up but the severe pain pulls him back to the cot.

"You're in the hospital. Apparently you picked a fight with one of the mules ... and lost."

Robert grins weakly, "Oh, yeah. I remember." He looks around at his surroundings. There are several cots set in two rows. Some with maimed survivors of the Confederate's booby traps. "How long——?"

"'Til you're better," answers Welker.

"You've been out goin' on a day," says Lawton. "You took a pretty hard blow. It's best you listen to the doctors and do what they tell you. We need you back with the company." Robert nods. Lawton looks to the rest of the group. "Let him get some rest." The men say good-bye and wish him the best as they file out. Jim and Will lag behind.

"You scared us," says Jim.

"We weren't sure if you'd pull through," adds Will. Jim swats him on the shoulder. "What?"

"Don't say things like that. It doesn't help."

A little embarrassed, Will looks back at Robert. "You sure missed a show yesterday."

Robert tries to prop himself up by his elbows, but falls back to his pillow with a grimace. "Why? What happened yesterday?"

"You remember that Loeb fellow with the observation balloon?"

"Sure."

"Well, a little before noon, he starts to inflate it to take flight," Will explains.

Jim says, "Thousands of men from around the camp poured out to see it."

Will takes over. "It took close to three hours to inflate it, but the funniest thing ... the balloon has a likeness of General McClellan painted on the side, which stared out at us as it filled up. He just kept getting bigger and bigger."

"The Rebs must have gotten a kick out of that," says Robert. "How far did it go?"

"Not very," answers Jim. "There were three men in the basket, held by two ropes, each controlled by scores of troops. We offered to help them, but they declined. They were from the Fourth Maine Infantry, and claimed they were specially trained to manage the lines. We took the hint and stayed out of their way."

"Yeah, they said it rose to nine hundred feet. Imagine that ... nine hundred feet," marvels Will. "They're up there for close to three hours. You sure missed it, Robert."

Jim swats him again. "Come on. I think it's time we let Robert get his rest."

Will rubs his arm and says to Robert, "Hope you're back soon." He turns to Jim, "Why did you keep hitting me?"

"I thought we had an understanding about you thinking before ..."

Robert smiles as his two friends pass out of earshot."

* * *

Federal observation balloon, *Intrepid*, being inflated, Fair Oaks, Virginia, May 1862
Alexander Gardner photograph
U.S. National Archives
111-B-680

The weather continues to warm as the days progress. The doctors keep a close eye on Robert as he slowly heals and starts to move on his own beyond the confines of his bed and the hospital tent. He has a steady parade of visitors from his battery as time allows them away from their duties.

Sergeant Welker and Corporal Wingate catch Robert alone, sitting on the edge of his bed. "Afternoon, Robert. How do you feel today?" asks Welker.

"Ready to get out of this place, that's for sure."

"Lieutenant Turnbull spoke with your doctor after he saw you last night. Wanted to get an update on your condition."

Robert looks at the sergeant skeptically. "Well, what did he find out?"

Welker reluctantly tells Robert, "You'll be placed on light duty for the foreseeable future. We moved Will into the rotation, and you are restricted until your injury heals."

Robert holds his left arm tight against his midriff as he slowly rises from the bed. "I'm pretty much healed already. I can do the job."

Welker lightly shoves his shoulder, and Robert groans as he stumbles back onto his bed. "I don't think you can."

"What did you do that for?" He holds his stomach as he struggles to get back up.

"I know that your heart's in it, but I need a capable body, and right now you're not. There's no shame in this. You'll be back on the line soon enough. Anything you need, or we can get for you?"

"Just out of here … but thanks anyway." The two NCOs leave him to his thoughts. Robert hasn't written his family since the incident. He gets a sheet of paper and envelope. He knows his mother will appreciate hearing he won't be in battle anytime soon.

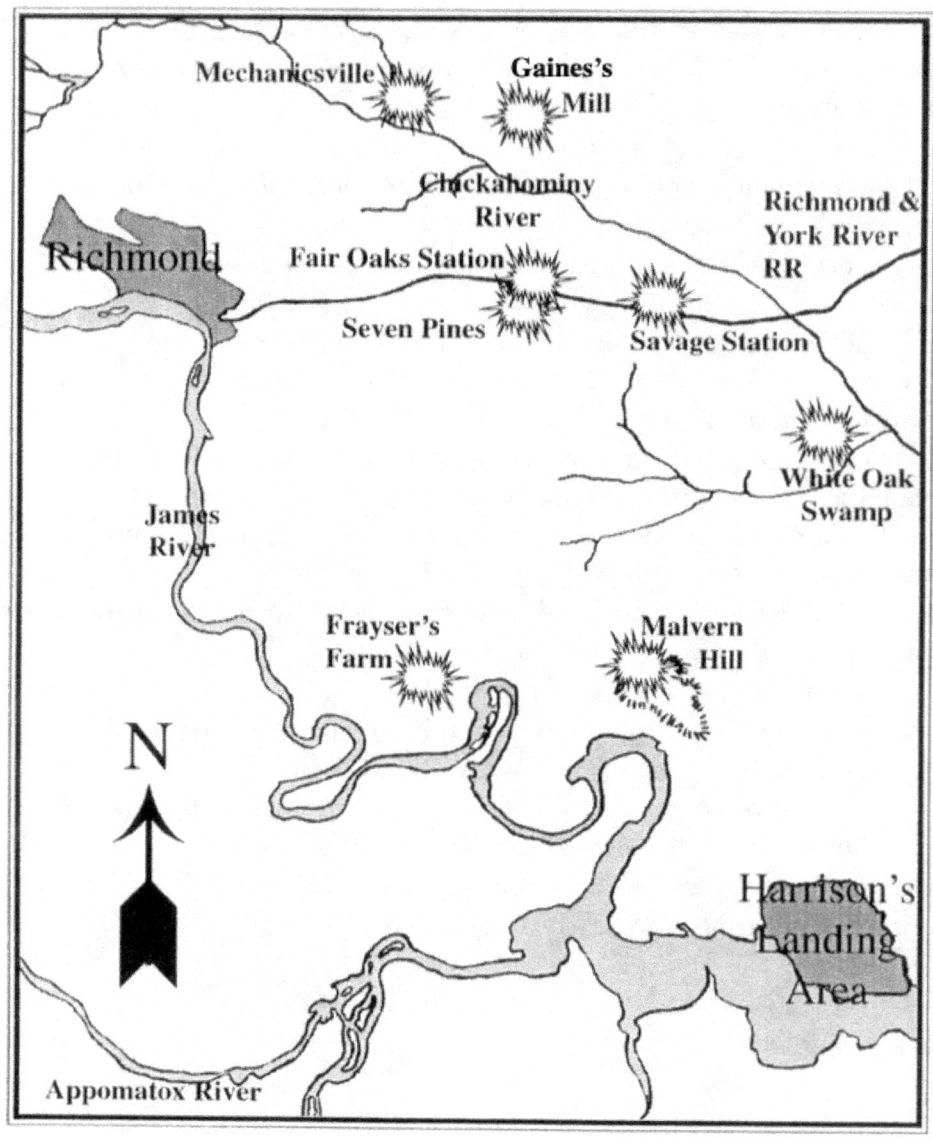

Seven Days Before Richmond Battles

on to richmond

Saturday, 31 May 1862

"Time to pack your things," Sergeant Davenport says to Robert. "General McClellan has called for reinforcements, and you're part of the movement."

"Excellent. Who will I report to?"

"Your regular command. The closer they get to the Confederate capital, the more the general wants to beef up his lines."

"It's about time. Any movement forward is better than being stuck in camp. We already missed out on Williamsburg."

"Better grab lunch and report back within the hour. We've got much to do before departure, then a couple of days ride ahead of us. You'll be driving one of the forage wagons."

He's placed near the tail-end of the large assembly as they start the trek toward Richmond. The rain-soaked roads are a quagmire, and negotiating them is slow and difficult. They only cover half the distance before darkness forces them to make camp.

* * *

The entire movement resumes early the next day. Unknown to them, the army has re-engaged the Rebels at Fair Oaks Station, now on day two of the battle. They are still several miles away, but don't know exactly where or how far, so the officer in charge of the movement sends a courier on horseback to locate them.

Once they reach the encampment, Robert secures the wagon and horses, and gets directions to his outfit. When he walks into the gathering around the campfire, he's enthusiastically greeted by his old friends.

"Hello, fellas," Robert says as he throws down his pack. "Been sightseeing?"

Jim responds. "While you've been malingering, we got to face hostile forces, *and* lob a few shells their way."

"How close are we to Richmond?" Robert asks.

Price answers, "I heard its nine miles due west of us. If you listen real quiet, you can hear the hourly bells from the city's clock tower."

Thursday, 26 June 1862

General Fitz John Porter's Fifth Corps holds the foremost position of the Army of the Potomac, at Mechanicsville, six and a half miles southeast of Richmond. Robert's battery is part of the Artillery Reserve.

He's been assigned steady duty in the stables when Sergeant Welker checks in on him. "How's your recovery going, Robert?"

"I'm shoveling shit with the best of them."

"You and the horses getting along any better?"

"The horses and I are just fine. It's those blessed pack mules I need to watch out for. How's Will working out with the team?"

"Are you're asking if there's an open spot yet?"

Robert looks down and lightly kicks at some of the spilled grain. "I guess."

"We'll be in more action once Richmond realizes the threat. Odds are there will be a place with the crew open up before you know it. Once there——"

"We've already been here three and a half weeks. What's the general waiting for?"

"Be patient. We hear Confederate General Johnston suffered a pretty grievous wound in the last battle and been pulled off the line."

"What's that mean for us?"

"He's been replaced by another General … Robert E. Lee." Welker continues, "I remember him from Mexico, General Winfield Scott's fair-haired boy, one of the few officers the commanding general depended on. Lee started as a captain, and was eventually promoted to colonel before the whole thing was over with. I hear he's been working with their President Davis as an advisor. I also hear he's not too popular with the troops. Some of them southern boys are callin' him 'Granny Lee'."

"Granny Lee?" Robert smirks. "Doesn't sound like much of a threat."

* * *

The east bank of Beaverdam Creek rises up a slope to a crest with a great view of the plain. Porter's troops are positioned in a defensive posture throughout the plateau with pickets extended forward. Thirty-six guns from General McCall's Brigade are situated along the crest where he directs their placement. The infantry is entrenched on good ground.

No orders are issued for the Artillery Reserve, which means Robert's crew must wait and watch. Not knowing when and where they'll be engaged works on the nerves of some of the men.

The distant sound of musket fire from the pickets puts everyone on alert. A little after 3:00 p.m., a horse gallops to a stop at the general's post. The rider rapidly dismounts, hands the reins to the guard, and enters Porter's quarters. Within thirty minutes, a single cannon shot serves as a pre-arranged signal to Porter that the Confederates are crossing the Chickahominy river and on the move. The messenger remounts and gallops off. Several officers emerge. Most move off to the north, where the bulk of Porter's forces are deployed.

Lieutenant Turnbull approaches his men. "You've talked a lot about getting into the fray. Well, General Porter has just received the signal from his picket lines. The Rebs are on their way. At present, we are to hold fast. You teamsters get the horses harnessed, and the rest of you ready your guns and wagons for deployment.

When Confederate forces advance into view around 5:00 p.m., Union cannon, along the crest, open up with deadly accuracy. Robert steadies his mount as the report from the first volley reaches them. Will looks side-to-side, and stands high in his saddle to get a better view. The only thing he can see is the smoke as it rises from the field.

Musket fire from both sides of the line erupts, accompanied by thunderous fire from the batteries. Another sound starts to rise above the gunfire——yells——reckless, high-pitched yowls unlike anything any of the men ever heard before. "What's that?" Will yells to the others.

"Relax, Will," responds Jim calmly. "It's just the Rebels making a whole lot of noise. No one's getting hurt from it."

It's apparent to everyone in the gun crew that he's losing his calm. "Take it easy, Will," Robert says as he reaches over to steady him.

Will swats his hand away hard. "Leave me alone!"

Sergeant Welker slowly rides alongside Will's horse. He reaches over to take the bridle from his hand. "Listen, Will. There's nothing to worry about." He points toward the field of fire, and adds, "Our men have the advantage." The sounds of the cannon's discharges change as the loads switch from shell to canister. "Right now a lot of Rebs are meeting their maker. They can't advance against concentrated canister fire like that."

Will is wide-eyed, his head turns from Welker to the sound of the guns and back. "How do you know that?"

"Because we're still here … in reserve. If the general thought things were out of control, we'd be moved into position. In the meantime, just relax. If we *do* get the call, you'll know what to do." The sergeant's calm settles Will back down. Welker hands the bridle back to him and slowly rides away.

As Will's adrenalin levels start to subside, he finds himself fighting fatigue. He shakes his head hard, and wrestles with the strap to move his canteen around to take a drink. He pours a little bit into a cupped hand to rinse his face.

He turns to Robert apologetically. "Sorry. I'm doing better now." Robert nods his acceptance, but keeps his eyes focused on the battle.

The reserves hold their stations throughout the evening. The gunfire lessens as darkness settles in. The diminishing sounds of the fight are replaced by groans and petitions of the wounded. The Union's guns exacted a terrible toll.

Turnbull makes his way to headquarters. An hour and a half later, he returns. "We've been issued orders to move back to our second line of defense."

"Where to, Lieutenant?" Price asks.

"About six miles east of here."

"East? Why are we withdrawing? Today considered a loss?" asks Ramsey.

"Decidedly not. General Porter has received new orders from the commanding general."

Robert stays with his harnessed team, and hears Will questioning the sergeant as they walk away. "I don't get it. If we won …"

gaines's mill

~~~

Friday, 27 June, 1862

In the early morning hours, Robert's battery arrives at the Watt House, a little over a mile southeast of Gaines's Mill. General Porter has requisitioned the small white clapboard building for his headquarters.

Boatswain's Creek runs east to west, then curls south of the Chickahominy. The Union forces establish a position on the crescent-shaped plateau atop the steep slope that faces west and north and overlooks the creek. This time Porter places eighty guns along the plateau.

At its crest, the Reserve Artillery is part of the third line of defense, seventeen batteries comprised of ninety-six guns in a line two miles long.

Sergeant Welker advises his men to grab some food and sleep while they can. He doesn't believe the day will be without uninvited company. Their rubber blankets are thrown on the ground and the men cover themselves with their overcoats.

Awakened a couple of hours later, most only need to put on their shoes, throw some water on their face, and fill their canteens with coffee. The men are tasked with preparing the ground fortifications. Robert's assigned to a group of men building abatis—trees are felled, their branches are sharpened to fine points, then turned outward—formidable opposition to advancing ground forces. Others in the battery help the infantry dig rifle pits; they are happy to contribute. By noon it's back to waiting.

The temperatures are warmer than the previous day, and the fight much hotter. By 2:30 p.m., the Confederate artillery provides cover fire for their troops as they advance. The Union responds with eighty guns firing in tandem. The cannonade resonates throughout the entire battlefield with a terrible, bone-jarring concussion.

Sergeant Welker stands next to the lead wagon of his battery to get a clearer view of the battle through his field glasses. The lines waver back and forth, charges and counter-charges.

"What's going on over there, Sergeant?" asks Will, starting to lose his nerve again. Welker lets the glasses drop to his chest, takes a deep breath, followed by a long sigh. He retrieves the cold remains of a cigar from his jacket pocket and lights it up. "Sergeant?"

He tries to formulate an answer to Will's question, without causing him further anxiety. "It looks like the Rebels are putting up a much stronger fight today than yesterday. But our boys, our *men* are holding their own."

"What do you propose to do about that, Sergeant?"

Annoyed, Welker ignores the question, retrieves his field glasses, and resumes monitoring the action.

Along the entire line the Confederates continue to progress up the slope, forward a bit, then back, then forward some more, throughout the afternoon and into the evening.

After an extended lull, the Confederates launch their fourth assault, and break through to the left of the Union center, directly in front of the Watt House. They are met by Union artillery lined up wheel-to-wheel. Double-canister fire blasts away, but rather than flee, the Rebels rapidly regroup and continue their advance.

Welker clearly sees some of the gun crews involved in a life-or-death struggle with Confederates wielding bayonets. The implements of the artillery——ramrods, handspikes, and sponge staffs are no match for bayonets and bullets in hand-to-hand combat. The sounds from the front are horrifying——the Rebel yell, ceaseless infantry fire, and shrieks of men run through with cold steel. The cannoneers try their best to limber up and escape, but the vast majority of their horses are either dead or maimed. A bugle call signals the Union cavalry to charge through the artillery line and into the fray with sabers slashing. The Confederates counter the charge with infantry fire, and decimate the ranks. The Rebels press forward and capture fourteen of the eighteen cannon.

The onset of darkness, and the arrival of two Union regiments bring about the end of the battle. Horrific casualties are suffered on both sides. Even though McClellan's army inflicts more damage in overall numbers, the Federals are ordered to withdraw from the field.

Lieutenant Turnbull gallops over to Welker and issues the order to join the artillery train as it rolls out. Robert's crew follows the exodus southeast. When the movement halts for the night, everyone disperses to find a place to grab some food, hot liquid, and rest.

Robert sits near the campfire by himself, with a mug of coffee, not tasting any of it. His thoughts are filled with how terrible the battle seemed. Even though his crew did not participate, he watched in horror as the two sides fought it out. *The artillery wasn't the "Long Arm of the Army" today. No guns throwing shells a mile away at a faceless enemy. That was up close ... personal ... deadly.*

Robert smells the cigar before his visitor gets within view.

"Evening, Robert."

"Sergeant," he says without looking up from his cup.

Welker exhales a large cloud of smoke. "I imagine that was a bit more than you expected."

Robert makes eye contact. "I'm still trying to sort through it."

"Changed your opinion of 'Granny Lee'?"

"Where the *hell* did they ever come up with that name?"

Welker shakes his head.

"What's next?" asks Robert.

"The lieutenant told me McClellan's convened a council with the commanders of the five corps tonight. I'm sure we'll hear the results before the morning's out."

Ramsey wanders over to them with his own mug of coffee. "Am I interrupting anything?"

Robert gestures for him to sit on the log next to him.

He does and says, "Nobody ever told us about fighting like that."

"Yeah," sighs Robert.

"Those Secesh are a mighty scrappy bunch," Jim adds. "Sergeant, how do you think Will's going to handle actual battle? I mean, he's thoroughly frightened, and we weren't even engaged."

"Can't say until we see him up against the enemy for real, not just watching from a distance."

"But——"

Welker cuts him off, "You'd be surprised. Young Will let his imagination get the best of him these last couple of days. It even rattled me just watching the spectacle today. As far as Will goes, well, we'll see how he does when it's our turn. Then we can draw the true measure of him."

"I guess, but what if he panics … what if he runs?" asks Jim.

"Look, any of us might panic when the time comes. We need to concentrate on our duty, and our training to get through these challenges. I take it he's out of earshot?"

"He's back in the tent, sound asleep."

Welker and Jim continue their talk while Robert retreats into his own thoughts. *How will I handle it when the time comes?* He eventually nods off where he sits.

changing bases

∞

Saturday, 28 June 1862
Savage's Station, Virginia

Ramsey shakes Robert's shoulder. "Let's go, Robert. We're on the move."

"Why?" Robert tries to shake off his few hours of sleep. He's stiff, heavily congested, and a bit off-balance when he stands. "What's up?"

"Word is circulating that the command will continue its move down the Peninsula."

It's before dawn, and Robert is still disoriented. "Yeah … sure … okay." He takes a gulp of his leftover coffee, and immediately spits out the cold, bitter drink. There's a pot on the fire, so he helps himself.

The wagons are hitched up and the men have gathered. Lieutenant Turnbull motions for everyone to draw closer. "The commanding general is 'changing bases' and having the supplies rerouted down the James river to a new location. He's already made arrangements to ship all that he can from his base at White House Landing, and burn what's left. Once we're relocated, we'll be under the protection of Union gunboats and await reinforcements from Washington." The men are left confused by the orders.

Jim sidles up to Robert, looks to see if anyone watches, then says, "They can call it a 'change of base', but if you ask me it's a retreat, plain and simple."

Robert whispers, "I think it's best you keep that to yourself."

Two corps and the Artillery Reserve are ordered to continue as the wagon train travels east on the Williamsburg Road. Three corps stay behind as a rear guard.

* * *

Robert and Jim sit astride the lead mounts of their gun carriage, now part of the general movement south, away from Richmond, away from the train depot at Savage's Station, but still in danger from the pursuit of the Rebels. Despite the heavy involvement of the batteries, General Porter continues to hold back the Artillery Reserve, much to the frustration of the men who want to get into battle, and to the relief of those who don't.

The day starts out warm, muggy, and heavily overcast. While they continue south, they can clearly hear the fire of artillery and muskets north of their position. At 4:30 p.m., the skies open up, and the men wrap up as best they can in their rubber blankets and continue on. Jim says to Robert, "Sounds like the rear guard has their hands full."

Hickman, who is on the mount in back of Jim, yells to Turnbull when he pulls alongside Ramsey's mount. "Hey, Lieutenant, you think we'll ever get a chance to fight them Rebs?"

"I'm sure of it. Just when, I can't say. That's up to the generals."

"Which of them do we answer to now?"

"All of them ... of course." Turnbull smiles as he spurs ahead to the next gun carriage.

* * *

The horses are put out to forage, and Robert wants to walk off the day's ride. "I'm a bit saddle-sore, Jim. Any desire to take the long way back to camp?"

"Sure. Let me see if Will wants to come along."

Hickman yawns as he catches up with the two of them. "Not tonight, fellas. I'm beat."

They part company and Jim begins, "Did you ever think we'd fight a war like this?"

"If you call this retreat a 'fight'."

"You mean 'change of base'."

"Take your pick. Watching them at Gaines's Mill scared the wits out of me, but to just sit there and then retreat is not what I thought we'd be doing."

"Yeah, I just don't get this being held in reserve. They sure needed us the other day when the Rebs broke through the lines."

From off to the right a loud guffaw catches their attention. Jim elbows Robert. "Wanna see what's going on over there? I'll bet they've got some coffee brewed up. Maybe they'd be willing to share some."

As they approach the campfire, they find five men gathered in a semicircle, who seem to compete with each other to see who can tell the funniest story. By the firelight, Jim can make out the red pin-striping of the artillery. He interrupts them. "Evening, fellas."

The men look up at the approaching strangers. "Evening yourself," says the oldest of the group. "Who you boys with?"

"Battery F, Third U.S.," answers Robert. "How about you?"

"First Rhode Island Light."

"Isn't that Captain Reynolds outfit?"

"How'd you know that?" asks the man closest to them, without looking up from the fire.

"He was one of our instructors at Fort Monroe. Good man."

"I agree. We're lucky to have him," answers the oldest.

Jim points to the man's mug. "Any chance we can share in some of that coffee?"

He looks over to the oldest who nods. "There are some mugs over by the pot. Help yourselves."

The two extend their appreciation, then join the conversation. Robert says, "We heard your laughter. That's what drew us here."

The oldest chuckles, then says, "We're just discussing the fate of General Reynolds." Laughter circulates around the group.

Jim asks, "Why? What happened to him?"

The men try to suppress their laughter as he retells the story. "Well, the general slept through his unit moving out, and no one," he chuckles, "no one from his staff took the trouble to wake him up. I guess that everyone thought someone else'd do it." He gets more animated as he retells the story. "Well … when the Rebels show up … where's the general? He's sound asleep." Everyone loses it and the guffaws start over.

"What do you think will happen to him?" asks Robert.

The oldest takes a more serious tone. "I imagine a few heads will roll when he's paroled. I think the Rebs will have their fun with him, make some noise in the press, and get a juicy exchange when the time comes. He'll be back. He'll be embarrassed, but he'll be back in the fold before too long. He's too valuable."

The one closest to the fire, a corporal, speaks up, "Weren't you fellas on the road today?"

"That's right," answers Jim.

The one who stands next to the oldest asks, "And you fellas ain't seen much action this week. Have ya'?"

"Right again."

"Why's that?"

Robert points back and forth between Jim and himself. "We've been asking ourselves that very same question. Think we'd been of some use, but the general wants to save us for something later I guess."

"Well, you missed a humdinger of a show today, ya' did," says the corporal.

"How's that?" asks Jim.

"They held us back as part of the rear guard action at Savage's Station. Guess there weren't that many Rebs available to fight cause they sent some under-manned probes our way. We out-numbered 'em 'n pushed 'em back easily enough."

The oldest of the group picks it up. "I think their general just wanted to show off his newest toy."

"Newest toy?" Jim asks.

"Around five, a bit after the rain started coming down, a locomotive pushed a double-flatbed into the field of fire. They had mounted a banded thirty-two pounder, and surrounded it with armor to protect their gunners. Bales of cotton stacked on the other flatbed provided cover for their sharpshooters. It got rolled into the midst of our troops, fired off some thunderous shots that sent our men into a mad scramble for cover, but did little damage. Then it just pulled back out. Looked like a small gunboat it did. Made a lot of noise, but no bother. Before long we were given orders to move out," he pauses to smile. "But not before we put on a show ourselves."

By this time the oldest lit up a cigar, and the man next to him followed suit. Taking a long draw, he says, "We didn't want to leave our supplies for the Rebs. Once we drew all our ammo stores from the coachhouse that we could carry, we torched it. When the explosion first lit up, everyone stopped to see the show, showers of sparks, somewhat akin to fireworks, the skies aglow with the exploding ordinance and barrels of whiskey."

"That weren't the best part though," interjects the corporal. "We filled a train with explosives, then lit a long fuse and sent it east, with no engineer mind you … along the tracks toward the wrecked bridge, 'bout a mile from the station. Just before it got there, the fireworks filled the sky, followed by the train that plummeted into the river. Why you could see, hear, and feel the explosions all the way to the depot."

"That musta been some sight," says Ramsey. "But what a waste."

"If we can't carry it, we can't leave it for the Rebs. Don't be surprised if you see more displays like this along our way south."

"Too much waste, if you ask me," says the man standing next to the oldest. "The troops are exhausted, and they can't lay down to rest else Johnny Reb'll get 'em. They started to shuck their outerwear—jackets, then their backpacks—sides of the road all lined in blue."

Robert glances over at Jim.

His demeanor and the tone of his voice lessen. "The men weren't the only ones exhausted. Some of the horses and mules started to stagger under their loads. Couldn't take another step forward. They just unhitched 'em and left 'em by the roadside." He hesitates for a long time. "Then the cavalry found 'em. Can't leave 'em for the Rebs to rehabilitate, so they destroyed 'em."

Robert drops his head, thinking of how precious their teams are to the gun crews.

"Worst part's about the wounded, though," says the oldest.

"What do you mean?"

"They left 'em. Told those able to walk to get to it, but the rest they left to fend for themselves. Some of our doctors and stewards volunteered to stay with 'em. Upwards of two thousand, I hear."

"More than that," adds the oldest.

"Lord," exclaims Robert.

"The curious thing about it," says the corporal, his voice elevates as he continues, "Well, they got over five hundred ambulance wagons they sent ahead ... *empty!*"

"Why empty?" asks Robert. "That makes no sense."

"I guess to save 'em for future fightin'. They didn't want 'em slowing us down. Figures the Rebs'd take good enough care of 'em."

"You believe that?" asks Jim.

"Not on your life. Neither did they," the oldest says as he tosses the remnants from his mug. He puts on his jacket and moves over to the fire pit. Once he steps closer to the light, the two notice that he's a sergeant major. He tops off his mug, then looks at the two visitors. "What do you two think of our 'great skedaddle'?"

Robert's taken aback by the question from the senior sergeant. The two of them look closely at the rest of men. They realize they've stumbled into a gathering of NCOs.

Intimidated, Robert points to his empty sleeves. "I don't know about such things, Sergeant. I'm just a private." Everyone laughs and waves him off, except the oldest.

"Did you men ever hear of a private without an opinion?" he asks.

"That'd be a first," adds the corporal. Their laughter gains momentum. "Never did hear of a private who didn't hold an opinion 'bout ... well, everything." The laughter grows louder.

Robert's embarrassed and flustered. "I think it's best we be getting back." More guffaws. Setting the mugs down by the fire, he adds, "Thank you for the coffee and hospitality."

Robert smiles and turns to leave. As they swiftly escape, they can hear the groups continued laughter. Ramsey says, "They seemed to be in good spirits."

"Wonder what's in their mugs besides coffee."

Henry Jackson Hunt
Brady's National Photographic Portrait Galleries
Library of Congress
Prints and Photograph Division
LC-DIG-cwpb-05876

colonel hunt

Monday, 30 June 1862

As they resume their trek, Robert points out four batteries deployed along the south bank just past White Oak Bridge. Welker stops to take a look through his field glasses. "Looks like men from General Franklin's Fourth Corps."

An explosion to the back of them draws their attention. Framed by the column of black smoke, several officers, including Lieutenant Turnbull, ride at a full gallop to catch up with their batteries. Sergeant Welker pauses until they meet next to Robert's limber. Turnbull slows to a trot as the others continue further ahead. Welker salutes and asks, "Are the Confederates closing?"

"We're still safe. Two divisions of Franklin's Corps are assigned to slow down the Rebs' approach. They just blew the bridge, which'll give us a considerable amount of lead time." As he speaks, a loud peal of thunder comes from their rear.

"Confederate guns." Welker stands tall as he looks back from his saddle. A thunderous report from Franklin's batteries, responds to the Confederates.

Turnbull takes a minute to catch his breath. "I guess the Rebs won't rebuild the bridge under that kind of fire."

"What's our goal today, sir?" Welker asks as they put more distance between them and the fight.

"We're on the way to a rise at a farm called Malvern Hill. Not much further ahead the road splits. Most of the supply train will take the left fork to an area ten miles south called Harrison's Landing. Make sure your crew stays with the group going right. Hopefully someone will be there to point the way." The lieutenant continues, "The commanding general has placed five divisions to defend our movement near a crossroads called Glendale."

* * *

As the Union wagons pass the Charles City Road, Sergeant Welker holds back to meet several men in blue who approach on horseback from the east. The lieutenant joins the discussion.

When Turnbull questions them, the corporal responds. "We are assigned to Slocum's Division, tasked with slowing the Rebel phalanx. We dropped several trees to slow them down a ways back. The trees weren't that big, but instead of just moving them, one of their officers ordered them to cut a pathway through the woods to get around the obstacles. That isn't the best part though. When we noticed what the Rebs did, we cut down more trees." They started to laugh. "We eventually ran out of trees, but them Rebs are still at it … still working their way around 'em, now we're lookin' to rejoin our outfit."

"Good job, men," Turnbull says with a chuckle. "Carry on."

"The Rebs must not be too anxious to meet up with us," Welker says to Turnbull. Artillery fire from the east puts an end to any talk about their lack of will. Robert's battery safely clears Glendale and continues toward Malvern Hill.

About a half mile ahead of the wagons, a Rebel battery unlimbers on their road, and makes ready to fire. Before they can open up, Union shells target them from positions on Malvern Hill, and Federal gunboats on the James river pour down hellfire in the form of hundred-pounder shells, the heavy gunners affectionately call 'lampposts'. The Rebs do all they can to limber up, and flee as fast as their horses can take them.

Robert points to the gunboats and asks Welker, "How did they know where to position their fire with that degree of accuracy? They pounded those Reb guns."

"See that brick farmhouse, right there on the southern part of the hill?"

Robert takes a look. "Yeah, got it."

"Now look up at the roof."

He raises the glasses slightly and sees a signal officer atop the building vigorously waiving two flags.

"He's directing the gunboat fire from atop the building. That's impressive." Robert takes another look, then hands the glasses back to Welker.

Turnbull rides alongside. "We best be getting up there before anyone else shows up."

* * *

The artillery units keep on the road to Malvern Hill, where a colonel directs the placement of incoming batteries. Chief of the Artillery for the Army of the Potomac, forty-two year old Colonel Henry J. Hunt has a small frame, a full, unkempt beard, and speaks with a high-pitched voice. Despite his reputation for having a mind keenly attuned to the use of artillery in the field, he is often subordinated under the command of the generals on site, but not today. The Artillery Reserve will not sit out this battle.

The colonel brings them to halt. The men are allowed to dismount. Colonel Hunt signals the officers and the sergeants to gather around. Robert stays with the horses, but within earshot.

"It's good you men are finally here," says Hunt. "I imagine some of you are anxious to get into battle. Well, I've been getting ribbing and complaints from others about our lack of involvement. That changes today. This field's a perfect place to take a defensive stand." The colonel has established a mile-long line of cannon spanning the crest of the hill, which includes the reserve units. The sloping terrain will allow placement of the infantry without interfering with the artillery's line of fire. He points to the slope to the left bordered by Turkey Run. "That ravine's too steep to allow any kind of assault." He points to the right, where the hill descends to a field of wheat, harvested and sheaved. "The only option open to the Rebs is straight at us from the front ... and gentlemen, we've got the high ground. Make sure your troops are in position and at the ready. Your teamsters need to be on hand to reload the ammunition cases when needed, which I believe they will be throughout the day. Any questions?"

Lieutenant Turnbull says, "General McClellan must be pretty pleased with this placement."

The colonel quietly replies that he has taken leave to move his headquarters to the gunboat, *Galena*, on the nearby James river. General Fitz John Porter holds command on the field.

The colonel notices more guns approaching and is ready to greet them when Turnbull speaks up. "Will we report to you directly?"

"General Porter has deferred the command of the artillery to Brigadier General Griffin. He will be in close contact throughout the day, and I will deal directly through your head, Captain Carlisle. Stay alert. After today, no one will be able to complain about the participation of the Artillery Reserve."

malvern hill

Tuesday, 1 July 1862

Two hundred and fifty Union cannon are in position, their crews doing what they can to brace themselves for the upcoming battle. It's sunny, bright, and heating up. Around 10:30 a.m., the Confederates start to move in the meadow beyond the rise of the hill. Rebel batteries are directed by their commanders where to unlimber and begin fire, without effect. As soon as they do, Union gun crews grab their hand spikes to turn their guns in the direction of the Rebels and fire with shell and case shot.

The Gunners are forced to wait seconds for the blanket of dark smoke to clear, to gauge their effectiveness. With longer range than the Confederates' guns, the accuracy of their fire has its intended effect— to disable the enemy and force them to move. The Rebels who find cover in the fringing woods are met with bursting shells tearing through foliage and men.

Throughout the day, oncoming Rebel infantry are first met by artillery shells. As they draw closer, a combination of Minié balls from the Union infantry, and the shotgun-like spray of lead balls from canister fire, cuts large swaths of devastation through their lines. They close ranks for the next round of fire to repeat its terrible business. With each explosion pieces of men and equipment are flung in every direction. The Rebs pull back to regroup, or find safety behind the cover of trees.

Fire from the Union guns continues to shake the ground with thunderous explosions so intense that the cannoneers can no longer hear verbal commands. The crews look to their Gunners for hand signals, facial expressions, head nods, anything to get the message—"Load" … "Fire" … "Reload". As Rebel infantry progress up the slope, Welker yells to the men at the limber to change the rounds from shell to canister.

As promised, the ammunition stores in the limbers start to thin out. Robert and other teamsters are signaled forward. They drive the caissons at a full gallop, to rapidly refresh their ammo stores. It's a steady demand that pushes them throughout the afternoon.

The Confederates continue their relentless advance. Some of their troops affix bayonets without stopping to fire, then work their way up the hill toward the batteries. Officers plead with the infantry to drive them off. Some are successful, others are not.

For a small and desperate few, it devolves into hand-to-hand combat. The overrun artillerists try to fight them off with only the guns' implements. Somewhat of a one-sided scramble, the Rebels drive their steel into the bodies of the under-armed men. It's not long before those Rebels are either driven off or killed by infantry answering the call.

Robert resumes his position by the caisson and awaits further orders. Only minutes pass before Lieutenant Turnbull yells as he approaches. "Sergeant Payton's been hit." He points him to the crew immediately to the left of Welker's, and says, "Follow me and see what you can do to help." Robert takes off on a dead run after the lieutenant's horse, and follows the two men who clear the downed NCO from the hub of activity. He's been shot in the groin, his pants soaked in blood. Lieutenant Turnbull assumes the sergeant's role as their Gunner, and directs the crew to resume the sequence.

Payton screams in pain as they carry him over to the side of a nearby building, shaded from the sun and out of the way. Private McCabe from Battery K, sits in the grass and leans against the building, his arm in a makeshift sling from a gunshot wound.

"McCabe isn't it?" asks Robert.

The wounded man gives him a slight nod.

"Has anyone sent for help? This man's in a bad way here."

Robert can barely hear his answer over the din of battle and the groans of the wounded sergeant. He moves closer.

"The musician's off to get stretcher bearers for me," he whispers. "Guess I'll need to wait my turn."

"Good man. I'll send for another as soon as they take the sergeant."

It isn't long before two stretcher bearers arrive. "Looks like you need more help. We'll be back after we get him to the field station."

"How long?" Robert yells.

"Soon," answers the harried private. "It's close by; it won't be long." Payton groans as they move him over to the stretcher, and again as they lift it and rapidly walk off.

Robert looks back to McCabe. "Can I get you anything?"

He leans in to hear his raspy answer. "I'm thirsty."

He looks about. "Where's your canteen?"

"Let me have some of yours." Robert slips the strap off his shoulder. The wounded man drains what he has left. He stays with him until the same crew returns. They load McCabe and hustle back to the aid station.

Robert has to resume his duties on the caisson, but he takes a pause to look around at the different batteries carrying out their duties. Through the deafening roar of the guns, the throbbing ground he stands on, and the thick, engulfing smoke, he comes to fully understands how their incessant drills prepared them for a day such as this. All of them efficiently perform the complicated formula to fire their weapons. It doesn't matter which crew he watches, or what type of cannon they fire, each team's in sync. He stares in awe at how seamlessly Lt. Turnbull fills in for the injured Gunner—just as brave, efficient, and faultless. The rapid *thoop, thoop, thoop* of Confederate Minié balls striking the ground at his feet, reminds Robert he has a job of his own to perform.

***

By 9:00 p.m., ammunition stores and daylight rapidly fade. For another hour, siege guns trace red streaks in the skies marking the paths to their targets. The Rebels seek safety out of sight, in the cover of the woods, while groans of the wounded fill the void left by the diminishing gun fire.

The men's adrenaline and anxiety are replaced by overwhelming exhaustion. Robert, Jim, and Will work their way through it to prepare their carriages to move out. The wounded animals in Robert's battery need to be dealt with first. Two horses too injured to continue, are mercifully dispatched. Two others, though wounded, have a good chance of surviving. They are tied to the back of the wagons to walk back without the pressure of a load.

As they mount the lead horses of the battery's first carriage, Will leans back toward Robert. "I've never been that scared, ever, specially after Sergeant Payton went down. I mean, some of the gun crews fought hand-to-hand ... the Rebs with their bayonets, and what did our men have? Nothing! They were being murdered! I can't believe *you* weren't scared?"

Shaking his head as he speaks, Robert says, "The empty limbers demanded my full attention. There wasn't much time to think about the goings on around me."

"Whooped 'em pretty good, though, didn't we?" says Jim.

"I guess ... but it cost us." Robert puts his hands over his ears and shakes his head, with hopes of expelling the constant ringing. It doesn't work.

As they continue down the hill to the fork in the road, which leads to safety, they pass a small train of wagons headed in the opposite direction. Will yells over to the teamster driving the lead wagon filled with men, "You're too late. The battle's over, fella."

"Yours, maybe, but ours has just begun." He points ahead, and says, "They're the ones that need our help now."

"How ya' gonna see? It's dark out."

He grimly responds, "Don't go frettin' 'bout us. We have enough light."

Jim leans back from his mount to face Will. He signals him to shut his mouth, and move on.

Will looks back to the caregiver, but his wagons have resumed their trek to the battleground. Throughout the night, with lanterns in hand, they scour the grounds for wounded, giving succor where they can.

harrison's landing

Wednesday, 2 July 1862

Located thirty-five miles southeast of Richmond, Harrison's Landing is a five mile long tract on the north shore of the James river, bordered by Herring Creek to the south and Kimages Creek to its north. Its deep-water dock can handle the endless stream of food and supplies required by the army. Gunboats *Mahaska* and *Galena* are part of the armada that protects the fleet of supply ships, and discourages the Confederates from thoughts of launching an attack against McClellan's troops.

Intended to be a place where the Army of the Potomac can rest and recover from the week of non-stop fighting they just endured, Harrison's Landing is less than ideal, with oppressive heat and humidity, poor water quality, swarms of insects, and non-existent sanitation. It's estimated a quarter of the men not hospitalized for battle wounds are sick.

Dr. Letterman, Chief Surgeon of the Army of the Potomac, takes over the Berkeley Mansion from the commanding general, for use as a hospital, instead of his command post. Scores of tents are needed for the overflow of the not-so-urgent cases.

The reserves establish their artillery park near the northwest corner of the camp, not too far from General Hooker's headquarters. Before any serious thought can be given to rest, back-breaking work needs to be done. The men are set to build breastworks of logs and earthworks along the western edge of the camp. Sally ports and redoubts are built into the breastworks and equipped with light artillery to overlook the vulnerable approaches, with abatises that fringe the entire camp.

* * *

Sergeant Welker wants an update from Robert on how the horses injured at Malvern Hill are progressing. The grounds are still wet and spongy from heavy rains, and the footing requires extra attention. Robert is gathering grain to supplement their feed when he catches up with him.

"They seem to be content, Sergeant." He points out a couple of the animals about fifty yards from them. "Those are the wounded ones. They've been treated, and we'll keep a close eye on them." He pauses, then adds, "I guess that all our questions were answered about how Will would handle himself under fire."

"Yeah, I think he surprised the lot of us. He stayed focused, and performed well. That's the other reason I wanted to talk with you. McCabe has already been released back to the company, but his wound will keep him out of action for a while. Private Price will replace McCabe, which leaves an open position for you."

"I appreciate it, thanks. Have you heard anything more about Sergeant Payton?"

"Lieutenant Turnbull and I just left his bedside at the Westover Church. He's under good care," Welker's voice cracks as he tries hard to keep his emotions in check. "But they say his wound is grievous."

"I'm sorry to hear that," Robert says in a soft voice.

"He's been a good friend. We've known him for a long time. He has a wife and two children. It'll be a hard loss."

"It's that serious?"

Welker nods. With a thick throat, he answers, "He lost a lot of blood."

"Sergeant, you've never mentioned *we* before. Do you have a family?"

Welker hesitates, then sighs. "I normally don't talk about them."

Robert senses Welker needs to talk to someone. He looks around at the entire field and says, "You know we're totally alone, and nothing will go beyond this point."

Welker is reluctant to open up, and he takes a long hard look at Robert before he speaks. "Her name was Kristen; her folks immigrated from Sweden. She took my heart the first time I ever laid eyes on her." His tears start to flow freely, and he periodically looks away to wipe them with his sleeve. "We had a boy two years after we married. He looked so much like her, and I adored him. Army life isn't easy on a family, but we kept it together." He breathes deeply to try to settle down. "We were sent to New Orleans a few years before the war. Then yellow fever swept through the city. I lost my boy to it first … Kristen shortly after that." He starts weeping.

Robert's tears flow freely. "I'm so sorry, John."

He clears his throat a few times, wipes his cheeks, and points his thumb toward headquarters. "I guess I best be gettin' back."

Robert nods, puts his hand on his back, then watches him as he walks away, and notices his posture isn't as upright as he's seen in the past.

Tuesday, 8 July 1862

When the President arrives from Washington to confer with McClellan, the gunboats render honors with their cannon. At the signal, the men come to attention and salute, and the bands fill the campground with music. The men wear newly issued uniforms, and white leggings. The cannon are scrubbed and shine like new. The men are ordered to stay at their stations as General McClellan rides alongside the President, who is assigned a ridiculously short mount for someone of his physical and professional stature, part of the posturing of the commanding general. They are trailed by their respective aides, assistants, and secretaries. The President wants to take a measure of the spirit of the men after their retreat, and the Corps' commanders wish to leave him with a favorable impression.

The temperature and humidity continue to climb and the skies grow darker by the hour. Despite the threatening weather and the dour sentiments of the men, Robert is excited to catch a glimpse of his

President. They stand at attention as the retinue passes. The general continues to the Rawlings' House where McClellan relocated his command post, and the President is quartered for his stay. By 6:30 p.m., the skies open up with a furious rain and hailstorm.

Thursday, 14 August, 1862

"Finally," Will says with excitement, as he throws his things together. "We're getting out of this hole." Issued three days rations, and under orders to return to Washington City, the other men are just as happy to be leaving Virginia for the foreseeable future.

Their return journey passes through battlegrounds experienced during their drive to Richmond. Houses have been burned to the ground, marked by remnant chimney stacks. Overgrown fields have taken over quickly marked graves of comrades and enemies that rapidly lose their identities to time.

* * *

Robert's battery has orders to return to Camp Berry. It's a short sail down the York river to the Chesapeake, then north to Washington.

"Fresh air feels good, doesn't it?" Welker says as he exhales a large cloud of smoke.

Robert stands at the rail, and takes in the sights of the bay, and tries to find some relief from the near ninety degree heat. "Happy to get back to friendlier territory, that's for sure."

"These orders could not have come at a better time as far as I'm concerned." Welker takes another pull from his cigar. "Hope to get some time to see the city and enjoy some good food for a change."

"Any news on Sergeant Payton?"

"Only that he was shipped out with the rest of the hospitals' patients. As it stands, the system makes it difficult to track him down. I am going to try though."

"At least he's still with us."

Welker nods his head. "That he is … that he is." The two of them stand together, and lean on the rail, look ahead at the bright skies, the calm waters, and speculate about their uncertain future.

George Brinton McClellan

M.B.Brady photograph
Library of Congress
Prints and Photographs Division
LC-DIG-ppmsca-19389

change of command

∞

Saturday, 1 November 1862

Once again Robert's battery heads south on the Potomac river. Not to Fort Monroe this time, but to Aquia Creek Landing en route to Falmouth, Virginia. Robert seeks his favorite refuge at the bow of the steamer. It's chilly once the ship gets underway, and not many others want to be exposed to the elements. Though he relishes the peace and quiet, he always enjoys Sergeant Welker's company.

"Regret not joining the Navy? I always know where to find you."

"Hey, Sergeant. You look a little tired. Seems like the process went a lot smoother than our Peninsula excursions."

Welker lights his cigarette as he answers, "Practice makes perfect, I guess. As much as they keep shipping us up and down this puddle we oughta be pretty good at it." Holding out his cigarette, he offers, "Go ahead and take one."

"No thanks. What's up ahead of us?"

"Winter quarters, I imagine. It's November. It's cold. The armies want to get their troops fed, rested, and trained before the big push this spring."

"Big push?"

"I can't imagine McClellan's sitting on his hands. He has to redeem himself in the eyes of Washington." Welker turns to leave, "I'm headed inside to get warm. Wanna join me?"

"Thanks, but I think I'll stay out here a while longer."

Six hours later the ship makes dockside.

Friday, 7 November 1862
Falmouth, Virginia

The men huddle around a campfire stoked up to a full-on blaze. Sergeant Welker joins his gun crew as they soak up the heat. They all helped themselves to hot coffee and most enjoy a smoke. They remain unusually quiet until Lieutenant Turnbull approaches.

"Good evening, Lieutenant," says Welker as he stands to greet the officer. The others start to stand until Turnbull motions them to sit back down.

Staring at the blaze, Turnbull says, "This looks comfortable."

Ramsey stands and asks, "Care to share a seat with us, sir?"

The lieutenant nods, and Ramsey signals the men to the left of him to move over.

"Coffee, Lieutenant?" offers Hickman.

"Thank you, Will. Sure." He declines the offer of a smoke and stares into the fire.

"What brings you down to this neck of the woods, Lieutenant?" asks Welker.

Turnbull hesitates, then answers, "I've got some news that directly affects us …"

After a few minutes, "Lieutenant?" coaxes Welker.

Another long pause before he answers, "McClellan has been relieved of command." Some of the men are shocked, and others outraged.

"Why'd they fire Li'l Mac?"

"Wasn't Antietam a victory?"

"Okay, stow it you guys. Who they gonna replace him with?" presses the sergeant.

"Oh, sorry. I'm still trying to think what this means for us. Burnside. Major General Ambrose Burnside has been appointed head of our army."

"What can you tell us about him, sir?" asks Ramsey.

Ambrose Everett Burnside
Brady's National Photographic Portrait Galleries
Library of Congress
Liljenquist Family Collection of Civil War Photographs
LC-DIG-ppmsca-40543

"I can tell you what I've heard, but you can treat that like any other rumor. He has an unforgettable growth of facial hair, but you'll get to see it soon enough. He's a graduate of West Point and good friends with the out-going general. His success in North Carolina earned him his second star and the head of the corps. His troops fought well at Antietam, but ..."

"But, you have reservations?" asks Welker.

"I've heard his initial reluctance to take the command *may* be because of his friendship with McClellan, or for other reasons. I know that any new general wants to make a favorable impression, and right now, well, the eyes in Washington are on us. The President replaced McClellan because he's not happy, which means he wants to see success at whatever arena we're in. You can expect movement orders ... soon." Turnbull stands up to spread the word. "Gentlemen, I hope this hasn't spoiled your time together."

Monday, 17 November 1862

With surprising speed, the Army of the Potomac has arrived at the heights on the north side of the Rappahannock river. Below them lies the historic city of Fredericksburg—George Washington's childhood home and burial place of his mother. Located forty-five miles south of the Union capital, and sixty miles north of the Confederate capital, the city is bordered by the river to its north, and backed by wooded, rolling hills to its south.

* * *

But the Army of the Potomac, and its new commander, are frustrated by the non-arrival of the pontoon boats, integral to the general's plans. Throughout the delay, the Confederates continue to build up their numbers, and consolidate their defenses.

Building pontoon bridge at Fredericksburg, Virginia
Harpers Pictoral History of the Civil War
December 1862

pontoons

Thursday, 11 December 1862
Fredericksburg, Virginia

It's 1:00 a.m., and the city is dead quiet. Fog bleeds over the river's edge, and blankets the shoreline and lowlands. The setting moon contributes to the cover the engineers need to start construction on the pontoon bridges.

They lead a train of a hundred and eighty-nine wagons of pontoon boats, and support materials, down the steep slope from Stafford Heights to the wide flood plain of the Rappahannock, and begin to construct three bridges to span the river. Six men in each of the thirty-one-foot-long pontoon boats take to the river, and have to negotiate the ice building on the surface, in some places an inch-thick.

To construct a pontoon bridge, the engineers align the boats side-by-side, and space them thirteen feet apart. The pontoons are cinched together with cables and beams as they cross the river. Once anchored on the other side, planks are laid down and the ramps graded to accommodate the troops, equipment, and horses.

A temporary break in the mist uncovers a sight terrifying to the engineers——Confederate infantry massed along the other side of the river. At 5:00 a.m., the Union's men are startled by two Rebel cannon firing a signal for the rest of their army to concentrate. Ten minutes later, the Confederate sharpshooters open fire from vantage points in cellars, ditches, and behind stone walls, in homes and buildings around the city, which force the construction crews to withdraw.

A hundred and forty-seven cannon under the command of newly-minted Brigadier General Henry J. Hunt, span Stafford Heights. They open fire. It's a back and forth between the engineers attempts to build, the enemy snipers' response, and the Union cannon shutting them down.

At 9:00 a.m., Hunt adds thirty-six cannon to cover the area where the engineers are at work on the middle span, for a total of a hundred and eighty-three guns, which he orders to open fire. Robert's crew is one of the thirty-six, now posted on a bluff immediately to the right of the railroad, near a building that once served as a home.

Now back on the gun crew, Robert's angst of facing battle resurfaces the doubts he was able to sublimate as a teamster.

"Ready your stations, men," yells Welker. The lieutenant has a fix on a building housing the riflemen. He points it out to Welker and slight adjustments are made to reposition the aim and elevation of the cannon's barrel. "Fire!"

Turnbull's guns institute rapid fire, and with each round, the guns' stock-trails dig into the frozen ground. Some of the batteries report them splitting, from defective, even rotten wood, and are taken offline.

Volunteer engineers are called upon to continue with the threatening work; the Confederate marksmen resume their fire.

At 12:30 p.m., Hunt passes on the directive ordering a firestorm on the city. For the next two hours, the artillery assails Fredericksburg with a devastating hailstorm of nine thousand artillery shells. Shards of wood explode from the sides of buildings and shattered bricks rain down, to leave gaping holes in the walls. Doors are torn from their hinges, and floors are ripped asunder. Buildings collapse exposing fireplace hearths like gaping maws open to warming rooms that no longer exist. Lines of smoke from the smoldering ruins drift straight up. The Rebel snipers resume their fearsome attack.

At 2:30 p.m., Burnside calls for volunteer infantrymen willing to cross the river in the unused pontoon boats to root out the sharpshooters building-by-building. Cover fire is laid down for thirty minutes until the volunteers get across. They move through the city, street to street, building to house, and into the yards. The fighting in close quarters is fierce and exacts a terrible cost to both sides.

As the soldiers carry out their assignments, the pontoon bridges are completed and the Union's troops immediately start to cross. It's each man for himself, careful not to walk in cadence. The harmonics of men marching in unison might cause the bridge to sway too dangerously.

By 7:00 p.m., the fighting tapers off——that's when the looting starts.

* * *

Early the next morning, Robert and a crew of five others are detailed to jury-rig the five cannon with damaged spike-trails to a harness team. They will be taken to Falmouth for eventual transport to Camp Berry for refurbishment. Robert and Jim are teamed to work the problem together.

"Can you believe that we razed the city like that?" asks Robert.

"I got no problem with it," says Jim. "Burn 'em out of house and home as far as I'm concerned. Them Secesh are our enemies. If they didn't want their precious city destroyed, they'd picked different spots for cover."

"I guess it's the idea of destroying their hearth and home. The battlefield doesn't bother me, but these are civilians."

"Those *civilians*, as you dearly describe 'em, provide sustenance to the soldiers with every intent of ending you. We hit 'em where it hurts, then maybe they'll think twice."

Once they're finished, the NCO in charge directs them back to their outfit. When they reach the base of the ramp, they see Turnbull as he stands beside his horse and looks toward the town.

"Reporting as ordered, sir." Turnbull ignores their salute.

"Disgusting."

"Sir?" says Ramsey.

"Oh, sorry, Jim. Not you." He points to the clamor at the center of the town. "Apparently, our troops decided to ransack the city."

They look over to the main source of the disturbance. The houses are being systematically emptied of any personal belongings. Men are running off with every bit of foodstuffs they can handle. Anything they can't carry, furniture, clothes, dishes, wall hangings, pianos, books, letters, and mementos are being dragged into the streets and either smashed, torn, or burned.

"Outrageous," Turnbull reiterates his disgust. "You men stay clear of that. The Provost has been summoned to deal with these hoodlums." He shakes his head, "Utterly shameful."

Turnbull sees Major General Couch approaching on horseback, followed by his staff. Turnbull salutes him, but the general focuses on the melee. He turns back to Brigadier General Winfield Scott Hancock and signals him alongside.

"General Hancock, I want this disgraceful looting to stop. Post guards at the city-side of these bridges with orders to let no contraband cross the river." Hancock salutes and rides off to carry out his orders. Without acknowledging the saluting lieutenant, General Couch and his aides return to headquarters.

Turnbull looks to Robert and Jim. "You men best be getting back to your battery and tell them to get a good night's rest. We will deploy early in the morning."

prospect hill

Saturday, 13 December 1862
Prospect Hill, Fredericksburg, Virginia

Union forces, under the command of General Franklin, deploy six miles south-southeast of Fredericksburg under the cover of darkness. To their left, the Rappahannock river has swelled to a width of over four hundred feet. To their right, a sizable plain leads to the heavily wooded region known as Prospect Hill. At the base of the rise, the tracks of the Richmond-Fredericksburg railroad run parallel to the river before they veer northwest into the city. The Federal's goal is the portion of the Confederate armies, under Stonewall Jackson, strongly ensconced in the wooded hills.

At 8:30 a.m., the temperatures are frigid, and a heavy fog blankets the flood plain. General Meade's infantry marches parallel to the river, then turns to face the enemy. Robert's battery is positioned at the far right flank of the Union guns in support of Meade's advance. The artillery sweeps the field with shellfire ahead of their troops, as they advance toward a thickly wooded break in the Rebels' line. Due to the heavy fog, the Rebels can hear the bands play and the troop's movements, but cannot clearly see them.

A Confederate artilleryman has his men limber up a twelve-pounder Napoleon cannon with hopes of harassing the Federals. They independently fire from a hollow at their far left, and effectively tear great holes in their lines, slowing their progress. Union batteries are ordered to return fire, but with little effect. Empowered by his success, the Confederate gunner orders a second cannon, a twelve-pounder Blakely, to join him. Again the Union guns respond, and disable the gun with a direct hit. The Rebel crew quickly moves the remaining cannon to another spot, and pours more fire into Meade's forces. He moves again and again, and stalls the advance for close to an hour, before running too low on ammunition to continue.

Atop the ridge, Rebel cannon open fire on the army, and trigger a full-on artillery duel that lasts for three hours. Staying focused on the process dominates Robert's attentions. Eventually, the Union batteries are ordered to cease fire for fear of hitting their own troops. The last shot, from a Union gun, punctuates the end of the duel with a direct hit on a Rebel caisson full of explosives. It's greeted by enthusiastic cheers from the Northerners.

Meade's men form a wedge and charge, exploiting a weakness in the Rebel lines. As they proceed through the dense brush, both sides eventually realize that Meade's forces are now surrounded on three sides. An intense cross-fire drives them back toward their original position, followed in hot pursuit by two Confederate divisions.

General Sickles's Third Corps enters the fray to defend Meade's retreat. The reinforcements advance, trying their best not to stumble over the already fallen and still maintain accurate fire. The Federals suffer heavy losses at the hands of the Rebel's counter-attack. The troops flee to the protection of the Union guns. In their pursuit, the Rebs find themselves within fifty yards of the Union's cannon before they realize their mistake. Eighteen guns, Robert's included, open fire.

He looks out over the growing panorama of death and dying on the grounds in front of them, called "The Slaughter Pen". A knot of anxiety rises from his gut. Bodies are spread about the field in utter confusion, both Union and Confederate, thousands of them. In seconds his eyes dart from one man to another, and records micro impressions of images——one whose limbs are in complete disarray, another with blank, lifeless eyes stares back at Robert, a frozen arm, woven in the mix of bodies, points at him, temporarily accusing him, but soon covered by another, dead before he hits the ground. Men lay on their backs with chests split wide open, twitching bodies, cries of anguish, looks of shock frozen on lifeless faces, limbs with no bodies spread about the cold, ice-hardened ground enveloped by growing pools of blood. The frozen barrier keeps the crimson reminder visible for everyone to witness. It's too much for Robert, and he turns away, and uses his ramrod to hold himself up; he vomits. As his stomach convulses, his head spins. *How will I ever be able to forget these sights, ever justify my hand in this before God?* There's nothing more forthcoming, yet he continues to dry-heave uncontrollably.

Ordered to shoot double-loads of canister, the ammunition runner, Anderson, removes one of the bags of gunpowder and places the other with the two tin containers of lead balls into the muzzle. He notices Robert bent over and staring out at the killing zone. Robert's head turns from one part of the field to another as he coughs, spits, and tries to refocus his senses. He's brought the rhythm of the crew to a halt. Anderson crosses in front of the muzzle to Robert's side of the cannon and swats his chest. "What are you doing, Canham? You've thrown off our entire crew!"

At the rear of the barrel, Ramsey stands with a leather thumbstall pressed over the vent hole to prevent a deadly premature spark. Something's wrong. He doesn't feel the back-pressure from the seating of a new round. He looks up to see Anderson and Robert face-to-face away from the cannon. "What are you two doing!"

Ramsey's plea breaks the concentration of Sergeant Welker who is focused on the enemy, timing his next firing sequence. He's forced to turn his attention to Robert and Anderson, both out of position. "Anderson, what the hell are you doing? Get back to your station immediately. Canham, get your head back in this, or both of you will shovel horse shit for the duration of the war!"

Anderson runs back to his spot, furious that Robert has gotten him in trouble. Robert recovers enough to refocus on his responsibilities. He raises his right hand slightly as he gets back on task. "Sorry, sorry." He seats the load of canister with his ramrod. This time a new voice in his head speaks with clarity. *Stay focused, not on the sights and sounds of the wounded and dying, not on those poor souls, just on your job. You're needed here, and now, with these men, who are counting on you.*

As the cannon fires and he continues through his paces, the concussions rattle Robert. He continually fights the urge to look out onto the field, but the *pings* of Minié balls off the cannon remind him he's still in a life or death struggle. Eventually, the urge to look out, to lose himself in the devastation, passes. There will be time to ponder after the battle. Back on track, Robert's battery continues its furious cannonade. Heavy resistance, and loss of daylight, force the Rebels to withdraw.

The agonizing moans of the wounded fill the void left by the silenced guns. Robert's crew huddles around the barrel, and draws heat from the gun in the chilling winds. None of the men want to look at Robert directly, but murmur amongst themselves about his conduct in the battle. He steps away from the glares of his battery mates, and the warmth of the gun, to retrieve his canteen. He takes a short draw to rinse out his mouth, then takes in a long pull and swallows. His stomach still convulses, but he knows the violent upheaval is over. Welker orders the men to put a lid on the carping about Robert and Anderson. As the talk tapers off, they look out at the field of devastation in front of them. The bodies blanket the area, some dressed in Confederate butternut, some in Union blue, mixed with reds from the Zouave regiments, and all awash in blood. Neither side has gained any ground.

The batteries are ordered to stay on the alert for another counter-attack. Robert drops to one knee as he watches the stretcher bearers work their way through the carnage, trying to find those who might be helped. They fail in their attempt to navigate the grounds without stepping on the fallen. He starts to silently weep.

Sergeant Welker notices Robert, breaks away from the rest of the crew, and places his hand on his shoulder. Robert, doesn't look at Welker, but scans the killing field. "How do you make sense of this? I mean, what's worth the price these men paid?" His arm points to the Confederate lines. "They still hold their position. We still hold ours, both pretty much where we started … less all these lives. Why?"

Welker listens as Robert vents. "We can't justify this, Robert, and shouldn't try. We follow our orders, do our jobs, and wait for the next set of orders. You can't take the burdens of war on your shoulders. It's too much for any one man to bear."

They are distracted by the sounds of musketry from the west, Robert says, "I guess others are paying the price over there ... but who?"

Welker looks to the source of the noise, and offers to help him up. "Come on, we best get back on line. We're not officially done yet."

That night the skies light up in a spectacular phenomenon rarely displayed this far south. For over an hour, waves of lights, an aurora borealis, adorn the heavens. The men take in the wonders of yellow curtains rippling in the vast darkness to their right, and waves of even brighter reds shimmer to their left.

Late the next night, word spreads throughout the Union ranks that they need to make ready to pull out. Under the cover of driving rain and hail, the Federals take great care to make as little noise as possible. With orders to withdraw over the bridges, Robert's battery carefully wraps the wheels of the wagons and carriages, and ties down their trace chains to silence them. The men secure canteens, cups, pots, pans, any metal that might possibly rattle as they move.

At the pontoon bridges, engineers spread dirt and brush on the planking to muffle the noise of those crossing. Once the crossing is complete, and leaving the Union's pickets, the engineers cut the anchors, and allow the currents to swing the bridges to the northern shore, where they are disassembled and carted off; the pickets are then ferried back in pontoon boats.

anderson & lew

∞

Wednesday, 17 December 1862
Falmouth, Virginia

Robert hopes beyond hope the others have forgiven him or forgotten about his conduct in the recent battle. But how can they? He let them down.

It's the break of dawn, and he's the first one at the stables. He wants to be left alone, but knows that won't happen. The job is too big, and last Saturday needs to be reckoned with. Robert hears boots crunch through the frozen mud as they approach the shelter. It's Anderson, fueled by a night of drink with several others. He can see that Anderson is worked up to a full boil, and focused on him.

"What did you think you're doing out there, *Canham*? You might have gotten us killed, but ..." His fists are now clenched, face-to-face with Robert, he pushes him hard on the shoulder. "What you *did do* is get us in a world of shit with the sergeant."

Robert's shaken, but steady. "Look, I'm sorry. I didn't know how bad——"

"Whatdaya mean you didn't know?" Anderson pushes him again.

The teamsters are the next to arrive, followed by the raw replacements who've yet to see action on the battlefield. Everyone circles around the two of them, excited at the prospect of a fight.

Robert looks around at the gathering crowd. As more men move closer, the goading and excitement grow to a fever pitch. Robert doesn't hear the yells. He knows what's coming next, but not from how many. He turns his focus on the man in front of him.

Anderson lunges toward him with a right roundhouse. Robert steps to his right and leans back. The punch grazes his shoulder. As Anderson's momentum carries him forward, Robert grabs under the armpit of his jacket and the waist of his pants, and drives him face-first into the partition of the stall. Anderson's feet never touch the ground. In a daze, he drops to a knee. As he starts to get up, Robert lets go with a hard overhand right on his left cheek, tears his face open and knocks him senseless. It's over in a matter of seconds. With his fists still clenched, he turns, ready for the next taker. As he scans the onlookers, he ends up face-to-face with Sergeant Welker.

"Stand down, Private! This fight's over!" Groans of disappointment circulate throughout the crowd. Welker singles out Ramsey and Hickman. "You two take care of that man," pointing to Anderson. "I'll deal with him later. The rest of you get back to work." He takes a moment to calm down before he addresses Robert. "You, follow me."

As the two men start to leave the barn, Quartermaster Sergeant Davenport, who witnessed the whole melee, grabs Welker by the shoulder and pulls him aside to talk with him privately. When he's through, Welker turns back to Robert. "Let's go."

Robert matches Welker's brisk pace to command quarters. He knows he'll get chewed out, likely court-martialed, and resigns himself to the possibility he will be removed from the crew, permanently.

When the two of them reach headquarters, Welker tells him to remain outside while he talks to the lieutenant. A few minutes later, Welker motions him inside. He stands at attention and salutes the duty officer. Lieutenant Turnbull looks over at Corporal Wingate and asks him to leave the office for a while. Disappointed, Wingate obeys.

Turnbull returns Canham's salute. "Stand at ease, Private. Sergeant …"

Welker notices Robert still at attention, his eyes track him as he circles around to Turnbull's side of the desk.

"At ease, son … relax. I've been in the same position under similar circumstances. It's been a spell, but I still remember." As the adrenaline in Robert's legs starts to drain, he places his hand on the desk to steady himself. Welker questions him. "Do you want to tell me your side of the story?" As Robert collects his thoughts, Welker adds, "Never mind about the incident in the stalls. Tell me about last Saturday. We've been too busy to chat 'til now."

"Well, I ..." He struggles to find the words. "I wasn't prepared to see——"

"The first time's always a shock. Trust me. Everyone has to cope with their first experience on the front lines."

"But how do you ... how did you deal with it? The wanton slaughter?" Robert's anxiety level peaks, as his memories start to play out in his mind. "Look at this field in front of us. You can't walk anywhere without stepping on someone, or be ankle deep in their blood!" Tears run down his cheeks. Welker looks over to his lieutenant, but Turnbull wisely defers to the older veteran who *has* experience with this.

"There's no easy answer. It's personal. You'll need to find a way to deal with it, then let it go. Clear your head, or it will render you useless to the team and to yourself."

Robert sighs as he nods.

Welker asks, "Lieutenant, anything you want to add?"

Turnbull looks at the sergeant, then over to Robert. "You are dismissed, Private." Robert comes to attention and salutes, then grins weakly to Welker before he returns to the stables.

The lieutenant looks to Welker. "Do we need to find a replacement for him?"

"He'll be fine. I've seen this before ... he's just sensitive, and he did finish well. Anderson, however ..."

* * *

Early that evening, Robert gathers wood for the fire and stokes the embers still aglow from the afternoon rations. He's alone and relishes the prospect of some undistracted time to think about all that has happened in the last couple of days. He wants the solitude to process it——the destruction of the city and the pillaging of the people's homes, the enormity of slaughter on the battlefield, and his hand in it. He wonders what the rest of the war will be like? He also questions whether he can do his job effectively. *Will there be more outbursts and confrontations from his battery mates? Maybe I am best suited to stay in the stables and tend the horses.* After his performance in battle, despite Welker's encouragement, he still has doubts.

Within the hour, Lew Billings approaches him. "May I join you Robert?" It's the first time Billings has seen him since the fight in the stables, and he wants to know what happened.

Initially annoyed by the intrusion, Robert realizes Lew's presence gives him a sense of calm, and he accepts his invitation. Robert points to the log next to him. "Sure, Lew, take a seat."

"Thanks. Ramsey has a pot of coffee. Would you like some?"

"That'd be great."

Lew Billings joined Robert's battery last April, a freshly-minted eighteen-year-old, with a uniform that drapes over his skeletal frame. Sun-drawn freckles compliment his wispy mustache, capped by a shock of blonde hair that constantly fights for freedom from his forage cap. He wears an ever-present smile, with a quick and infectious laugh that breaks the ice with warmth and sincerity.

Robert indoctrinated him on the regimen needed to keep their livestock healthy and battle-ready. They enjoy an easy rapport. Lew often seeks out Robert for advice, and their talks would sometimes stretch into the early morning hours. Lew makes Robert laugh, and he fills the role of Lew's older brother, believed taken prisoner at the Battle of Gaines's Mill.

It's much darker and the campfire is now fully ablaze. As he waits for Billings, Robert comfortably soaks up the heat. At the sound of footsteps, he expects to see Lew with the coffee, but instead it's Anderson. He immediately stands, tense, and reacts like another physical confrontation is imminent. Alone this time, Anderson stops eight feet short of Robert. He takes off his hat and asks him if they can talk. Robert notices the results of their earlier encounter. The crescent shaped cut on his upper cheek has been crudely sewn together, more likely by a steward than a doctor. When Anderson nears the fire, he sees his left eye is swollen and discolored. "What do you want here, Anderson?" asks Robert.

"I'm here to say I'm sorry. I made a mistake blaming you. I got … well, I got confused and took my mind off my own job." Robert doesn't say anything at first, and Anderson takes that as a sign he needs to leave, and starts to turn away.

"Hold up, Anderson … look, I made the first mistake." He taps himself on the chest with each pronouncement. "I didn't expect it to go like that out there … I was overwhelmed and froze up."

Anderson lets out a sigh of relief. "Yeah, I was so focused on not making a mistake with the ammo, that I didn't think to look ahead of us. I see now how it got so confusing."

Robert looks at him in a different light. "I guess I screwed things up for the entire crew."

Anderson continues, "'Sides that, I should'a minded my own business. It wasn't up to me to get in your face during the battle, and certainly not afterward. You aren't my enemy … them damn Rebs are." He holds out his hand to Robert. "I'm askin' if you'd forgive me?"

Robert walks to him and takes his hand. "Of course. No hard feelings."

"I think you may wanna know," adds Anderson. "I've been reassigned to another gun crew. There is an opening with the Battery K boys. They asked for an experienced replacement, and the sergeant was only too glad to get rid of me."

"Best of luck to you then."

"Yeah. Be seein' you around."

As Anderson leaves, he passes Billings, who waits in the shadows with their coffee. Billings hurries to Robert and hands him his rapidly cooling brew, and the two of them sit back down.

"What was that about?"

"He wanted to make things right."

Lew stares at Anderson as he departs, and says, "I never did trust him."

"He's okay. Just temperamental. But, hey, sounds like there's a place on our gun crew. Any interest in joining us?"

"And fight alongside you? Sure. You can make that decision?"

"No, but Sergeant Welker can. No guarantees, but I'll put in a word for you, if you like."

Billings has a hard time containing his enthusiasm. "That'd be great." Then he remembers why he joined Robert to begin with. "What happened out there? Why's Anderson angry with you?"

He looks at the young man. "I committed the one sin that you cannot do in an artillery unit ... I froze in battle."

Burnside's Mud March

Alfred R. Waud drawing
Library of Congress
Morgan collection of Civil War drawings
LC-DIG-ppmsca-22444

mud

Tuesday, 20 January 1863
Falmouth, Virginia

Morale is dangerously low throughout the Army of the Potomac. The slaughter they suffered at Mayre's Heights, and the harsh winter they've had to endure, have contributed to the loss of confidence in their commanding general.

Lieutenant Turnbull dismounts and hands the reins of his horse to Corporal Wingate. The men are told to stand at ease while they wait for his return with the orders for the day. They are dressed heavily in their their wool uniforms and winter overcoats. Heavy winds and dark skies foretell the promise of tumultuous weather. Robert hears an undercurrent of murmurs throughout the parade grounds as other units get their instructions.

Lieutenant Turnbull returns and directs the men to pack three day's rations, break down the camp, and ready their equipment. They've been ordered to cross the Rappahannock river at U.S. Ford, due north of Chancellorsville. Once across, Burnside's forces will move on Lee's left flank, and engage him in conditions more favorable than what they faced five weeks earlier.

* * *

At the front of the long train, the engineers' battalions tow pontoon boats needed for the bridgework, but their wagons are tearing up the roads for everyone else.

Robert and Lew ride two of the six horses that pull their cannon. It's been impressed upon them that any breakdown can mean a huge bottleneck for those who follow. Robert notices the mud build-up on the carriage wheels. They labor to keep up with the unit ahead of them. "We won't be able to keep on like this," Robert says to Welker. "The horses already complain about the increased weight and unsure footing."

"There's six of them, and they're strong," Welker responds. "Don't you think they can handle this?"

"I don't know. They struggle just to slog through this already torn up road."

Lieutenant Turnbull catches up with them. "A change of plans. We will soon turn due south for Bank's Ford. Apparently the general has moved up to reconnoiter the area, and believes we will be more successful crossing there."

"Yes, sir," they respond. Robert tries to point out the growing encumbrance of mud, but Turnbull is focused on the unit to their rear, and moves on without looking.

Deep into the afternoon, the skies fulfill their promise and start to deliver a torrential downpour. The road conditions usually range from hard and dusty in the summer, to frozen and slick in the winter, but are now a deep slurry of soaked clay and sand. The longer the storm continues, the more the movement bogs down. Gale-force winds drive the rain and sleet hard against the men, horses, and the canvassed wagons, but they continue on throughout the night.

* * *

By the next day, the conditions of the roads have deteriorated to the point where the weight of the vehicles can no longer be supported. Robert's cannon sinks to its axle, and brings everyone in back of them to a complete halt. Sergeant Welker quickly orders Robert off his mount and Lew to stay in place.

Robert gropes his way to the trail of the cannon to retrieve the rope from the prolonge hooks. He attaches it to the axle of the cannon and hands it off to six men who are there to help pull. Robert and Will take a place by each of the carriage wheels to help their rotation. Men are positioned in back of the limber to help push. Welker tells Lew to spur the horses forward as men push on the back of the limber, pull on the rope, and try to turn the wheels of the carriage and limber. It's no use. The men slip, slide, and sink in the mud. The wagons are down as deep as they can go. The horses wail their frustration.

Turnbull returns shortly. He shouts to Welker, "There are about a hundred and fifty men from an infantry unit on their way to help get us out of this mess."

Welker orders Robert and Lew, who have now dismounted, to requisition the harnessed team of six horses from the cannon in back of them. The gun crew's sergeant has his teamsters unhitch the team and lead them ahead of Welker's. In addition to the men, there will now be twelve horses to pull the cannon. The teamsters stay with their charges after they combine the two. Jim and Will retrieve as much rope as they can from the supply wagon. Welker directs four others over to a fence that borders the road.

"Get as many of those split rails as you can carry over to the front of the wagon. Save four of the poles for us to use as pry bars on the axles."

Logs are placed in front of the wheels for traction. Men on each side of the wagon are setting the poles to lift the axles and advance the wagon wheels. Jim returns with three more long lines and attaches two of them to the limber and one more to the cannon carriage. By this time the infantry units start to arrive. The soldiers are told to ditch their knapsacks and grab a place along one of the tow lines.

After briefing everyone on the process, Welker positions himself at the side of the horses. The secret——establish a rhythm for the men to follow. Robert and Lew hold the lead horses by the cheekpiece and wait for the signal. It's difficult to communicate with the heavy winds. Welker yells out, "Ready, pull." Like a metronome he drops his arm down emphatically, raises it, and repeats, hoping to establish a rhythm. "Ready, pull … ready, pull … ready, pull …" The mud doesn't give up easily, and the horses balk at any prodding. The men are strained to the limit, but pull to the beat until the mud reluctantly gives way. Hickman falls flat on his face. Welker yells at him to get off his knees and help out.

"I'm not *on* my knees, Sergeant," he protests. "I'm sunk down *to* them." Welker laughs and directs a couple of men from the infantry to help him out. One of them fights through the mud, and irretrievably loses his shoes. Eventually, they free Will. Thoroughly caked in the mire, his attempts to scrape off the excess mud from his face are fruitless.

Robert's wagon is just one in an endless line of vehicles victimized by the quagmire. All along the lines the conditions are the same—stuck wagons, animals exhausted to the point of collapse, and angry, frustrated men.

At the front of the column, the engineers try to keep their charges from tying up the wagons behind them. Some of their teamsters disconnect the trace pins of their pontoon wagons to free up the boats from the encumbrance of the wheeled carriage, then ride ahead, as the pontoons skim over the rain-soaked ground.

Other units lay down logs to make corduroy roads, but the rains and mud swallow up the wood as soon as it's laid down. The relentless storm wreaks havoc on the men for four days.

The engineers, who finally reach the river, start work on the bridge, and by the time Burnside arrives, fifteen pontoons are in place, but twenty are needed to cross. Burnside issues orders for the artillery units to move up to protect the area, but the artillerists' endeavors are helpless to make any semblance of further progress.

Across the river, Confederate sharpshooters add to the element of danger by using the engineers and their pontoons as target practice. Burnside had ordered five bridges built to span the river. At this point, he'd settle for at least two. The element of surprise has, once again, been taken out of his hands.

The Confederates raise large banners. One reads, "This way to Richmond!" Another says, "Burnside's Army Stuck in the Mud." Their pickets and scouts delightfully yell and jeer at the hapless Yanks. It becomes readily apparent there will be no bridges, no more forward progress, no surprise attack.

The entire army has only advanced five miles in yet one more humiliation. With resignation, Burnside realizes he's made another costly blunder, and orders a return to camp——a trip equally arduous.

He can't help but notice the abandoned equipment along the entire route, including dead and dying horses and mules. His men apoplectic with frustration.

Bad luck, maybe, or the reality Burnside knew before accepting high command——that of his own limitations.

Joseph Hooker

Matthew Brady photograph
U.S. National Archives
111-B-326

another change

Falmouth, Virginia

A couple of days later, Ramsey asks Welker, "Are the rumors true, Sergeant? Another new commanding general?"

Welker nods, discouraged with the constant turnover of high command, and the uncertainty of what that means.

"What can we expect?"

"I can't imagine it any worse than what we just experienced. I think the morale of this army will be General Hooker's top priority."

"Don't they call him 'Fighting Joe'?"

"Careful you don't make the same assumptions we did with Lee."

Friday, 30 January 1863

The men in Robert's shelter are awakened by the rustling noises in nearby cabins, the clatter of cookware, and louder than normal bickering. Sergeant Welker peeks his head into Robert's cabin. Like the others in camp——its mud-dappled walls are four feet high, with a small fireplace and their canvas field tents serve as a roof. "Good morning, gentlemen. We got a little task for you to do today. Everybody up. We'll talk outside."

Within minutes the four of them, in various stages of dress, stand in front of their impatient leader.

"What's going on, Sarge?" asks Will.

"Orders from our new general in charge. As soon as I leave here, you will clean up this filthy cabin and bedding, then take off the canvas roof to air this place out. I'll be back to see that you've done it properly. If not, you will get to do it over again, and we will go through this little exercise weekly ... inspections included. Your refuse needs to be burned daily. I know that you enjoy campfires, use 'em for something beside warming your butts. Any food-related garbage must be tossed in the pit behind the mess tent. Any questions?" Without waiting for a response, he says, "Good. Then, you are to take your filthy carcasses and get yourselves bathed. That you will do twice a week ... starting today." He puts his index finger flat under his nose. "Do you get my drift?" The embarrassed men look down. "You are also directed to wear your hair cut short. Get used to the thought of being each other's barber." The men take a closer look at one another to size up what that might entail. In a lighter note he continues, "You are then to report to the supply sergeant to get a new issue of clothing. Whatever you need for apparel: uniforms, coats, shoes, socks, underclothes, caps. You name it. Compliments of the general."

* * *

As the men leave their cabins to start the day, something's different, the aroma. Corporal Wingate places a sack near the fire.

"Fresh bread!" He no sooner gets the words out of his mouth than it's a mad scramble to empty the sack of its contents. The men tear through the bread as they stand and listen to what the corporal has to announce. "The general has decided that we need to eat better."

"Here, here," adds Hickman.

Wingate continues. "Huge bakery ovens are now on site so we can have fresh bread four times a week. Added to that, we'll get fresh, not desiccated, vegetables at least twice weekly. The commissary will be stocked with potatoes, fresh beef, peas, and rice."

"Wonder how long this'll last?" asks Hickman.

"Doesn't much matter. Not none of us can cook worth a whit anyway," says Ramsey.

"Glad you brought that up, Jim. Each company will be assigned a cook to prepare your food properly. There will also be coffee, sugar, and candies."

"I don't believe it. This is too good to be true," says Will.

"On the other hand, there is latrine duty." The group collectively groans. "I know, it's disgusting, but the rotation means you won't do it that often. Just cover your nose and mouth with a kerchief and bear with it. The trenches will need to be dug eight feet deep. There will be an NCO assigned to oversee the work. Each evening the pit will need to be covered with six inches of dirt." He continues, "Look, fellas, the general's trying hard to advocate for our health and well-being."

"It'll take more than a hunk of bread to convince me," says Will.

"Give him a chance. I think there'll be more good news to follow."

* * *

Lieutenant Turnbull is standing with six other men at the head of the assembly. He addresses the troops. "These men are from the Paymaster's office. General Hooker has pushed Washington to get us paid. You will each be issued six months of your backpay." With that, a cheer erupts from the crowd. Turnbull continues. "I suggest you avoid the usual pitfalls that always seem to accompany large amounts of cash. Next on the list, the general promises that we will now be paid on the first of each month." Another cheer goes up. "Settle down, there's more. We are authorized to issue furloughs for those of you who wish to visit your families. Before you get too excited, there are some restrictions. We can't let everyone go at once, and the furloughs are for a few days only. If you live any kind of distance away, I'm afraid you're out of luck. Those of you who want to take advantage of this, please submit your requests through your sergeants."

The Paymaster and clerks set up tables where the men line up corresponding to their last name——A through F, etc.

"Looks like ole' Joe's keeping his word," says Price.

Ramsey adds, "He's sure doin' right by us in my eyes."

Robert nods. "It's been a long time. We can sure use this alright."

* * *

Sergeant Welker stands next to Lieutenant Turnbull at roll call. He holds up a red cloth patch two inches long and shaped like a diamond.

"You will be issued patches similar to this one. Each corps gets a distinctive patch to easily identify who they belong to. For instance, the Eleventh Corps' is shaped like a crescent moon, whereas our Third Corps' is a diamond. Within each corps, the divisions will get their own color. The first division will be red, just like this one. The second will be white, and the third blue. Artillery units will be a derivation of that."

A question comes up from the ranks. "What'll we do with 'em, Sergeant?"

"Sew them atop your forage caps. Those of you who wear slouch hats will sew them on the front. Wear them with pride men. Show the Rebs just who they're up against." The men let out an enthusiastic cheer.

As the days move forward, variations of the patches start to appear on different uniforms. Letters home sharing the news bring a response of ornate homemade patches that the officers allow as substitutes. Some of the more well-heeled men order enamelware pins made up to proudly adorn their uniforms. Men now know by sight who belongs to what unit.

General Hooker's changes have a positive effect on the men. Corrections in their sanitation and hygiene have cut the sick call list by half. Better food has done the same and helped the men regain their strength. Steady pay and furloughs radically reduce the desertions, and those little two-inch patches give them a sense of pride, identification, and accountability with their units. The men are kept busy with drills as well. The discipline, combined with the personal attention the men receive help revive their morale.

new IDs

Falmouth, Virginia

As Robert's crew enjoys the warmth of the campfire and the shared camaraderie, Sergeant Welker makes an unexpected appearance bearing gifts. "The general has provided us with a sizable ration of tobacco for those of you who'd like some." The men enthusiastically respond, each fills a small pouch. Some roll their own immediately and light up, while others set theirs aside for later. The sergeant pulls up his shirt sleeves and lights one up for himself.

Lew elbows Robert and gestures to Welker's forearm. He has a tattoo of crossed cannon over his name.

"Interesting tattoo, Sergeant. There a story behind that?" asks Lew.

"When this melee broke out, me and a number of the other veterans got these markings. If we fell in battle, we'd be easier to identify ... good for our families to know."

"Where'd you get 'em?" asks Jim.

"At a parlor near Camp Barry. We got pretty liquored up first. Helped with the pain," he winks. The men chuckle.

"Too bad we're not near the city," says Jim.

"If you're serious, there's a sutler set up on weekends near the train platform. He comes in from Aquia Landing on Fridays and stays through Sunday evening. From what I hear, he does a pretty good job."

Looks are exchanged with the tacit understanding they are getting tattoos.

* * *

The foursome head to the train platform. True to Welker's word, the sutler's cart that offers tattoos is one of many. He has samples of his drawings and invites the men to take a look through his selections. He's in his forties, but looks closer to sixty. His skin has a gray pallor, his fingers are heavily stained with ink and nicotine, and he wears a proud display of work on his arms and hands. Some of the samples are large, ornate, and expensive, while others are smaller, not as detailed.

"Whatdaya boys have in mind?" the sutler asks with a raspy voice.

Jim tells him the story Welker shared with them earlier in the week. They are looking for something small, that might still serve to identify them. They wanted to get the same design, but couldn't agree on a choice. The sutler grabs the samples and spreads out a selection of well-worn pages.

"Instead of arguin' 'bout it, I think it's best ya' each choose yer own."

It takes a while for them to make their decisions. Someone has to go first, so Jim points to the crossed sabres and says, "My granpops fought as a dragoon in the War of 1812. I'd like that one. How 'bout a price for the four of us?"

"Sorry, lad. Each tattoo takes its allotted amount of time. You wouldn't want it to affect my work, would ya'? This here is two dollars … and none of that Confederate script, neither."

"Okay, okay," says Jim. "Let's get started."

The sutler lights up a smoke before he sets up the needles. The finer lines require three number twelve needles tied closely together at an angle. He uses black India ink. He starts by drawing the design freehand as a template, then begins the tattoo. Jim winces as he punctures the skin at an angle just below its surface. The sutler takes his time, but works methodically and neatly. It's apparent he knows his profession and takes pride in his work. When he's done, he wipes the blood and excess ink off Jim's arm with a bit of brandy and offers him a swig. He then takes a swig from the bottle himself before he looks to see who's next.

Robert has made his choice. He points to the serpent.

"Why that one?" asks Lew.

"I like the look of it, a harmless reptile, but with a potent bite." He stares at the sutler to get his attention. "And I want 'R CANHAM' beneath the serpent." He writes his name on a slip of paper to help the tattooist spell it correctly.

"Good idea, young man," encourages the tattooist.

Robert looks over to Lew and raises his eyebrows. "Here we go." He grimaces as the artist starts. When finished, the sutler wipes down his arm. It burns a little, but Robert figures that comes with the territory. He passes on the offer of the brandy. The tattooist doesn't.

Will and Lew both want the same tattoo that Welker displayed.

"That'll take a little longer and be three bucks each." They nod okay, and he starts on Lew's.

The other three stroll around the carts, to look at their offerings. One sells rot-gut whiskey, which Will patronizes. Another sells newspapers, and yet another a selection of baked goods, which includes small pies and cakes. Robert buys a small berry pie and holds onto it for later. No one is around the tintype photographer's cart.

When Will's finished, they gather together and proudly hold their arms out to compare the work. Their tattoos are red and a little swollen. The sutler warns them, "Yer arms are gonna get itchy, but don't ya' go scratchin' 'em. Everything yer seein' 'n feelin' will pass in a few days. Just leave 'em be."

The next morning they are quick to show Sergeant Welker their arms. He looks at each one carefully, then at the four of them collectively. "Fine workmanship. Let's just hope you never need to use 'em."

Sunday, 5 April 1863

One man is reported absent for roll call. The pie that Robert bought from the sutler left him indisposed. Lieutenant Turnbull makes a note of the absentee and speaks up, "Captain Clark would like to share some news with you."

"Good morning, gentlemen. The general is proud of how his army has responded to the changes he has implemented. In fact, he invited our Commander-in-Chief, to get a first-hand look at you. He was due to come in today, but surprised us by showing up yesterday with his family and other VIPs." The men start to speculate with each other how this might affect them, but are soon quieted by the captain. "Let me continue. The general has asked us to get you ready for a review. The cavalry will conduct a parade for the President tomorrow." Pointing to the parade grounds at Falmouth Heights, he goes on. "As our space is relatively limited, and we are so many, the review will be spread out over a period of days. In the meantime, he will want to tour the encampment and meet the troops. Make sure the grounds are spotless, your cannon polished, and you look sharp and professional."

Pointing over the river, one of the men asks, "Aren't we kind of vulnerable being in full view of Bobby Lee?"

"That's just the point. The general wants the Confederates to know we are not going anywhere. In fact, we've gotten stronger than ever, and General Lee needs to know that."

* * *

The next day, eleven thousand members of the cavalry, led by Major General Stoneman, put on a great show for the President. Lincoln, bare-headed, wearing a black military cloak, and mounted on a beautiful steed selected especially for the day, is positioned to watch the parade next to his wife and dignitaries. On the other side of him, mounted on his bay horse, sits the proud commanding general.

The Second, Third, Fifth and Sixth corps are reviewed two days later——fifty thousand men, two companies wide in lines a quarter mile long. They are accompanied by bands playing and enthusiastically cheered by the rest of the men watching the spectacle. As the troops pass by in review, the company guide-ons are dipped and the sabers are raised in salute.

General Hooker makes a point of singling out how sharp Major General Daniel E. Sickles's Third Corps looks. The President knows Sickles well, a politically appointed officer and the general's intimate friend, but with a notorious background.

In Lafayette Park, directly across the street from the Executive

Mansion, he shot to death the son of Francis Scott Key, composer of our national anthem, for having an affair with his much younger wife. He's the first man to ever beat a murder rap by pleading temporary insanity. Sickles's defense attorney was Edwin McMasters Stanton, now Secretary of War Stanton. Unlike most political appointees to generalships, Sickles is an able and aggressive military commander, and in Hooker he finds a friend who likes the bottle and women as much as he does.

When it's time for the artillery to demonstrate, they appear three hundred cannon strong, each wagon drawn by a team of six horses. The batteries are led by their respective officers astride their mounts, swords drawn in salute to their Commander-in-Chief.

Robert has fully recovered, and sits atop the limber between Case and Lew, and controls the reins of the team. He wants to get a good glimpse of the President, but has to keep the horses under control. Nevertheless, the Grand Review measures up to the participants' expectations.

Over the course of the next couple of days, Lincoln does make his rounds, visiting as many units as possible. Wherever he goes, the men congregate tightly around him. Relegated to the stables during the time Lincoln calls on his unit, Robert misses the man he dreams of meeting.

The President and his entourage return to Washington on the tenth. The time for parades and reviews is finished. General Hooker now has to take his well-drilled, but unproven army into battle.

Catharine Furnace
      graphic courtesy Fredericksburg and Spotsylvania National Military Park

the furnace

Friday, 1 May 1863
Chancellorsville, Virginia

The Union army successfully crosses the Rappahannock and proceeds with orders to seek out and engage the enemy. A heavy fog provides cover for the troop's movements. Early on, Hooker's forces run into Lee's advanced guard, and push through with minor losses.

Robert's battery arrives at the conjoining of Plank, Telegraph, and River Roads, west of Fredericksburg. The impressive two-and-a-half story red brick farmhouse, owned by John Chancellor, dominates the other buildings at the crossroads. With a front porch supported by large white columns, the home is surrounded by clear grounds two to three hundred yards in any direction. The area is named in his honor—Chancellorsville.

Despite the secure positions attained by three of the Union's corps, Hooker makes the decision to halt the advance, which confounds his senior commanders. He establishes his headquarters in the Chancellor House, and has his forces assume a defensive posture, handing the offensive over to the Confederates.

Saturday, 2 May 1863

Lieutenant Turnbull carries out his orders to incorporate his guns into part of a defensive line comprised of six batteries totaling twenty-two cannon along a rise called Hazel Grove. They are placed along an elevated area devoid of trees that present a formidable line more than three hundred and seventy-five yards long.

The Third Corps' Artillery Chief, Captain Randolph, in company with Captain Clark, ride over to Lieutenant Turnbull. "Good morning, John. Crisp morning we're having here." The lieutenant nods in agreement as he salutes. "We are here on a matter of some importance——" A cheer starts to move down the line and interrupts Randolph. "Never mind. Here we go."

Generals Hooker and Sickles make a first-hand inspection of the line. The men seem genuinely pleased to see their commanding general up close. They want to show their appreciation to the one who has done much to restore order and morale. Robert joins the others and raises his cap high to acknowledge them.

After the two generals start back toward headquarters, the captains ride in response to a summons from General Birney. A messenger rides up and engages them in animated conversation. The officers follow the messenger south to a copse of tall oak trees where a couple of scouts were sent high into the branches.

The men in Robert's battery finish their gun emplacement and gather around Sergeant Welker. Hickman asks, "What do you think they're up to?"

As he pulls out his field glasses Welker answers, "Lemme get a better look." What he sees has piqued his curiosity. "Looks like they're talking to the lookouts who keep pointing to the west."

Welker turns to the men gathering around him. "Better get back to your posts." The men grumble as they start to leave. Welker continues, "Don't worry. I'll fill you in as soon as I know anything."

Immediately west of Robert's battery, at the far left flank of the artillery line, the commander of Battery B, New Jersey Light Artillery is invited to join the group talking with the scouts. Several minutes later, the four officers ride back at a full gallop. Welker hopes to get more information from anyone, but they all ride to the far end of the line.

A full two hours since the lookouts were sent aloft, Turnbull signals the men from the surrounding three guns to gather around. "There is definitely movement. Rebel columns are on the march. What we don't know is how many there are, where they are going, or why. The commanding general believes they are in retreat. The guns to our left will lob some shells in their direction to see if they will engage or move along faster."

The lieutenant finishes when three guns open fire. Lieutenant Sims has repositioned their cannon and loaded long-range shells. His ten-pounder Parrot guns can effectively reach sixteen hundred yards with a great degree of accuracy. Despite their distance from Robert's crew, the ground reverberates with each report. A slight breeze clears the smoke to the west.

The shelling is ineffective, but the Rebel column moves much faster now they know they are in an exposed position. Messengers on horseback are sent back and forth to General Hooker's headquarters.

General Birney addresses Turnbull, "Get your cannon limbered up, Lieutenant. I want you ready to move out by the time I return." He repeats the order to Battery E, First Rhode Island. By the time the general arrives with their guns in tow, Lieutenant Turnbull has his crews ready.

The artillery barrage from Sims's guns continues until Sickles receives permission to move his troops. General Birney is ordered to take possession of the road where the Confederate movement has been spotted and harass them as much as possible. They penetrate the woods until they come upon a cluster of buildings centered around a tall rock stack known as Catharine Furnace.

"What is this place, Sergeant?" Hickman asks Welker.

"A furnace for smelting ore."

"Like what, gold or silver?"

"No, iron ingots. They feed the ore down the top of the stack."

"Why's this——"

"Just keep your focus on your job, Private," says Turnbull.

Pointing to the movement of Confederate troops, Welker asks, "Where's that road lead, Lieutenant?"

"None of us know. It's not on any of our maps."

Incoming artillery rounds cut the conversations short.

Welker notices the Rebs fan out through the complex. "Heads-up fellas. It's going to start getting hot in here."

Because of the confined area, there's some confusion where Turnbull's crew should be placed. Captain Randolph joins the lieutenant to help them get situated.

Robert looks over at his friend facing his first battle on the front lines, and wonders how he will perform under fire. Lew tries to stave off the waves of nausea rolling around his gut by breathing deeply through his mouth. He catches Robert's gaze, and doesn't appreciate the close scrutiny. He uncomfortably forces a smile, then gestures Robert to keep *his* eyes forward.

Sergeant Welker orders his crew to load up with spherical shot. They draw ammunition from the limber, which Billings places into the muzzle of the cannon. Robert slides the load down the muzzle with the ramrod until it seats properly. At the rear of the cannon, Jim inserts a thin pick down a shaft located at the top of the barrel to prick open the gunpowder bag. Opposite him, Will inserts the firing pin. By the time Welker gives the command to fire, Robert turns away from the muzzle to cover his ears. Will pulls the detonator cord, which releases a spark from the mercury fulminate and ignites the gunpowder. The resulting blast sends the shell airborne. Robert sponges out the muzzle to dampen any sparks while Welker looks through his field glasses to see the results. In twenty seconds the cannon is reloaded and ready to fire.

It's a lively, nerve-wracking fight that taxes the men and their resources. After a spell, Welker says, "Lieutenant. We can't keep up this fire much longer. Our ammo's running low."

"How's that, Sergeant? Where's our caisson?"

"Back on the line where we were ordered to leave it."

Turnbull relays the news to Captain Randolph. "Sorry, John. I already sent a message to the commanding general who replied he 'can't make ammunition'. You'll need to return to Hazel Grove. I'll bring the Rhode Islanders forward."

By the time the new crew is ready, the Rebel artillery and infantry abandon the foundry and rejoin their movement, but not before losing several to capture.

Turnbull's guns resume their assigned station at Hazel Grove. Despite the successful skirmish, the men sense this isn't the end of it.

battle

Saturday, 2 May 1863
Chancellorsville, Virginia

Immediately in front of the line at Hazel Grove, an open field extends a quarter mile to the edge of an ominous forest, heavily populated with new and old growth trees, stunted oaks and junipers, and carpeted with thick undergrowth and vines that make it barely penetrable. Impossible to negotiate in a timely manner, the inhospitable region is called "The Wilderness".

The sense of danger is palpable, but Robert's gun crew remains calm, confident in how they acquitted themselves in earlier conflicts. He stands in the number one position, to the right of the muzzle of his cannon. With a clear view of the battlefield, it isn't lost on him that he's one of the most exposed of their gun crew. To cope with the heat, and his nerves, Robert takes off his forage cap to allow the evaporating sweat to cool his brow. After a few quick waves of his hat, he replaces it and adjusts the brim to shade his eyes. He leans his ramrod against the gun, uncorks his canteen, and takes a long drink of warm water. He pours some into his hand, dampens his face, then resumes his position.

Lieutenant Turnbull wraps up the conference with Randolph and Sims to rejoin his battery. He beckons the crews from the three nearest guns to gather around him. Still on his horse, the lieutenant speaks out. "I know we got the run-around this morning at the furnace. General

Hooker believes the Rebel troops are in full retreat, but Bobby Lee has never shown his backside to us before." He pointing ahead to the forest and adds, "On the other side of those woods, our right flank may be vulnerable. Warnings were sent to General Howard's headquarters at Dowdall's Tavern, but he agrees with the commanding general. Be prepared for any possibility."

Facing the opposite direction, Union infantry are dug in against those of Confederate General McLaws, remnants of the forces under General Lee withheld to turn the Union's attentions away from his divided army's movement through Catharine Furnace.

* * *

As they face the distant woods, Lew points to the treetops and gleefully yells, "Look, look at 'em go!" A thick black cloud of birds has taken to flight, noisily orchestrating their distress. The huge flock starts toward the batteries, banks east over the ridge toward the river, then out of sight.

There is movement from one side of the woods to the other, at first distant, then ever closer to the edge of the forest. Rabbits, foxes, raccoons, squirrels, woodchucks, and quail, that haven't sought the relative safety of their dens or nests, flee in panic. As they emerge from the protection of the woods, they skirt along the perimeter between the trees and the open ground, and search for access to new cover. Emerging deer deftly leap over the border scrub, avoid the smaller critters, then sprint across the open field, darting left, right, and back again. The men shout out taunts at the panicked critters.

Welker tries to refocus his men's attention back toward the woods. "Heads up fellas. That has to mean something's up."

Men are the next to emerge. First a few, then by the scores, finally by the hundreds. Having ripped their way through the nearly impassable undergrowth, they take off on an unfettered run across the open fields, waves of blue flowing over the ups and downs of the uneven ground straight toward the Union batteries.

Sergeant Welker shouts over the confusion of the mass panic, with an experienced warning, "I don't know what outfit these boys are with, so get ready. This could go really bad, really fast."

Line of battle at Chancellorsville to cover retreat of the 11th Corps, disgracefully running away

Alfred R. Waud drawing
Library of Congress
Morgan collection of Civil War drawings
LC-DIG-ppmsca-22527

At a distance, it's hard to tell who the horde belongs to. The fastest ones carry no weapons, no canteens, no jackets, and some are in their stocking feet. The few who wear forage caps display the insignia of the red crescent moon which identifies them as part of the First Division of Major General Howard's Eleventh Corps. The others are clad only in their blue pants and sweat-stained, bloody shirts. Their clothes and skin are badly torn from the bush and brambles of the thicket.

Robert looks back at Welker and yells, "I thought these guys are supposed to cover our flank!"

Welker shakes his clenched fist, and with one finger pointing at Robert, he yells, "You keep your attentions on what's happening in front of you. We might just survive this day."

Next to emerge are the Rebels at a full run, firing their muskets and fueled by the familiar whoops and high-pitched hollers of the Rebel yell. In their flight, the pursued start to fall, stumbling over the uneven ground. Others run into and over one another, taking both down. More fall when Confederate Minié balls find their marks. They stagger in their flight with either slight injuries, disabled from more serious wounds, or drop in their tracks, dead before they hit the ground.

Close on the heels of the first wave of refugees are others from their company with the presence of mind to keep their uniforms and canteens, muskets, and cartridge pouches for use when the lines might possibly re-form. The canteens slap hard against their hips, and clatter rhythmically in sync with the pace. Men who pause in their flight to fire at their pursuers realize little success, and often become easy targets for the Rebs. They are either wounded, or killed——there's no time for taking prisoners.

As he watches the panicked throngs approach the Union lines, Robert holds his staff at a forty-five degree angle in front of him to fend off anyone heading through their position. He catches the eye of Lew and points to the other pole mounted under the cannon's carriage. "Grab the other staff, Lew," and demonstrates a parrying move.

Lew grabs the pole, looks to his right and mutters, "Heaven help us."

Their chorus of threatening shouts grows louder as the mob closes in on the batteries.

"*Machen Sie den Weg frei!*"——"Clear a path!"
"*Macht schnell!*"——"Move!"
"*Aus dem Weg!*"——"Get out of my way!"
"*Hilfe!*"——"Please help!"
"*Um Gottes Willen, schiesst auf se, haltet sie auf, irgendwas!*"——"For God's sake, shoot at them, stop them, anything!"

No one understands. They are recent German immigrants assigned to Colonel Leopold Von Gilsa's First Brigade. They are the first troops to encounter the charge of the Confederates, and the first troops to run——forever identified as the "Flying Dutchmen".

Both Robert and Lew redirect the flow around their gun crew, but one corpulent young boy, with wild-eyes, plows straight into him with a loud *OOOF*, and topples both of them. Robert angrily pushes the boy off to the side. He starts to yell at him, then notices that his hand feels sticky. It's covered in blood. A bullet has pierced the base of the youth's neck, taking away the balance of his years. Robert resumes his station, still angry, and distracted by the dead youth. *What's a boy this young doing on a field of battle? Why isn't he still at home, in school, playing with his friends?* To avoid the mistakes he made at Prospect Hill, Robert quickly shifts his attention back to the arena.

Even though most of the panicked soldiers head for the left side of the artillery line, their sheer volume spills across the entire line of guns, effectively disabling the artillery by blocking their line of fire. Cannoneers are bumped, jostled and some are knocked over. Many of their cannon are pushed out of position, including one that's completely upended.

Teamsters flee the hot pursuit driving their wagons through the area at a full gallop. As they continue toward the rear they pass the gun crews' limbers whose teamsters try to keep their horses from joining the wild exodus.

Behind the artillery lines, mounted officers do their best to stem the tidal panic. General Hooker gives the officers orders to shoot the deserters, which they ignore. Major General Hancock slaps men on their backsides with the flat edge of his sword to get them into line. A confused Major General Howard retrieves a Union flag, balances it under the stump of his right arm, and tearfully pleads with the panicked men to set up a new defensive line of fire. The men who kept their weapons, are grateful for any kind of direction, and re-form with others to return fire.

The unarmed men ignore the petitions and keep running, having left any semblance of personal pride back at the camp along with their abandoned gear. The most panic-driven pass the artillery, and continue through the dug-in Union line. The entrenched infantrymen marvel as they see their own troops jack-rabbit toward the enemy. Some don't stop, scramble through another killing ground, only to end up in the arms of the Confederates who take them prisoner. Others seek safety to the left. Eventually, the adrenalin of the panicked horde starts to give out. They drop in their tracks, and desperately gasp for air, utterly spent.

Artillery officers gallop back and forth along their line to rally their gun crews and get them ready for the enemy's assault.

"Back to your stations."

"Resume your positions."

"Look to your Gunners."

As the professional calm of the leaders settles their crews, the balance of the men resume their stations. The Gunners redirect the aim of their cannon, and order the guns to be loaded with double-rounds of canister. When the Rebels advance to within two hundred and fifty yards, the bugles sound out the command.

"Fire!"

The tremendous explosions rattle the constitutions of the gun crews. Smoke diminishes the artillerists' vision; a minor hint of a breeze slowly carries away the dark curtain.

Lieutenant Turnbull, unable to see through the haze, stands high in his stirrups to evaluate their fire. The unforgiving spread of iron balls and shrapnel rips gaping holes in the Rebel lines. Ten, fifteen, sometimes twenty-plus men fall with each volley, some wounded slightly, others disabled, and the unluckiest of souls are hideously torn apart. Death in their cases, though ghastly, is mercifully swift.

The cries of the wounded are interrupted by the staccato sounds of the Rebel guns, as rounds *ping* off the cannon and chip away at their carriages. Robert realizes that the men in flight are no longer the primary targets of the Rebel muskets. *He is!*——as well as each man up and down the entire artillery line.

The artillery fire reduces the Confederate numbers as well as their resolve, and persuades some to take cover, but the battle is far from over. In a renewed surge, the Rebels lay down deadly fire on the Union lines in an attempt to dislodge them. It's a pandemonium of deafening cannon fire, bugle calls seeking to find their voice, terrified solders, ceaseless musket fire, and the shrill cries of panicked and wounded horses.

The Rebel infantry, energized by their belief in their leaders and each other, continue forward, leaning into the defensive maelstrom as if fighting against a severe wind storm, drawing closer, ever closer. Flanking infantry fire combines with the Union artillery to break the onslaught. The Rebel lines are reluctantly forced back to the relative safety of the woods. The guns continue their cannonade.

As Billings turns to start his run for the next round, a shell explodes some thirty feet above them. A stinging blunt force knocks the pole out of Robert's hand and spins him around. The concussion from the blast lifts him away from his position, knocks him flat on his back, forcing the air out of his lungs. As he gasps for breath and struggles to regain his footing, the din of battle diminishes and his vision starts to tunnel in, growing ever darker … his knees buckle and he helplessly surrenders as his world goes black …

wounded

With daylight fading, the battle slowly tapers off. Robert's cannon and crew are out of commission. The only sounds now come from the petitions of the wounded soldiers, leaders try to restore order, and the occasional pistol shot as hopelessly wounded animals are put out of their misery.

Dull, relentless pain begins to pull Robert slowly back to his senses. Still in a stupor, he places his hands on the ground to help himself sit up, but his right arm responds with a searing jolt of pain, and he collapses to his side with a groan. In his confusion, he looks down at the blood-stained sleeve of his jacket. He shakes his head from side-to-side trying to clear his senses, when Lamb, one of the company's musicians doing double-duty as a stretcher-bearer, tries to help him out of the danger zone.

"Please soldier, we need to get you out of here. Can you stand?" The shock from the explosion and repetitive cannon fire has temporarily deafened Robert. He waves him aside. Lamb moves on to help other wounded.

Robert sees the cannon has been displaced to the right, and under its muzzle lies his friend, Lew. The concussion from the blast pushed Lew into the barrel where he fell, bent face-down at the waist. Robert's heart drops as he sees him, his forage cap blown away and his blond hair thickly matted with blood. A piece of shrapnel is hideously imbedded deep into his skull. Lamb checks for a pulse, but he's unresponsive. He looks over to Welker and shakes his head, then moves to the next man down. Robert eyes fill with tears.

Ramsey and Hickman are both on their backs to the rear of the cannon. Jim comes-to first and crawls over to check on his friend. He looks to Welker. "I'm okay, Sergeant, but Will's still out of it."

His own shoulder severely lacerated by shrapnel, and bleeding from his left ear, Welker redirects Lamb to the lieutenant, who is flat on his back and starting to stir. "See if you can help him, but make sure he doesn't get up until he's ready." The blast knocked the officer from his mount; he's stunned, but otherwise unharmed. Lamb picks up the lieutenant's hat and sword, then helps him stand up. Turnbull tries to brush the dirt from his uniform, and finishes composing himself. Corporal Wingate locates and returns the lieutenant's horse. As he gestures at a man ready to help, Turnbull says, "Corporal, take that private there with you. We need an accurate count of the casualties."

Fifty yards west of the artillery line flows a small creek called Lewis's Run. Its four-foot embankments are lined with laurel bushes. Turnbull says, "Then take whomever you can gather, and move the wounded to the creek west of us and try to dress their wounds as best you can. Make sure they've got full canteens; it may be a long wait before help arrives."

Captain Randolph inspects the condition of Turnbull's guns, which includes Welker's destroyed cannon. He moves his horse alongside the young lieutenant's. "How are you, John?"

"I'll be alright, sir."

"You accounted for your losses, yet?"

"We're still trying to get ourselves sorted out. The injured are being moved to protective cover until help arrives."

Wingate runs over with the report, "We have one dead, six wounded, and one man missing, sir."

Randolph's face takes on a more somber look as he listens to the corporal. "Looks like no one got away scot-free. Lieutenant Sims's crew also took pretty hard losses. As good as these grounds are, the commanding general wants us back at the heights of Fairview, closer to headquarters. Our forces are still in jeopardy and need to be safely evacuated. Unfortunately, we need to leave the wounded to the will of the Lord and the mercy of the Rebels."

Lamb returns with a new man, and starts to help Robert regain his footing. Oblivious to Robert's wound, he tries to duck under his right arm. Robert lets out a scream, flinches, and knocks his hat off. With apologies, he backs away, and retrieves his hat. The shock snaps Robert fully awake. The two of them try again by putting their arms around Robert's waist, careful to support his injured arm, and make their way to the creek.

Lamb breaks out his knife and lets Robert know he needs to assess and bind up the wound.

"You don't plan to cut on me with that, do you?"

He shakes his head. "No, no, but we do need to take a look and see what we've got here." The new man carefully holds Robert's arm as Lamb starts to cut the red piping along the seam of his shell jacket, up to its elbow. When he tears away the shirtsleeve, he sees the entry-point of the bullet, but oddly enough, no exit wound. Lamb slowly, carefully turns his arm palm-side up, and notices a large lump below his ring finger. "I think I found your bullet."

Robert looks at the hole in his arm as it slowly oozes blood, then makes eye contact. "I can't feel anything when you touch my hand."

"I'll wrap around the entry point, but a doc will need to tend to you further." He folds a couple of layers of bandages to cover the wound, binds it up, then fashions a loose sling that extends from his swollen wrist to the edge of his elbow. "That'll hold you. I don't expect you'll have much use of this for awhile."

About that time, Sergeant Welker is gingerly placed next to Robert. Next is Will who is carefully laid on his back, still unconscious. Lamb pours a little water from his canteen into his hand to clean the blood off Will's face. It wakes him with a start. Not recognizing the unfamiliar face, Will desperately looks around until his panicked eyes settle on Ramsey.

Jim says, "You've given us a bit of a scare, Will. This here's one of our musicians, John Lamb, who's tryin' to help. You can trust him."

He tries to sit up, then gives up the effort with a moan. "My head. What happened? Where are we, Jimmy? Where's the rest of our crew?"

"Just relax. Seems the Rebs took the whole lot of us out with one of their shells." Jim waves his thumb over his left shoulder, "The sergeant's right here with Robert. The rest of the gang's back some fifty yards, trying to get things in order." He lifts up Will's head to get him to take a drink from the canteen. "You'll be safe here, but we gotta get back. The lieutenant's expecting us." Jim stands, motions to Lamb, and reluctantly leaves his downed mates. He looks back to say, "Take care. I'll try to find ya' as soon as possible."

The embankment is lined with wounded and soon, the dead. As others are being helped to the side of the creek, the over-looked do their best to drag themselves to relative safety. The petitions for help, prayers, and groans of the individuals unite in a chorus of agony to anyone within earshot. The collective pleas lessen as the stretcher bearers try their best to help them with water and reassurance. As the evening loses its hold on the light, many surrender to their exhaustion, while others slowly bleed to death.

left behind

∞

As the sun breaks the horizon, cooling fog rises from the creek, envelopes the bordering laurel bushes, and flows over its embankment to surround the men with soothing moisture. Reality soon breaks through the idyll as artillery fire from the distant north startles those left by the creekside. The Confederate guns find their mark forcing the Union batteries to rapidly abandon their line at Hazel Grove for safer ground around the Chancellor House, a mile southeast.

Robert's arm throbs mercilessly, but keeps him fully aware of his surroundings. He realizes they are left behind, too weak to follow, much less stand.

Sounds of approaching footsteps fill the area. Rebel infantry cover the field previously held by the Union's guns. Ground troops wade across the creek, clear paths through the laurel, and crest the embankment to find it lined with the Union's wounded and dead. Robert doesn't know what to expect, but at present there's no threat, the Rebs are focused on their goal of the high ground at Hazel Grove.

As the Confederates drive off the Federals, they quickly move twenty-eight cannon in place, facing the opposite direction. Ahead of them, the ground slopes down to a valley which gives them an unobstructed view of Fairview two-thirds of a mile away. The Rebels open fire immediately.

Robert looks over to the now-awake Welker who's closely watches the Confederates at work. He gently nudges him. "You have to admire how efficiently those Rebs set up and started laying down fire." Welker gives him an appalled double-take, ignores his observation, and turns his attentions back to the enemy's movements.

Late-arriving infantry, not solely focused on the heights, stop to taunt the wounded:

"Stay put, Yank, we'll be back fer ya' soon enough."

"Yer invited to join us in Richmond, once we send the rest of ya' Yanks to hell or home."

"Still lookin' fer a competent general? I reckon ain't none to be had up yer way."

A pair of stragglers make their way over to the line of dead bodies. One, a lad no more than fifteen, barefoot and dressed in ragtag butternut, the other is older wearing corporal's stripes. The younger of the two starts to remove the boots from one corpse, when the older hits his shoulder and points to Robert and Welker. Noticing his stripes, the youth forgets the boots and starts to yell at Welker, "Y'all had yer way with us back there," pointing to the battleground littered with bodies from the evening before. His face reddens as his anger takes over. "Thems 'r boys we knew," he yells, "and best I can tell, y'all had a hand in killin' 'em." He raises his rifle to waist level, pulls back the hammer, and places a percussion cap on the gun's nipple. When he takes aim at Sergeant Welker, Robert helplessly raises his left arm to cover his own head. Welker takes a deep breath before the corporal deflects the rifle, sending the shot skyward. "Whatcha doing? These here killed our boys!"

He tries to reload, but the corporal quickly relieves him of his rifle. "We ain't doin' no murder. These men are unarmed. They been doin' their orders." He points to the troops ahead and says, "We best be doin' ours." He pulls the youth away by his collar and leads him to the front.

With a quivering voice, Robert says to Welker, "I thought he was going to kill us for sure."

"Think he might've, if the corporal hadn't stopped him. Your raised arm was a good help," he jests. "Think that'd stop his bullet?"

"I guess I just panicked."

"Yeah, I figured I'd be meetin' my Maker real soon, too."

"You're a braver man than I."

"Brave nothin'. I suspect I'll need to be cleanin' my drawers soon enough."

The growing staccato of the muskets, the intensity of the artillery fire, and the infernal Rebel yells are tell-tale signs of how hot the battle rages. It continues for hours without let up. The sounds that accompany the Confederate advances signal how successful they are in driving the Union from the field.

"Wonder if we'll ever experience victory like that. I'd kind of like to know what it feels like."

Welker is a bit puzzled at his observation. "You've forgotten Malvern Hill already." He then points to one of the ragged Confederates who didn't make it much further than the reeds. "Notice his feet?" The bare feet of the corpse are caked in dirt and dried blood. "By the looks of these fellas, we've got the better of the equipment. We just need to find the general who knows how best to use us."

Robert looks over at Will who has fallen back asleep. "Think we'll be getting some help anytime soon?"

"This day has to be decided first and the way it's goin' …" Welker stares off. "It surely won't be from the Rebs, and it may not be for a good long while. How are you holdin' up?"

"Okay … I guess."

"You handled yourself like a seasoned trooper yesterday."

"Did you ever experience anything like that before? Those people, our people, running right through us. I didn't know what to do."

Welker recollects the moment. "From what I hear, it was pretty similar to Bull Run, 'cept the civilians that came out for the show got caught up as well. Must'a been some sight, seeing them high-tail it outta there back to the capital."

"It got so bad, I didn't care who we fired at. Good thing you were calling the shots."

"What I'm tryin' to say is you did well. You've put your past experiences into proper perspective." Welker turns back, tries to get comfortable, and despite the noise of battle, nods off.

With unsure footing, Robert shakily stands. "How are you doing, Will? Where'd you get hit?"

"I don't know. Nothing's achin' 'cept my head, and as soon as I raise it, the world starts spinning and I can't get my bearings."

"Can I get you anything?"

"How 'bout a ride home." He gropes around blindly to find his canteen, tries to take a drink, and is reminded it's empty. He holds it up to Robert, "Can you get me a refill?"

"I'll try." He negotiates the heavily-worn path through the bush to the roiled-up creek. The effort makes him a little dizzy, but he manages his way back.

Will notices, "How bad's your arm?"

"Don't honestly know. It hurts like hell, but I can't feel anything I touch."

Will takes a sip then gives in to the weight of his eyelids. Robert places the canteen by his hand and returns to Welker.

He's starting to feel the hollowness in his own gut, as he hasn't eaten since resupplying their ammo, and then only some dried beef and hardtack. He carefully sits back down, and soon follows Welker to sleep.

* * *

He awakens when the sun breaks the horizon, and props himself up with the idea of finding anything edible. Instead he runs into a Confederate foraging party of four men, one of them the corporal from the day before. This time their rifles are held at waist level, aimed straight at him. They notice his immobilized arm, realize he's no threat, and lower their guns.

"Got any food Yank? Ain't et nothin' in three days," says the corporal. Robert shakes his head.

The man with a gray-streaked beard next to him, points at Robert and sneers, "If you'd leave us alone, and get the hell off *our* land, we'd need not be havin' to forage for our vittles. You neither." Robert doesn't respond, so they leave him standing there, and move on to frisking the dead and wounded for anything worth taking.

* * *

The relative silence is replaced with the singing and conversations of grave diggers as they start to clear the fields of the fallen, shovels and picks working the dirt, clearing way for the shallow graves. As the hours pass, a couple of black men pass by with large carts encumbered with Confederate bodies intermixed with severed limbs, their tools stacked atop the load.

The showers start that evening, and later into the night mix in thunder and lightning. The rains smell cleansing. Robert forces himself up and grabs a couple of the blankets used to cover the dead, exposing the bloated bodies. The sickeningly sweet smell of decay starts to permeate the area. He quickly replaces the blankets. They spend the night in the storm, uncovered, and nodding off whenever they can.

* * *

As another day and night pass, neither Robert nor Welker can muster the strength or wherewithal to forage. In the distance, they hear another noise——more carts for the dead, this time for the Union fallen, pushed by other black men.

A group of three, two young and another much older, stop their cart by the artillery victims. Their makeshift clothes are ragged, and supplemented with pieces of uniforms they salvaged from the field. The old man, unshaven, and wearing the forage cap of an infantryman, directs the others to start loading the now swollen corpses onto their cart.

Robert boosts himself up, takes off his hat, and with a soft, quivering voice says, "Bye, Lew."

"Friend of yours?" the grave digger asks. Robert nods.

As Robert struggles to contain his emotions, Welker shares the moment. "Their days of pain and anguish are over now. May God grant them a peaceful rest."

Soon afterward, stretcher bearers arrive to begin removing the wounded. It's a laborious process, and difficult for the men being rescued. Late in the day, one of the drivers stops near Robert who looks at him with a sense of relief. His look soon turns to disappointment. The driver explains, "Sorry, but your sergeant is in worse shape than you, and," pointing to other wounded, "they be needin' help more'n you." They carefully take Welker, who lets out a groan when they load him up.

The driver reaches back in the wagon and grabs a blanket and tosses it to Robert. He thanks them, then points to Will, "How about one for him?" They toss him another, then goad the mule forward. Despite his disappointment, Robert yells after them, "See you soon, Sergeant." There is no response as the wagon pulls away.

Robert moves over next to Will, helps him get a drink, then covers him with the blanket.

"Why are we still here, Robert?"

"Guess others need help worse than us." He sits next to him. With his one good hand, he tries to wrap himself in the blanket. It's raining again, and now they are alone.

* * *

The rains continue until mid-afternoon the next day, and with temperatures hovering around fifty degrees, the two are still wrapped up. Around the time the rains stop, their turn arrives.

"Looks to be you boys been out here for some time?"

Will doesn't acknowledge him, and Robert just nods his head. The bearers make sure they both have water, then carefully transfer them onto stretchers, and move them to the wagon already loaded with others. The driver says, "This won't be a long ride, fellas. We'll be takin' ya' to the field hospital near the Chancellor House, where you'll be fed and the doctor can take a look at ya'. It'll be a bit bumpy. Can't help it none."

Taking more than an hour, the muddy road slows the ride, each bump amplifying the pain in Robert's arm. They pass by an alarming number of unattended dead and wounded scattered about the fields. Will remains quiet. They finally arrive at the field hospital, where Robert asks about Welker to no avail.

Field hospital on the battlefield at Chancellorsville

Edwin Forbes drawing
Library of Congress
Morgan collection of Civil War drawings
LC-DIG-ppmsca-20538

field hospital

Robert and Will are carried to a shaded clearing. In the background they can see the smoldering ruins of the commanding general's former headquarters. The one-time family mansion has been reduced to a few partial brick walls, overshadowed by precarious chimney stacks with heat still emanating from the stonework.

One of the two stretcher bearers gives them a fresh draw of water and tells them, "Just sit tight, soldiers. Someone will be over soon." It's several hours before anyone comes to examine them. One of the medical orderlies has Will removed to the doctor's tent. He turns his attention to Robert, and removes the bandage. Doing a perfunctory exam, he finds somewhat of an enigma: an entry wound but no exit hole, a severely swollen wrist, fingers completely limp, laying over the lump in his hand.

"I think we can take care of that now for you, but it'll be painful as we are out of chloroform and ether. The general didn't leave us much to work with for supplies."

Robert holds back the orderly's hand. "Where'd you take Will? Where's Welker?"

"I don't know about this fella Welker," says the orderly, "but your friend needs a closer look by a real doctor."

Robert frees his wrist. "Don't take offense, but I want this to be looked at by a surgeon before any cutting happens."

"You and a thousand others. Look, the surgeon's too busy to deal with the likes of your injury. If you won't let me do it, you'll be forced to wait until you get to a hospital in Washington City. That'll be a spell and infection or gangrene can cost you the arm, or worse. Still wanna wait for someone 'more qualified'?"

"I'll take my chances."

He starts to redress the arm for the trip ahead. "We're gonna send you up north where a 'proper surgeon' can take a better look at you. There'll be a wagon to take you across the pontoons, then over to Falmouth."

Robert's eyes widen.

"Don't worry. We're under the protection of a truce. The Rebs can't handle their own wounded, and they sure as hellfire don't want you. A train will take you on a short ride to Aquia Landing. Then, it's a luxurious cruise into Washington City. Better food will be waiting for you there. But before that, someone will bring you coffee and biscuits soon."

As he walks away, Robert props up on his good elbow and yells, "Can you find out about my sergeant? Welker's his name." The orderly doesn't look back, waves him off, and keeps on walking. Despite deep hunger pangs, Robert has no appetite. Exhausted, he falls asleep.

* * *

Early the next morning, Robert finally gets some warm coffee and biscuits which help revive his spirits. The rain continues throughout the day, and it's still cold when the stretcher bearers approach.

"We're here to transport you to the train station at Falmouth. The roads are in bad shape and getting worse by the hour. Once we get to the corduroy roads, the footing will be more solid, but yer gonna be bouncin' like crazy, and the ride isn't a short one. Don't worry about the train. You won't be headed north 'til tomorrow even if we don't break down."

The others in the wagon do nothing to mask their discontent. Like Robert, they've waited close to a week without food or much sleep. Once underway, the complaints start and get louder with each bump. The men, drivers included, have to absorb a steady stream of bounces that aggravate the already weakened passengers' injuries. After a prolonged spell of non-stop carping, the teamster finally stops and turns to face them. "If ya' can't 'preciate what we're doin' here, I can let ya' walk. What'll it be?" He continues to stare at them until the undercurrent dies down; he then snaps the reins and rolls on.

The train depot is a welcome sight, filled with clerks holding journals, contraband labor working over a fire pit, and volunteers who wait to serve. The clerks work their way around to the new arrivals. Each man now has a medical case card attached to him with his name, unit, injury severity, and hospital of destination.

A bone thin corporal in his late forties approaches. Robert greets him with, "Did you see a Sergeant Welker come through here? Where's Will Hickman? Can you tell me how they are? Where'd they end up? No one will tell me anything."

The corporal patiently listens, then says, "I can't either, young man. There have been thousands of you boys come through here the last several days. We just collect the information that'll be given to the Sanitation officer."

"Sanitation officer? What's that?"

"He's part of the United States Sanitation Commission. They're here to keep things organized. Good people. Not Army or government, just civilians here to help make life better for you. You'll be seeing a lot of them here on out. These are the people who track everything we write down. You need to conserve your own energy, as there's a lengthy journey ahead, and I assume you're hungry. We'll get you something to warm you up."

About ten minutes later he reappears and hands him a mug of brewed coffee. It tastes as good as it smells. He sits down beside him, and says, "If it means anything to you, my name's Franklin. My friends and family call me 'Stick' on account of how I look. You can call me that too, if you like."

"Thank you, Stick." Robert gives his newfound acquaintance the information he needs for his journal. "Can we get some food?"

Waving his thumb toward the inbound train, "'Fraid not. When you arrive at Aquia, about an hour up the tracks, they'll take good care of you." As the corporal stands, Robert holds out his good hand. Franklin shakes it warmly, then moves on.

The train cars are shockingly open——flatbeds——no seats, no walls, no overhead. Franklin stands atop a wooden box under the small awning to forewarn everyone what's ahead. "As you can see it's still drizzling, so plan on getting wet." The soldiers respond with derisive no-kidding laughter, and an undercurrent of complaints. "Listen, I'm trying to be honest with you here. This will not be a picnic, and it's better you know what to expect."

"It'd be better if we'd at least had some cover," an anonymous voice shouts from the back. "We're hurtin' and still hungry." Another grumble from the men, this time in agreement.

Franklin answers, "You're right, but there's nothing I can do about that." More complaints, but this time malicious. The already rattled corporal continues, "Please. It's only fifteen miles northeast, and you'll be there in little more than an hour. You'll soon be in comfortable beds, getting warm food, hot coffee, and no threats of battle."

* * *

The train slows as it make the gradual descent to the tidal plain that leads to the landing at Aquia Creek. As they pull into the depot, the men are angry, hungry, and anxious to disembark; some don't wait for assistance.

A tent, at the far side of the platform, provides cover from the elements for those in charge. A middle-aged officer stands atop a crate and watches the chaos, ready to give a brief and field the inevitable flood of questions.

"Your attention men. Quiet! There are volunteers from the Commission making their way around. I promise you'll be feeling better soon. Your ship will be at dockside in the morning, but let's get you fed first, then we'll talk about tomorrow's trip." The officer climbs down from the crate and starts to circulate among the troops to answer their questions and give reassurance where needed.

A woman approaches Robert with a plate of hot food. She's older, late thirties or early forties, dressed in a plain gray outfit, and a bonnet to protect her from the rain. She asks to sit next to him, hands him the meal and checks his name tag. "Hi, Robert. I'm Susia. Do you need help with this?"

field hospital

Bringing wounded soldiers to the cars

Arthur Lumley drawing
Library of Congress
Morgan collection of Civil War drawings
LC-DIG-ppmsca-20792

"I don't know, ma'am."

She starts to feed Robert and continues to speak. "It was my husband, Franklin, who saw you men off at Falmouth."

"Oh, sure," he says with a mouthful. "I know who you're talking about."

"We've been married close to twenty-three years now. Got a boy a little younger than you, desperate to get into the fight. Daughter, too. Franklin wants to keep him home because our youngest had already died from the fever. What brought you here?"

"A bullet and a Rebel shell. Sorry for your loss, ma'am."

"It's been a number of years, but thank you, Robert."

He keeps the conversation going between bites. "I understand what your boy's feeling, but he ought to know it's no picnic out there. I couldn't wait to get into it. Nothing back home, just farm work. No money. Sounded like it'd be an adventure. I had no idea the fight the Rebs would put up, or how long this would last. I don't mean to worry you, but do your best to keep your boy at home."

"We may not be able to with the draft. President Lincoln keeps raising the numbers."

The mention of Lincoln brings new enthusiasm to Robert's demeanor. "Got a chance to see him a couple of times, but not to speak with him or anything. Once on the Peninsula, and again at Falmouth."

"I imagine those are times you'll never forget," Susia adds. "He passes through here when he comes down to pay a visit to one of your generals. So tall, so impressive, and kind. He came around and shook our hands on one of his visits. Seemed like a right humble, appreciative man." She stops and reflects on the memory, then with a satisfied grin adds, "Franklin's a little jealous he never got that close. Where are you from?"

"Originally England, ma'am. My family came over about ten years ago. We moved to a small farming community in western New York. How about you and Stick, I mean Franklin?"

She smiles. "Oh, he shared that with you? Doesn't give that name out to many people. He must a taken a likin' to you. Right now we live outside of Washington, but his duty and my work keep us in the city most of the time."

"Sounds like it isn't easy."

"I'm grateful that at least Franklin isn't in the field. Close enough right here."

Robert tries, and fumbles using a fork in his left hand, but manages to finish his meal—a good-sized portion of bacon, potatoes, a mug of beef broth, and a large slice of corn bread. Robert hands her the empty dishes, and says, "Thank you. I imagine you have others to see to."

"I do, but it's been a real pleasure, Robert."

"You too, ma'am." He relaxes with a fresh mug of coffee. He places the empty mug alongside the stretcher and despite the activity and volume of noises around the depot, falls sound asleep.

Friday, 8 May 1863

The pain in Robert's arm awakens him before sunrise. Early on, Susia is there to hand him coffee which he gratefully accepts. His eyes follow her as she walks away until he notices the transport. It's not as big as the one he rode from the Peninsula, but completely fills the dock.

After a brief from the same officer, black men come around to load the patients. When a couple approach Robert, one points to his stretcher and asks, "Gonna be needin' that, or wanna walk?"

"If you'll help, I guess I can walk. Just watch my arm. How'd you boys end up here?"

The first of the two looks to the other, then says, "Most not wantin' to hear our story. We both escaped from the fields, from our masters an' their whip. Come here for work and find some way to get our families. We got work here, place to sleep, and food 'nough, just no money. Commission people right helpful, but they got no money for us neither. Seems nobody's got no money up in these here parts."

They carefully escort Robert aboard the ship, adroitly maneuver him around the others already in place, and find him a partial bale of straw by the rail to sit on. It's in the high fifties, but cooling, so the men tuck him in with a woolen blanket. "This looks like it'll be comfortable, 'n you'll get a good view," says the one. As they turn to leave, Robert thanks them. They nod and move on.

* * *

Washington City's Sixth and Seventh Streets docks are a vast hub of ceaseless activity. Ships of various sizes line the piers, loading and off-loading cargo, wounded troops, and passengers. The piers are filled with onlookers, some out of curiosity, others to offer their sympathy to unknown faces. A large contingency of volunteers from the Sanitary Commission, stewards, aides, and scores of ambulance wagons crowd the docks to assist the wounded.

Unloading the ship is a masterwork of efficiency. The men, wrapped in an assortment of bloody, make-shift dressings, await assignment. Some take seats on the pier, others on the dry grounds.

Medical orderlies assist Robert relatively soon. He notices their gray armbands with an embroidered yellow symbol of two snakes twisted around a wand with wings at its top. He points to the insignia on the younger of the two and asks, "What's that? Never seen one before."

The older one answers. "It's a caduceus, the symbol for healing. They're new. We like 'em. Gives us some status with the men."

With their help, Robert stands and unsteadily makes his way to a line of ambulance wagons waiting to take them to their destination hospital. Three men are already seated, the stretchers soon follow.

It's a slow ride to Carver Hospital, located on Meridian Hill in the northern part of the city; the grounds are part of Columbian College. The carriage passes along Fourteenth Street where the full hospital complex comes into view. North of the road, there is a large array of tents, home to the "Invalid Corps", that looks more like a field encampment than a hospital. Once past the grounds of the college, the main hospital comes into full view. Army barracks, now converted into wards, line the south side of the avenue with more that surround the perimeter of the grounds.

A young man in a different style of uniform is flanked by several hospital stewards and a nurse. "Please stay seated. Welcome to Carver Hospital. My name's Sergeant Stroud. As soon as we can get you checked in, you'll be assigned a temporary bed. Those of you who can get out and walk, please follow me. The rest of you will be carried in by the stewards."

Over the next three months, Carver will be Robert's new home.

Carver Hospital, Washington City

Library of Congress
Prints and Photographs Division
LC-DIG-ppmsca-33660

Carver Hospital

U.S. National Archives
111-B-173

carver hospital

Saturday, 9 May 1863

The hospital steward leans over the cot and gently shakes Robert. "Come on, soldier, it's time to wake up." There's no immediate response. He checks his registration card for his name and tries again, this time more emphatically. "Robert, it's time to get up."

He begins to stir. It's been his first night of real rest in any semblance of a bed for weeks. "Yeah, thanks, I'm awake." Even though his bed is little more than a wooden frame with stretched canvas, it is major step up from the cold, wet ground.

Through sleep-fogged eyes Robert looks at his billet. There are several cots similar to his filled with the men who rode the ambulance wagons from the wharf. The room seems bright, and clean. There is much coughing and a little groaning as one-by-one the men are awakened. The stench of untreated wounds, unwashed men and uniforms, coupled with the pungency of disinfectant, assault Robert as he regains his senses.

"Good morning, soldier. You can relax, now. We'll give you a good deal of our time and attention today," says the steward. "One of the commission volunteers will be around to talk with you, and one of the staff will be here to get you cleaned-up. A surgeon will follow sometime later to see what we can do to treat your arm. After that you'll be assigned a ward."

Within minutes a nurse in his mid-thirties, overweight, and balding, stops by Robert's bed. He's empty-handed.

"What's it take to get some food around here?" Robert grouses.

"Excuse me? My name is Benjamin. Yours?"

"I'm sorry. My name's Robert. I'm just hungry."

"I understand, but you're scheduled for a surgical procedure this morning. They will administer an anesthetic. Any food or water eight hours prior to that might be aspirated."

"What's that?"

"Well, say there's food in your stomach, and you get nauseous from the chloroform, a relatively common occurrence. You throw up, inadvertently inhale some of the vomit, then choke on it."

Robert is more than a little alarmed. "Do I need to be worried about it then?"

"Just in combination with food, which won't be an issue now that you know."

"Thanks … I guess."

"Don't worry, you'll be fine." Trying to take Robert's mind off the upcoming surgery, Benjamin asks, "Where's home for you?"

"New York."

"City boy, huh?"

"No, no, western New York, not too far from Rochester."

"That's good. Those big city boys are usually a handful. Look, we'll give you a sponge bath, put you into a fresh bed shirt, then take your uniform; don't worry, you'll get it back."

"Considering the condition it's in, you can toss it, but I will need to get a replacement." Benjamin chuckles. "Where are *you* from, Ben?"

"Call me Benjamin, please," he says. "Not too far north of here in Maryland."

"I thought a lot of you Maryland boys lean toward Secesh sympathies?"

"A lot of 'em do. I'm not one of 'em … never have been. I hate what they're doing to our country."

Robert holds out his good hand. "Glad to meet you, Benjamin."

The nurse smiles back. "You too, Robert. I'll be back shortly to get you cleaned up."

He turns to walk away when Robert asks, "How long before the doctor gets here?"

Benjamin stops short and sighs. "Best to start having some patience now. Things don't happen here as fast as they do in the field. The doctor will get to you when he does. He's a good man and thorough. Count yourself lucky."

"That took a lot of grit, to say that about the Maryland boys." Robert looks to see a man in the bunk next to him. They are only four feet apart, but he hadn't noticed him before he spoke up.

"What's your name?"

"Jimmy from Hoboken," he answers with a wide smile.

"Where's that?"

"New Jersey. You farm boys don't get out much do you?"

"Guess not. How'd you know I come from a farm?"

"Lucky guess." He grins.

"What are you here for?"

It's an effort for Jimmie to shift position. "Took one in the foot at Chancellorsville. Left me in the field for close to a week. How 'bout you?"

Robert holds up his arm. "Same deal. Just got in last night."

His new acquaintance gets a little more serious. "They think I may lose my foot. Got a bad infection. Been in one of their field hospitals to keep an eye on me. Decided I'd get better care here."

"Tough break. Some orderly out there wanted to do surgery on me, but I wouldn't let him. Still carrying the bullet."

"Where?"

"In the palm of my hand. Can't feel anything. I guess it can't be that bad."

Benjamin arrives with a deep pan filled with soapy water, a clean cloth, and a small towel draped over his shoulder. First he cuts off the remainder of Robert's jacket, shirt and field dressing. Before he can object, Benjamin says, "We'll see what we can do to get you that replacement you asked for."

He starts to wash his face, then moves on to the back of his neck. The cool, clean water is a welcome relief. His skin tingles from losing the last couple weeks of caked on grime and dried blood. Benjamin asks

Robert to lean forward, and does the same to his back, then vigorously washes his left arm and hand that are close to black with filth.

"Ohhh, this feels great, Benjamin."

"This will start to start get a little tricky. Tell me if it hurts." He gently lifts his arm, and gingerly scrubs his chest and under the right arm.

"How's that?" he asks.

"I'm alright."

Benjamin takes the towel draped over his shoulder and carefully wipes off the areas he just washed. He holds up the nearly black towel, and says, "Your next bath will be much more thorough. Just need to get you presentable for the surgeon who will be here shortly."

Within minutes, a major, dressed in full army blues, stops by with a steward who carries a pen and a journal.

"I am Dr. Cross. You may call me Doctor, Major, or Sir. We may not be in the field, but don't get the idea you're no longer in the army, soldier. Now let me get a look at your arm."

As he lifts Robert's arm, he says "Tell me if you feel this." Robert nods with a grimace.

He starts to dictate to the steward, who's recording. "Looks like a Minié ball entered the upper right extensor compartment, traveled along the ulna, and through the wrist. Judging from the redness and swelling, the bullet's track stopped at the base of the fourth metacarpal in the palm of his hand. The wrist appears to be fractured." He carefully moves each of Robert's fingers, and notes they are completely flaccid, then looks at him and asks, "What do you feel when I do this?"

"Nothing. My hand has been numb since the battle. My arm aches, but I can't feel anything in my hand when you touch it."

"Can you move these fingers?"

"No, sir."

The doctor looks back at the steward, then remarks, "The right hand may also be fractured, and there is tendon and nerve damage from the bullet."

He asks Robert, "Why didn't they take care of this in the field hospital?"

"I wouldn't let them."

"You wouldn't?" he replies sharply. "If this infection doesn't respond to treatment you can lose this arm. Frankly, it's a miracle the bullet didn't take it off to begin with."

Robert gets defensive. "The only person who looked at me at the field hospital was an orderly. We were outdoors, in the rain, and I wasn't about to let him cut on me there."

The doctor nods. "I understand, but we need to attend to this as soon as possible. I will send a couple of stewards to take you to a surgery ward where we can treat you properly." The doctor sees him start to tense up. "Listen, you are in qualified hands here. You will not feel a thing. You will be put to sleep, and while you are out, the procedure will be a quick one. When you come to, you'll be in a much more comfortable bed. I'll stop by later in the day to fill you in on what we found."

Robert nervously asks, "Will you be able to save the arm?"

"No promises. It's too soon to tell."

The steward continues to fill out the chart then adds it to the color card at the foot of his cot. Robert tries to take his mind off the operation, and asks, "What's the card for?"

"It just tells us what kind of foods we can feed you. Different colors designate whether you're on a low-, half-, or full diet, and right now, with the surgery, you're not allowed any food or drink for the next few hours, and having an anesthetic, you won't want much to eat anyway."

As Robert waits for the stretcher bearers, Jimmie pipes up.

"Man you're lucky. Getting top brass treatment like that. They haven't done nothin' for me yet."

Robert raises his eyebrows and tilts his head to the side. "Guess you needed to come from a farm."

surgery

Within the hour, two stewards arrive with a stretcher and transfer Robert, sheets and all. They take both cards from the foot of the cot, toss them atop his legs, then carry him into a long corridor for the short trip to the surgery room.

"Don't try to get up. The surgeon's assistant will be in soon. He'll see to your needs."

He's left alone in the room, but not for long. A young lieutenant enters wearing a white apron. "Good morning, soldier. My name is Dr. Rucker. I'll be assisting Dr. Cross who examined you earlier."

Within minutes Dr. Cross enters, also wearing an apron. He's followed by the same steward. "It won't be too long before you will feel much better, Robert. Just relax and lay back." He looks up at Dr. Rucker and nods.

The young lieutenant holds up a device that looks like a cone with a sponge affixed to it. He opens the lid of a tin container and starts to slowly pour drops of the liquid into the cone. As the sponge absorbs it, he slowly lowers the device over Robert's mouth and nose.

After a few minutes, and a few more drops, he asks, "What's the smell like, Robert?"

"It's kind of sweeee ..." he tries to answer but goes limp.

* * *

Robert awakens in new surroundings. Once his head clears, and before he looks anywhere else, he checks to see if he still has his arm. With great relief he thankfully finds a light bandage around his hand and forearm.

The hospital pavilion is well over a hundred foot long, with walls and rafters painted bright white. Tall windows frame each pair of beds, with prominent displays of the Union flag, both large and small. The roof is peaked at an angle and supported by cross beams. It's fresh, airy, and seems well-ventilated for the number of patients in the ward. Even though a hospital, it beats anything he's been in for months. He lays his head back down and surrenders to his fatigue.

* * *

Later that evening, Robert sits upright, and enjoys some buttered bread and fresh coffee. His bed is an iron frame with a mattress supported by wooden slats, an unexpected luxury. Dr. Cross approaches him with Benjamin in tow.

"How did it look, Doctor?"

"Better than I'd hoped." He then tries to illustrate the operation using Robert's good hand as a guide. "I made a relatively shallow incision an inch long, from the base of your ring finger toward the wrist. Once opened up, the Minié ball popped out of your hand, not surprisingly followed by a fair amount of pus." The doctor reaches into his pocket and pulls out the bullet. "I thought you might like the memento."

The doctor waits while Robert looks it over closely, examines it from every angle, gauges its size, and feels the distorted features from the impact. "Thank you, sir."

The doctor continues on. "A small piece of your jacket floated out with it, a pleasant surprise. If it didn't, we'd need to probe around for it, a more invasive procedure. We irrigated the wound then bandaged it up. You were out of surgery and here in bed about twenty minutes after you fell asleep."

"How many stitches?"

"None. The opening's relatively small, no bleeding to speak of, but we will need to keep an eye on it to make sure it heals properly. The suppuration of pus is a good thing. Shows the body expelling the dead tissue that surrounded the bullet. Once the swelling goes down, we'll get a board splint put together, and you can start to get up and about."

"Food?"

The doctor looks to Benjamin. "Right. Let's change his card to half-diet. He'll tolerate food well enough. Next day or two we'll put you on full rations."

"Thank you, sir, for everything."

"You're welcome. The hospital will be your new home for awhile. Benjamin will stay on with you for a bit this afternoon to let you know the daily and Sunday routines, along with our expectations. Focus on getting yourself well."

As the doctor leaves the ward, Benjamin changes Robert's diet card, pulls a chair over to the side of his bed, and finishes his progress report. He places the new cards at the end of the bed and smiles. "I assume you're a lot more comfortable now?"

"I guess, but I haven't taken the time to think much about it."

"As the surgeon said, there's a routine here. It's the same six days a week, except Sundays. You'll be expected to follow military protocol. After breakfast, he makes his rounds followed by a nurse and your ward-master. You'll recognize him by his uniform and chevrons, different than yours. Don't sell him short. He's in charge of the patients. It's mostly an administrative position, but you don't want to cross him. He can make your stay uncomfortable. Everyone who's physically able is expected to come to attention, and salute. The surgeon will let you know when you can sit. Don't worry, he never keeps anyone up for long. For the next couple of days, just sit upright in your bed, like you did earlier. The surgeon will check your wounds, dictate what he finds to the ward-master, and let him know what treatment, medicines, or changes to your diet."

"How many patients are here?"

Benjamin points to the far end of the pavilion. "See down to the end there? We are but one of scores of pavilions in this complex. Over thirteen hundred beds. Our doctor isn't responsible for everyone, but more than what's in front of you."

Robert nods. "You mentioned Sundays."

"This whole place will be cleaned and spruced up. For rounds, we'll be in full dress uniform——surgeons, stewards, and patients. It's supposed to be a good reminder that we are still in the Army, but in reality, it's a show when the ward is open for public visitation."

"I thought by the looks of things that it's open every day."

"There are volunteer caregivers who come in to visit and see to the needs of the soldiers. Many are family and friends. Some are just people who want to help. You'll get to know who they are soon enough. Sundays are more for the general public. There will be church groups, fraternal organizations, Freemasons, and the like. They usually bear gifts, baked goods mostly, so we put on a good face."

"You said the place is cleaned once a week for the public?"

Benjamin grimaces. "More than that now. We got in trouble a short while back. Apparently an inspection was published that listed ours as one of many hospitals in the city cited for less than sanitary conditions." Everything looks so immaculate, Robert never noticed. "We're ashamed to admit that we, the staff, got cited for negligence, we failed to pick up bandages from the floor, empty bedpans in a timely manner, and change patients' soiled clothes. To be fair, it gets overwhelming at times. Regardless, our surgeon-in-charge got us together and royally dressed us down. I don't expect that will happen again. Every single day the floors get washed. Twice a day we inspect each ward to police it up, then twice weekly it all gets thoroughly scrubbed. Another crew checks around the grounds to police the trash."

"Another crew?"

"We call them the 'walking wounded'. *You.* You and others like you. Once you get ambulatory enough to pitch in without hurting yourself. You'll be outside in the fresh air, with plenty of company. There will be a few shirkers, but for the most part everyone pitches in. Things get done in short order."

"Whatever you say."

John G. Turnbull
 photo courtesy Massachusetts Commandery
 Military Order of the Loyal Legion
 and the US Military History Institute

captain turnbull

Sunday, 10 May 1863

The ward is immaculate. Its wide, wood-planked floors are still slightly damp from the early cleaning. Most of the men are in uniform and sit next to their beds to read, play cards, and keep each other company. The surgeon enters and looks resplendent. The patients are allowed to sit, but each stands as they are personally approached, and render honors. Robert tries to swing his legs around the side of the bed, but the doctor tells him to relax and moves on.

When all returns to normal, a woman in her late thirties approaches. "Are you Private Canham?"

"Yes, ma'am."

"There's a visitor for you."

"Who knows I'm even here?" By now she's out of ear-shot.

He looks to the foyer-side of the pavilion and sees Lieutenant Turnbull as he enters.

John G. Turnbull, a Washington City native, has been with his unit since 5 August 1861. He received an 'at large' second lieutenant's commission at the age of seventeen, and at nineteen, promoted to first lieutenant. Initially the men didn't know what to make of him. Not a West Point man, but one of the exceptions——a civilian volunteer with extraordinary leadership ability: calm under fire, clear-headed, and decisive. He defers to veterans, yet shows no favoritism, and recognizes and rewards the men on their merits. The three hundred men of his combined batteries feel lucky to serve under him.

"Lieutenant!" At first, Robert is shocked then takes a second look, sees the new bars on his shoulders, and corrects himself. "Captain? Congratulations, sir. When did this happen? How'd you find me? You can't know how happy I am to see you."

"Hello, Robert. It's good to see you looking so well."

"Thank you, sir. How are you? The other men? Any news about Sergeant Welker or Will?"

Turnbull holds up both hands to slow him down. "Let's take things one at a time." He pulls a chair over by the bed and sits. "First off, I'm here to see how *you're* doing."

"Pretty well I guess." He lifts his arm, "They took the bullet out of my hand yesterday."

He's shocked. "Yesterday?"

Robert nods. "I wouldn't let them cut on me at Chancellorsville."

"Why didn't they take it out sooner?"

"I just got here the night before last. They removed it first thing in the morning."

Turnbull slowly shakes his head as he speaks. "I'm sorry we left you in the field. That must have been rough on you."

"I understand the battery comes first. The sergeant and I kept each other company, and after they took him, Will and I stayed together until they picked us up."

"Well, they returned Will to us once we settled back in at Falmouth. He suffered a pretty bad concussion. He's on light duty and starting to come around."

"How about the sergeant. Hear anything about him?"

Turnbull sighs. "I did, Robert. They got him to Washington as soon as possible, and put him up at Armory Hospital. His wound didn't seem that bad, but after they removed the shrapnel he developed gangrene."

"Oh, Lord."

"He died last Thursday ... the hospital staff said he passed peacefully."

Robert's eyes begin to well up. The captain puts his hand atop his.

"I'm very sorry, Robert. I know that you two had a closer relationship than most. He always spoke highly of you. We'll all miss him: his accessibility, his leadership, and his sense of humor. He was a good mentor to both of us and a good man."

Robert can only nod as he struggles to keep his emotions in check.

Turnbull tries to lighten things up. "The men asked to be remembered to you. Ramsey, in particular, wanted me to order you to, 'Quit your skylarking, and get back to work.'" They both laugh.

"Have they given you any idea how much longer you're going to be here?"

Robert answers, "No, sir. Nothing definite. If my arm heals okay, I'll be splinted up for a spell. They're won't tell me much more than that."

"Can I do anything for you in the meantime?"

Robert looks at him. "It's been great to see a familiar face, and I do appreciate the news ... better to know than not, I guess."

As he stands, Turnbull says, "I'm in town to visit my folks, then I need to start to make tracks back to Falmouth. Lee's not giving us much of a break. We're going to move out pretty soon."

Robert holds out out his good hand. "Thank you again, Captain. And, congratulations, you certainly deserve it."

"Hope to see you back with us soon."

It's hard to see him leave. Harder still to digest the news about Welker. Robert spends the remainder of the day by himself—and remembers.

Monday, 11 May 1863

After rounds, the chaplain makes it a point to visit each patient in the ward. Robert looks forward to more than the superficial conversation they had when he first arrived. "Good morning, sir."

"Good morning to you, too." He looks at Robert's name tag then comments, "Please call me Chaplain or Chaplain Bill. 'Sir' just puts too much distance between us, Robert. I want you to know that I'm here to help in any way I can."

"I do have something that I just found out yesterday. The captain of our artillery unit informed me that my Gunner, Sergeant Welker died from the wounds he received in the same battle that brought me here."

"I'm sorry to hear that. Were you two close?"

"I considered him a friend. He helped me through a lot, and I miss him." Tears start to flow down his cheeks.

"News like that is never easy on anyone, especially when you're a patient."

"Did he tell you the cause of death?"

"He did ... he died of gangrene."

"Oh, dear. How do you think the other men in your outfit will take the news?"

"I think it will be hard on all of them. He was a very special man."

The chaplain doesn't respond.

"I do have a question, Chaplain. Do you think he suffered a lot?"

"It's hard to say, but I don't think so. In these cases, the men seem to be in a state of quiet peace. It's like they just fall asleep."

Robert motions the chaplain to move his head closer, then lowers his voice, like they would share a deep secret only between the two of them. "Sergeant Welker was a good man. Do you think ... do you think he's in Heaven?"

"None of us knows that. That's between your sergeant and his Creator," he answers. "I think you need to be more concerned about *your* relationship with Him."

Robert is a little taken aback. He never heard talk about God from a personal standpoint, just stories from the Bible, church hymns, and the sermons the minister preached. "I don't know how to respond to that, Chaplain."

He sits back up in his chair, but speaks softly, "I'm not surprised. I carry a booklet with me that might be of some help. It came out in the forties, but His truths are eternal. You're welcome to it, if you like?"

"I guess so. Sure."

"If there are any questions, please let me know, and feel free to keep the tract. It's a gift."

"Uh, okay, Chaplain, thanks."

He slips the booklet out of his pocket. *Come To Jesus*, by Dr. Newman Hall. Robert starts to leaf through it, but sees it will take some time to read it thoroughly, and places it on his nightstand.

"Is there anything I can do for you? The men often ask me to write home for them."

"No need right now. Benjamin got a couple of notes off to my family the other day." He holds up his arm, and adds, "I'm right-handed, and this makes it a little difficult, but I do like to read."

"It was nice to chat with you. I am sorry for the loss of your friend. I'll pray for you, son."

President Abraham Lincoln

Alexander Gardner photograph
Library of Congress
Prints and Photographs Division
LC-DIG-ppmsca-19215

mr. president

Thursday, 21 May 1863

After rounds, Robert notices a much more frenetic mood from the staff. He finally catches Benjamin in full stride. "What's going on?"

He stops, a little bit irritated with the interruption. "Rumors are, and they're usually pretty reliable, that we may entertain some important visitors in the next couple of days."

"How important?"

"It may be Mr. Lincoln, himself!"

"You sure that's not just scuttlebutt?"

"It's been floating around, but like I said, it's from a pretty reliable source."

"What can I do to help?"

"We'll need you with the outside crew. The grounds need to be immaculate."

"Sure. Anything."

Benjamin adds, "Let me finish what I'm doing here, and I'll get back to you."

Robert has been with the "walking wounded" crew outside since Monday, and doing light duty around the ward. His hand continues to heal nicely, the infection has cleared up, and the swelling has diminished. An assistant surgeon devised a board splint for the back of his hand and arm, which Robert keeps in a sling. The ache in his arm has subsided, but his fingers and hand are still numb. He's grateful for the opportunity to move about, even if only doing menial tasks.

Work parties of close to a hundred men join those already outdoors. Robert closes his eyes and deeply breathes in the fresh air. Their well-ventilated ward is still a hospital ward with the miasma associated with wounds, pus, and medicine. No matter how frequently or thoroughly it's cleaned, it doesn't compare to the pure aroma of fresh air. Robert continues to inhale deeply, until he gets a little light-headed He looks about at the thick, healthy grass and shade trees at the periphery, and takes in the perfume of nature.

A first sergeant steps up to give the men a brief and sets them about their task to police the grounds outside of the pavilions. Robert thinks the staffing is overkill until he sees how vast the grounds are. There are seventy-five pavilions spread about a forty-six acre campus. The job will easily take up the balance of this day and the better part of Friday.

At the end of the work detail, Robert returns to find a brand new uniform: shirt, pants, and the shell jacket of an artilleryman, topped by a forage hat, complete with his unit's insignia. Robert holds the hat and looks around until his eyes catch those of the woman who announced his visitor. "It's from that officer who came to see you the Monday before last. Seems so young to be a captain. He asked me to hold on to it until the time's right. I figure that's now."

Robert smiles and expresses his appreciation.

"He must think an awful lot of you," she adds.

"He has always looked out for us. Will you be here for the visit?"

"I wouldn't miss it. I just hope the President makes it to our ward."

"Why wouldn't he?"

"Well, consider the size of this place. You've seen it from the outside."

"I'd be disappointed if he didn't make it here." He pauses to work up the courage to say, "I've seen you in passing, and I'm sorry, but I don't know your name."

"My name's Pauline. Pauline Baker. Mrs. Baker to you, Robert."

He takes a closer, longer look at her. Even though she's close to twice his age, he finds her attractive. There are hints of age lines that radiate from the corners of her eyes which she playfully uses to endear herself to the men. She presents herself as a woman with few cares in her life, self-confident and genuinely happy.

"I know you're wondering … my husband, Nicholas, works with the United States Sanitary Commission, responsible for the coordination and redistribution of the many donations that come our way. He works at the Sixth Street docks."

"That's where I arrived from Aquia Creek."

"As did most of the boys in this ward. His committee usually oversees reloading the boats for their return trip."

"Sounds like a big job."

"It is, but he has good people working for him. They've gotten quite proficient. It's just that the needs are great, keeping the Army in goods."

"Any children?"

Walking away, she replies, "That's for another day, Private."

Saturday, 23 May 1863

Everyone's up early anticipating the President's visit. The grounds outside are seemingly spotless, the ward has been thoroughly scrubbed, and the men are freshly bathed and fed. Their beds made and taut.

The patients take special care in their personal grooming. Those not fully able to care for themselves are attended to by the stewards and nurses.

Robert dresses as much as he can with his one working hand, but he needs help and the staff passes him by. He can't find Benjamin, so he walks out to the foyer to see Pauline at her desk. Her dress is much more festive in coloration, though not ostentatious, with black, brown, and gold stripes. Its closure at her neckline is accentuated with an heirloom cameo. Her hair is tightly braided, pinned up with a velvet lace snood, and held in place by a decorative hair comb.

Robert's untucked, unbuttoned, and holding his jacket. Pauline looks up and laughs. "You're a sight, young man. Let's see if we can get you fixed properly." She buttons his shirt and left sleeve, and rolls up the right sleeve over his splint. She helps tuck in his shirt, slips the suspenders over his shoulders, and finishes buttoning him up. She slips on his jacket, and leaves the right sleeve loose.

"Where's your sling?"

"Going to try it without."

"Let's take a look at you."

She gives him the up-down once-over, and says, "Wait right here a minute." She reaches into her bag and produces a brush. As she's pulls back his hair, she asks, "When was the last time you got this cut?"

"It's been awhile," he concedes.

"I'll send one of the girls over in a couple of days to get that taken care of." She inspects him again, "My, you're a handsome sight decked out in your new uniform."

Robert blushes. "You, uh, look nice as well today, ma'am."

Pauline gives him a big grin and a nudge toward the ward. "You best be getting back by your bed. Can't be having you little chicks about when Mr. Lincoln gets here."

Warmth slowly permeates the ward with temperatures expected to reach into the nineties.

Within the hour a commotion starts in the foyer, and soon the visiting party enters the ward. The retinue is surprisingly small. Benjamin holds the door for the President, followed by Major Cross and an unknown civilian. Lincoln carries his stovepipe hat and hands it to the stranger, who waits by the door as the party works its way around the ward. The doctor introduces each patient and gives the President a quick recap of their maladies. Lincoln shakes the hand of each one of them, shares a few words, and moves on.

Robert is the eighth stop in this ward. He stands at attention, salutes, and says good morning to the President. Six inches taller than Robert, Lincoln has a kind visage, a gentle voice and demeanor, but looks to be carrying the burdens of a nation at war. Dr. Cross takes Robert's splinted arm.

"This is Private Robert Canham, Mr. President. He was hit here with a .58 caliber Minié ball." He follows the track of the bullet with his finger, and continues to describe the extent of his injury to the President, explaining how it's a miracle he still has his arm.

Lincoln smiles at him. "Robert's the name of my oldest son."

"Yes, sir." Robert is not used to looking up when speaking.

"What brought you here?"

"Chancellorsville, Mr. President."

"See much action there?"

Robert reluctantly smiles. "Enough I guess."

"Where's home for you?"

"Western New York, sir."

Lincoln emits a subtle laugh. "Seems you New York boys like to make that distinction between the city and the rest of the state. They treat you well here? Anything you need?"

"There's nothing that I need, sir. They take real good care of us."

Lincoln gestures to shake Robert's hand. "An honor to meet you, Mr. President. Got to see you when you reviewed the troops on the Peninsula and last April at Falmouth. Little disappointed I didn't get a chance to see you more up close, though."

Lincoln smiles again. "Hope you aren't disappointed. Folks sometimes set such high expectations, actual meeting me can be a big let down."

"Oh no, sir." Robert smiles. "It's been a pleasure."

Dr. Cross gives a nod of approval to Robert and extends his arm toward the adjacent bed. The party moves on.

Robert remains standing, still high on the adrenaline of meeting President Lincoln. He eyes the men as they work their way down the ward. *The folks back home are never going to believe this.*

elizabeth & hannah

Sunday, 31 May 1863

Late in the afternoon, Pauline approaches Robert who sits next to his bed reading *The Last of the Mohicans*. It's a book he has taken a personal interest in, with its narrative that centers on colonial New York. "There are people here to see you."

He shoots her a quizzical look. "Who?"

"I think it best you get up and come out to the foyer and see for yourself."

Out of guesses, he leaves his book on the bed, throws on his uniform jacket, and follows her out the door.

He's in a state of disbelief. "Mother! Hannah! How … when did you two get in?"

With that he throws his arm around his mother for a tearful reunion. After a long and tender hug, he kisses her on the cheek, looks over at his sister, who patiently waits, and gives her a hug.

"I'm shocked but delighted to see you … but how?"

Hannah answers. "Father's been squirrelin' away money fer just such an emergency. My husband figured it'd be best I come along with mother and fronted my train fare."

"What about your kids?"

"William's folks are watchin' 'em while I'm gone. They're always complainin' they never get enough time with 'em. I 'spect I won't be hearin' that no more after this trip."

Robert looks at her quizzically. "Where will you stay?"

Hannah nods toward Pauline who interjects, "Your father wrote the hospital when they first heard of your arrival, to see if coming here was appropriate. We invited them to stay at our place."

Robert looks at Pauline. "I'm humbled you'd open your home to my family, and a little sore you kept this a secret."

Hannah's eyebrows lift up. "Nice surprise though, huh?" Robert nods.

"Mother, Hannah, please come on in. I'll get some chairs."

As the three of them enter the ward, Robert makes a general pronouncement to the other soldiers within earshot to introduce the two. It's a good day. They jabber throughout the balance of the afternoon and into the evening, until Pauline says it's time to leave.

***

At rounds the doctor starts with, "I understand you enjoyed a couple of visitors yesterday."

"Yes, sir. My mother and my sister are in town."

"That's good, Robert. I'll pass the word along to one of the doctors to show them how to change your dressings, and reapply the splint."

"How much longer will I need to wear this thing?"

"At least for another couple of months. Your hand is healing nicely, but the fracture in your wrist was pretty severe. There may be some residual problems with your fingers. It's just too early to tell how much you'll get back."

"One other question——"

"They'll need to know how to change them when you're home on furlough."

"Furlough! When? How long? When?"

"Calm down, Robert. Once we ascertain your hand won't need such close attention, and your wrist is strong enough, we believe it'd be best you convalesce in the care of your family, and frankly, we need the bed space. It won't be for a couple of weeks yet, but I think you'll be glad to be out of here."

"Yes, sir!" It's hard for him to contain his emotions, and lets out a big *whoop*, much to the dismay of the doctor. The other patients are already jealous of him. This certainly won't help.

* * *

Robert's family arrives early in the afternoon, with a batch of fresh baked cookies. He sticks his face in the bag and takes in a large breath of the molasses and cinnamon.

"Oh, these smell great."

Pauline interjects, "Why don't you pass them around. They're supposed to be for everyone."

"An you'll be thankin' yer sister who baked 'em for ya'," says Elizabeth.

He squeezes Hannah's arm, grabs a handful for himself, then dutifully goes from bed-to-bed, letting each one take a cookie. He touches base with everyone in the ward. The last man grabs his wrist as he starts to leave, pulls the sack closer, grabs at the remnants of the treats, and with a smile releases his grip.

"Thank you, Canham. Nice family you got there." Robert does a double-take at the man as he moves back to his own bedside.

He hands the empty sack to Hannah. "I'm sure the guys appreciated that. I feel badly none of the staff got a taste, though."

Pauline speaks to him in hushed tones. "There's another whole bag to give to them and the two doctors in our dining area. Don't share that news with the others. Understand?" He nods.

Once he sits down, his mother takes his injured arm and carefully pulls it over to her lap. "How ya' gettin' along, son?"

He places his other hand atop hers. "I'm doing well as can be expected, mother. These things take time."

"Mrs. Baker has filled us in on your recovery." Her voice starts to quiver. "Sounds like you've been through a time of it."

"I'll be okay. The doctors, the staff, I couldn't ask for better care."

Too emotional to speak, Elizabeth just nods her head.

Hannah interjects, "Pauline says they're gonna show us how to change your dressin' and such, and that yer gonna' get a chance to come home soon. Did ya' hear Will's gettin' out … first part of the month!"

"I did. He wrote me about it. Father'll be glad when he's back."

His mother has composed herself and answers. "He's missed ya' too, and anxious to be gettin' *both* of ya' home."

Hannah says, "Pauline has offered to have her husband show the two of us around the city today."

Robert looks at her quizzically. "When is this supposed to happen?"

"As soon as Pauline tells us he's here."

Robert feels a bit disappointed, and jealous he can't go.

"Don't go frettin' yourself. We'll be back in the mornin'."

Tuesday, 2 June 1863

True to plan, the women wait in the foyer until the doctor finishes with Robert. Pauline escorts them in.

"Good morning, folks. I'm Doctor Rucker. I've been one of Robert's attending physicians. Are you ready to get started?"

The women set their things on the bed, and find a spot where they can get a good view. Another steward brings a chair over for his mother before the doctor begins. He unwraps the bandages and drops them into a bucket. He begins to dress the forearm first. Pointing to the entry-wound, he starts, "You'll notice the granula——"

Elizabeth stands and stares at his tattoo. "What's that, Robert?"

"Mother?"

"I told ya' before ya' left not to keep company with hooligans. I knew where they'd lead ya'."

"Mother, please. The boys in my battery——"

"I suppose ya'd been drinkin' and who knows what else."

Hannah takes her mother's arm. "Let 'im finish, mother. Hear what he hasta say." Elizabeth looks down at Hannah's hand, and shoots her daughter a mind-your-own-business look.

"Well, young man?"

"Mother, the others and I wanted to make sure that if we fell in battle, people could identify us, and let you know where we ended up."

His mother starts to cry. "Wicked, evil war."

The doctor excuses himself, "I'll give you folks some time to talk this out."

Robert looks up and helplessly nods. "Mother, please try to understand. We thought it'd be best for the families."

A patient in the bed next to Robert chimes in. "Ma'am, tattoos are pretty common——" He's stopped cold by the glare from Robert's mother. He swings his legs back over to the other side of his bed and doesn't repeat that mistake.

"And the snake? The devil it is."

Robert gives her a conciliatory nod. "Yeah ... probably pushed it too far with that, but the others got symbols over their names as well."

"I warned ya' not to keep that kind of company. Men that's led ya' down a dark path. I just don't like it."

When they finish with their back-and-forth the doctor returns. "You ready to continue? No more surprises?" They all nod, and he progresses through the redressing process. Hannah and his subdued mother take their turns at it.

Once he's trussed up, the three of them go out for a walk around the campus. "This is somethin'," Hannah exclaims. "How big is this place?"

Robert motions with his arm to take in the pavilions. "This section holds roughly thirteen hundred beds." He then points to the hub of the college, now converted into another hospital.

"And that one holds another eight hundred and fifty."

"Are they filled?" interjects Hannah.

"They've been at full capacity since I got here, and there are scores of hospitals throughout the city."

His mother sadly shakes her head.

* * *

Hannah's engaged in conversation with Benjamin, when Elizabeth points to the booklet on Robert's night stand. "What's that?"

"The chaplin gave it to me. It's called, *Come to Jesus*."

"It sounds good, son. What's it say?"

"It's a pretty involved Bible study, intended to lead the reader into a meaningful relationship with the Lord."

She flips through the pages, and asks, "Ya' read this, all the way through?"

"Truthfully, no. I just received it and it looks like it will take a bit of time to read, look up the Scripture references, and think on them."

"Are ya using that fer an excuse? Seems to me, ya' got nothin' but time to spare while yer here."

"I'm not ready yet, mother."

"Just look at where ya' are, son. Yer in a hospital from bein' shot! The Lord protected ya' this far. Do ya' wanna go back into battle not knowin' if yer saved?"

"It's a lot to think about, mother."

"I just hafta say this one more thing." Robert rolls his eyes. "I know, I know, but it's important. I see yer arm, and think of the evil around ya'. I think it's important to yer soul to get yer life right with God. I'll be prayin' fer that. That's all I gotta say."

"Thank you, mother. I love you too."

* * *

Robert is up early the next day. The women have a train to catch. He chats with his sister non-stop to the station. His mother stays quiet, dreading the trip ahead, but mostly leaving her youngest. Their goodbyes are heartfelt, full of gratitude, and promises to reunite soon. He doesn't say much on the return to the hospital.

Thursday, 18 June 1863

At rounds, Drs. Cross and Rucker examine Robert, then Dr. Rucker continues on while the major stays behind. "Here's your pass to cover your train fare back to your home, and your return." As he reaches for the pass, the doctor pulls it back.

"This is important, Robert. There's some men who've taken advantage of this——enjoyed the comforts of their home, then took it upon themselves to stay there. I need to remind you about your obligation to us and to your country."

"I understand, sir. Can we talk about my arm for a minute?" The doctor nods. "Well, how much can I use it while I'm home?" Pointing to the splint, he continues, "What can I expect when this comes off for good? Will my hand be crippled? Will I be able to stay in the army?"

The doctor looks down at his chart, then sighs. "I wish we knew the answers to all your questions, but nerve damage has unpredictable results. Until your wounds are fully healed and you start to get sensation back into your hand, we won't know."

"And while I'm home?"

"Try not to over-exert yourself or hit it on anything, and make sure it's kept clean. Look, son, in the next five weeks, get yourself home, enjoy some of that home cooking I've heard so much about, heal that arm of yours, then get back here by the twenty-fourth. After that, we'll be better able to tell what the coming months will bring."

"Yes, sir, I'll try my best."

"Now, grab your bag. There's a wagon waiting to take you to the station. And don't forget, back here no later than the twenty-fourth."

Benjamin's there to take his bag and help him out the door. Nicholas waits in the wagon, and Pauline comes out to say her good-byes. Much to his surprise, Pauline gives Robert a hug and a light kiss on his cheek. She says, "Be good, young man," then returns to the building without looking back.

Robert looks to Nicholas, who shrugs his shoulders. "You're like the son she never had."

furlough

The early morning sunlight pushes through the east window, tracks down the wall, and awakens Robert as it crosses his eyelids. He rolls over and covers his head, with hopes to catch more sleep, but it's too late. His mind starts to race with thoughts of decent food, fresh, healthy air, and no daily rounds, doctors, stewards, nurses, ward-masters, or other patients.

The trip from Washington to Medina, New York, ended up an exhausting odyssey of transfers, and delays. With Lee's troops on the move into Pennsylvania, the railroads cancelled certain runs and rerouted others. It turned into a nightmarish journey of precious days he'd much rather have spent with his family.

Surprised, but not shocked, they greeted Robert's arrival with hugs, kisses, handshakes, and endless questions about his arm, and the trip. He stayed up as long as possible, but once the adrenalin wore off, he wanted to climb into bed——his bed. The family understood, and redirected his brother to the couch for the first night.

His room has a double-bed the brothers have shared since childhood, and a modest four-drawer dresser that also serves as a nightstand, with an ewer of water and wash basin that compete with a single kerosene lamp for space. Robert unsteadily pours water into the basin and tries his best to freshen up with his one good hand. He looks in the dresser for something to wear, other than his Army blues. As he pulls on his pants, he realizes he's lost weight. His shirt wears like a drape and his pants need suspenders. He catches a hint of the aromas from the cookstove, and smiles with the thought that his mother wants to put some meat back on his bones.

He opens the door to the narrow stairway and descends the steep steps stabilizing himself with his good hand on the austere walls of white-washed plaster over lath. Once downstairs, he kisses his mother on the cheek, pulls up a stool, and sits at the table. She lays out a platter of fresh eggs, bacon, and biscuits to start the fare. Coffee and flapjacks with hot maple syrup soon follow.

"Some coffee, son?"

"Yes, ma'am, please."

"After breakfast, I want to take a look at that hand of yers, and replace them filthy rags with some clean 'uns. Happy bein' home? Sleep well?"

"I can't remember the last time I got such a good night's sleep. Waking up to something other than the hospital ward … well, it is good to be home. Father out back?"

"Both he and Will are hard at it."

"How's Will enjoying being home?"

"He's gettin' along just fine, but a little restless. I think he wants to get set up with a place of his own. Talks 'bout bein' a carpenter."

Robert smiles. "Any job prospects?"

"There aren't as many men around, and you'd think there'd be work, but pickin's are slim."

"I'll get up earlier tomorrow to help with the chores."

"You'll do no such thing! Ya' need be gettin' better first. The doctor sent ya' home for just that. Told me and Hannah that's our job. Don't want ya' to hurt yer arm helpin' out 'round here. Your father and I talked and he agrees with me. Though I s'pose you'll be gettin' some needlin' from yer siblings, but don't ya' make no never mind 'bout that. Can I get ya' anythin' else, son?"

"Thanks, mother, but I'm good for now. Well, just some more coffee I guess."

Elizabeth tops off his mug, pours a fresh one for herself, refills the pot, and sits down across from him. "I wanna talk 'bout things we couldn't in the hospital."

"Like what, Mother?"

"Were ya' 'fraid much ... in battle I mean."

He hesitates a long time before answering. He nurses his coffee to stall, and wonders how much will suffice to allay her fears. He wants to protect himself, not revive deep-seated horrors buried in his own mind. Yet he doesn't want to lie to her, either. "For a bit, we all are, but then we focus on our jobs. No time to think about fear then."

She looks at his arm, and asks, "What's it like gettin' shot, son?"

"I honestly don't remember. The first thing I recall, they were taking us to a safe area."

"Been prayin' for ya'. Me and your father both ... seems like we're always prayin' God will keep ya' from harm ..." She starts to well up.

"Looks like your prayers are answered, mother. God has brought both of us home, safe and sound."

"It's been hard not knowin' where ya' two were, or what was happenin' with ya'. Yer father reads the news reports, hear the rumors, and tries to find our people in 'em. The letters weren't often comin'. Made things hard. Tried not to worry, but when things get quiet at night——"

"Morning, Robert. Glad to see ya' join us," his sister Hannah jibes as she walks through the back door. She gives him a hug and a kiss on the cheek then heads to the stove for some coffee.

Their mother stops her, "Take a bit 'fore the next batch is ready. Emptied the pot a few minutes back."

"Guess we best be gettin' used to this with these two 'round." Hannah hugs him. "Glad yer back, brother."

Though married and raising her own family, she has a close bond with her parents and brothers, and frequents the farm to help out.

"Where are the kids? I want them to get to know their uncle before I head back."

"Good luck with that, son. They're shy at first, and once they're over that, they're so full of energy ya' can't see much of 'em no how."

"They keep you busy?"

She answers with rolled eyes. "What are yer plans while yer here?"

"Hope to visit some friends and go into town a bit. Want to keep up on the news, you know."

"That's good, but not much has changed since you left, 'cept for more of the boys gone off to fight. There are lotsa folks been askin' bout ya', hopin' to see ya'."

Elizabeth offers, "There's a couple a families want to hear 'bout yer time in the army. Asked us over for a meal. The Harmers for one."

"Of course. How's their father?" asks Robert.

After their mother hesitates, Hannah lets him know. "He's been havin' trouble with his heart."

"Serious?"

"Got the women folk worrin' somethin' awful," says Elizabeth as she pours Hannah her coffee.

"Would you be interested in paying them a visit with me, sis?"

Hannah glances at her mother, and suppresses a grin. "Yer interested in George Harmer's health are ya'? Truth be told, I think ya' wanna go see their Susan."

"Come on, sis. She's just a young little girl."

"Ya' forget how long ya' been gone. Susan's full-grown now. Ya' ought'a wear yer uniform. It's quite strikin' ya' know."

"This is just an informal visit."

Elizabeth adds, "Won't be when we go over for dinner. You'll need to look yer best that night."

"Yes, ma'am," he answers.

"How about tomorrow morning then?"

"Okay. I told my husband I'd be spendin' more time here while yer home anyhow."

Robert starts to pick up his dishes, but Hannah intercepts him. "Yer still healin', brother. Let us spoil ya' now, cause no one will once yer arm's better."

"Thanks, sis." He heads out to the barn to see his father and brother. Situated northeast of the house, the modest barn serves as the hub of activity year round. Corn, hay, and soy are the usual crops during season; their livestock always requires a fair amount of their time.

"Morning, father."

James slides over an empty crate with his foot. "How'd you sleep?"

Once seated, Robert answers, "Just great, slept straight through."

"How's that arm of yours?"

"Hard to tell all strung up like this."

"Your mother tells me you got yourself a tattoo."

"Oh, boy," he mutters. "Did she tell you *why*?"

"She tried, but got to crying. Hannah told me what she thought. Why don't you tell me your side of it?"

Robert thinks about how to answer him. "A bunch of us in the battery thought it'd be good to get a permanent way to identify ourselves, in case we fell in battle. That way you'd be told where we ended up."

"Don't you boys carry papers? Identifications?"

"Sure, we do." He starts to get edgy, hesitates, then goes on. "Look. Do you really want to hear this?"

"Yes, son. I do. Your mother probably shouldn't, but I do."

Robert continues. "Okay, it's not uncommon for the Rebs, or the Union boys for that matter, to rifle through the pockets of the men who've fallen. Lots of men end up in unmarked or mass graves, no way to be sure who they are. We figured it might help them to identify us properly."

As Robert looks off to the distance, James says, "No need to be apologetic with us. We can't imagine the horrors you faced out there."

Will enters the barn. "Mornin' there, sleepy-head."

"Hey, Will."

He clears a space on the workbench and sits on it. "Am I interrupting something?"

"No, son. Just getting caught up with your brother."

Will points to Robert's arm. "Let me get a look at that much talked-about tattoo of yours."

"Here we go," Robert mutters again. "It's covered with bandages."

"When they get changed, I want to see the hole Johnny Reb left you with, too."

"Great."

"How long you here for?"

"I need to be back by the 24th. They want me to get good and healed before my return."

"Not bad. String it out as long as you can."

James heads back to the house.

"I plan to go over to see Mr. Harmer in the morning with Hannah. Heard he's been having heart issues. Interested in going along with us?"

Will jumps down from the workbench as Robert stands. "Someone has to do the work around here," he chides.

※ ※ ※

After a sumptuous dinner, Hannah asks Robert if he'd like to take a walk with her. He jumps at the opportunity to spend some undistracted time together. As they step off the back porch, Hannah wraps her arm through his and they head out.

The three siblings are close. Hannah was born the year after William, Robert the year after that. Their family emigrated from England after selling their farm in the early-1850s in hopes of making a better life here.

"Good to be back?"

"You never realize just how good you've got it until you don't anymore. How about you, sis?"

"Been worryin' a lot 'bout the two of ya'."

"I appreciate you bringing mother to Washington."

"She's been beside herself with worry. News was sparse, and once we heard 'bout yer woundin', there's no keepin' her here. It helped father, too, knowin' he'd hear 'bout it first-hand. It's been hard on the folks. Especially with Will gone. Then the frightful news we're hearin' 'bout the battles." Hannah pauses, not knowing how sensitive he'd be talking about the Confederate's successes.

Robert stays quiet and looks over the field as they continue down the lane. It's too early for corn, but the stalks are getting high and carry promises of fresh, sweet corn—and mother's fritters—before he has to leave. They both enjoy the quiet for a bit, but Hannah's curiosity gets the best of her. "Wanna talk 'bout it?"

"About what?"

"Ya' know. Yer arm."

Robert pulls away from her and sighs. "You were at the hospital. Besides mother, you've seen more of it than Will or father."

"I mean 'bout how'd it happened?"

He doesn't answer her and Hannah doesn't pressure him. They come upon a large fallen tree at the far end of the property, which provides them a good place to sit. Robert glances at his sister, then looks out at the corn fields. "It's painful to have to rehash it over and over. The terrible losses, the things that we did ... that I've done to other people." He hesitates and tones down his voice. "Good friends no longer here, not knowing who, or if any of us will be here tomorrow." He sits silently, tears stream down his cheeks. Hannah sees how much pain he's in. She puts her arm around his shoulder and he leans his head on hers and calms down.

"I do need to ask ya' one other question though."

He wipes his face with his shirt tail. "What?" he says tersely.

"The more ya' get out there with others, the more questions yer gonna be asked. How are ya' going to handle it?"

"I guess I'm either going to ignore the questions, or change the subject. It may be awkward for them, but they'll need to deal with it on my terms."

"Aren't ya' 'fraid people will think yer tryin' to hide somethin'?"

He tries to control his frustration. "There are stories of the crowds that 'attended' the first battle at Bull Run. It was supposed to be fun and entertainment to see the men kill each other, until they fled for their own lives when things turned in favor of the South. Same thing with the crowds at the docks in Washington. They watched the wounded as we were unloaded——the morbidly curious, strangers not caring a whit for the injured. So ... let them! I don't care. That's their problem."

"That'll do for most, but what about those closest to ya'?"

"Who are you talking about?"

"Well, not just us, but those you've known yer whole life, like our our oldest friends, the Harmers. They're like family to us."

"Yeah, about that, I hope you and Will will cover for me with what you know, and that should be enough for them."

"That's fine, but what about when you get a wife?"

He pauses to think about it. "A wife? It's true that spending time with Pauline and Nicholas in Washington woke up a desire in me to find someone to build a life with. I want that, but she'll need to be someone I can trust. Someone who will allow my past to be buried with those men in the fields of Virginia."

Hannah looks at her brother, grateful for his transparency. "I'm sure there's someone who's gonna to fill that role."

He stands up and gives his sister a tender hug. "I think it's time we got back."

the harmers

Robert is up later the next day. He'd gone to bed early and slept undisturbed throughout the night. He's starting to adjust, to feel whole again. After he cleans up and puts on a fresh shirt, he navigates the narrow stairs and finds the entire family around the kitchen table.

"Oh! Morning all. What's the occasion?"

Will speaks first, "Well, Brother Van Winkle, we've been up for hours. The chores are done, and we're deciding whether we need to evict our new tenant for lack of carrying his load."

"William!" scolds his mother. The rest of the family laughs.

Robert chuckles as he goes for coffee.

"Never ya' mind 'bout that. I'll get breakfast on the stove for ya' shortly," says his mother.

"Well, it's close to 10:00 a.m.," chides Will. "I didn't even get this kind of treatment when I got out."

Hannah elbows him. "Yer forgettin' yer parade?"

Robert takes the mug from his mother and pulls up a chair. "Well, Will, you always told me you thought the folks loved me more … you were right."

He resumes sipping his brew, and looks over the cup at his brother. Will swats the back of his head lightly as he heads for the barn. Hannah smiles as she stands to leave. "I'll help Will hitch up the wagon if we're still going to the Harmers'."

"Okay, I'll be with you after a quick bite."

* * *

"Climb on in, brother, and hold on." He gets into the wagon with a little difficulty, and uses his left hand to grip the side of the bench seat. Hannah looks at how he carries himself.

"Forget somethin'?"

"What?"

"Your sling."

"Not today." He sits, and rests his arm in his lap, and holds onto the seat with his left.

Hannah snaps the reigns and they pull away from the farmhouse. They turn onto the Ridge Road, one of the main east-west thoroughfares in western New York. Its importance became outdated with the construction of the Erie Canal, and the expansion of rail service, but it still serves as a main rural route for the locals. It's a relatively short ride to the Harmers' even under the worst conditions.

Robert looks ahead as they approach the farmhouse. Their thirteen-year-old son, George, greets them. "I heard you're back."

"Good to see you too, George. You've sure grown. Do you mind taking care of the horse and wagon for us?"

"Dad already set me to that. They're inside waiting for you."

Robert quizzically glances at Hannah. "The Harmers stopped by last evenin' after ya'd gone to bed. Told 'em ya' wanted to see George Sr. I lied." She laughs and flinches when he pokes her in the ribs as they head up the porch.

Mrs. Harmer, Ann, opens the door to greet them. Hugs are exchanged and she sizes up Robert and his arm. "Looks like you've lost some weight, young man. Don't they feed you in that army of yours?"

"Yes, ma'am. Just sometimes not as regular as we'd like."

"I imagine that your mother plans to correct that. Well, come on in." Robert follows Hannah inside. The farmhouse is modest. The front door opens to the dining room. A small parlor to the left has a fireplace against the west wall, and is furnished with two sitting chairs, a small round table with a lamp, a sofa, and is accented with a brocade rug.

George Sr. sits in the parlor, and starts to rise as they enter.

Robert holds up his hand. "Don't get up, sir." He strides over to greet him. "It's good to see you again."

George gestures for him to sit on the sofa, and says, "You look well, Robert. Looks like army life agrees with you."

He overlooks the irony of the comment. "It *is* good to be home, sir."

Susan walks in from the kitchen with her mother. "You remember our Susan, don't you Robert?"

He scans her from head to toe. "I don't know that I do. You've grown up!"

She's noticeably taller than he remembers, and has the curves of a young woman. Her hazel green eyes are expressive with a warm and welcome smile. As the oldest of their children, Susan assumed the many responsibilities for her siblings. She's clad in a plain brown dress with the sleeves partially rolled up, and covered with an apron.

"It *has* been two and a half years." She stands on her tiptoes to give him a quick hug.

"Susan!" her mother half-heartedly scolds. "She's been in the kitchen preparing you a special treat."

"I didn't expect you to go to a lot of trouble."

"Oh, it's no trouble, not for you," her mother adds, then leads Susan back out to the kitchen by her elbow. Hannah looks back at Robert with a wink, then follows the women.

Robert turns to George Sr. "Sorry to hear you have some health issues, sir."

He entertains thoughts of lighting up his pipe, then places it back on the table with a sigh. "Guess my heart's startin' to feel the strain of life on a farm. I get awful tired, awful easy. Enough about me, how's that arm of yours doing?"

"Okay, I guess. I'll know more when I get back to Washington City and see the doctor."

"What's being in battle like, getting——"

"Okay, gentlemen," Hannah interrupts, "treats on the table." She gestures toward the dining room. The men get up and Robert defers to George as he leads the way in. Robert gives Hannah an appreciative nod.

There are five place settings with a hot pie in the middle. Robert bends over the dish and inhales the aroma of baked quince, raisins, cinnamon, nutmeg, and brown sugar.

"Mince meat." He looks over at Susan without straightening up and smiles. "My favorite." He takes in another whiff before Hannah nudges him aside.

Robert patiently waits as Susan cuts the pie and passes around the plates. She cuts his piece half again larger than the others. Hannah watches him closely as his eyes follow Susan out to the kitchen. A minute later she returns with a block of cheese. "It's cheddar. Hannah says you like that best with your pie."

He looks at the plate ravenously, and wonders how long he has to wait before he can dig in. As he grabs his fork, Hannah holds down his wrist and whispers, "Wait fer Susan to join us."

"Oh," he says, and replaces the utensil.

Susan serves the coffee, and once seated, Robert dives into the warm dessert.

"Ohhh ... my."

"Don't they give you pie in the army?" asks Ann.

He chuckles at the suggestion. "No, ma'am. We get pretty basic stuff in and around camp. Sutlers' wagons are set up nearby, selling their wares and foodstuffs. If men want something besides pork and beans, they usually buy it on their own. The quality of the food they sell can best be described as questionable." As he stuffs in another mouthful of the dessert, he begins to speak before he swallows. "There's nothing like this in any camp I've been to." He finishes his bite, and beams at Susan. "Thank you. What a treat." Susan appreciates her efforts are not wasted.

Embarrassed at his gluttony, Hannah doesn't comment except to tell Susan how good it is. For the next hour the five of them sit around and reminisce about life back in England, their experiences here, and what life has been like while he's been away. When anyone tries to ask Robert about his experiences at the battlefront, Hannah redirects their conversation to George's health, her trip to Washington, and the Baker family.

Eventually, young George comes in holding onto his younger sister's hand. Ann introduces her to Robert, and says, "Come on, child. Time for you to take a nap."

Young George informs their guests that their horse has been

watered and fed.

"He's quite a young man," Robert says to George Sr.

"He's a handful."

Robert and Hannah thank their hosts, and Susan gives him a small bundle wrapped in a cloth tied in a knot. "For your ride back," she winks.

He bends over and gives her a quick hug. "Thanks again, for the treat."

brother

Wanting to spend some private time with his brother, Will asks, "You up for some hunting today? Got a lot to get caught up on."

"Be happy to, but I won't be much use with a gun."

"Great. I'll hitch up the wagon, grab my rifle, and we'll head out."

When he walks through the door, Will catches Robert doing a double-take at the gun. Will grabs it, takes Robert by the arm, and leads him out the door.

Robert points to his rifle. "That's government issue."

"Let's get on a piece and I'll tell you about it. And some other news as well."

They ride out to their favorite hunting grounds a couple miles north of their family's farm. Their destination, a thickly-wooded area with plenty of trails and deer runs, a faint reminder of the Wilderness at Chancellorsville. Will ties off the horse, and grabs the gun.

"What's the story with the rifle, Will? Did you steal it? How'd you get it here?"

"Give me a little credit. I salvaged it. Bits and pieces of three damaged guns left to rot on the fields at Winchester."

"Look, brother, it's none of my business, but I know the government posts notices that any arms left on the field are government property, regardless of their condition. I just don't want you to get in any trouble."

"I appreciate that." Will seems unfazed. "I spoke to my sergeant after I retrieved the pieces, and he said to keep them. He understood the posting as applicable to the civilian populace."

Robert doesn't argue the point.

"Besides, when we got out, they offered us the opportunity to buy our rifles. Ended up I saved about seven dollars and used it to buy ammo, among other things." Will points to the various parts of the gun, as he gives Robert an impromptu demonstration. "One had a destroyed gunstock and the workings jimmied up, another with good workings, but the barrel'd been hit by a Minié ball and bent on impact, and the third with an undamaged barrel. I wrapped them in my blanket and brought them back with me." He holds up the gun, and exclaims, "Here we are, one good working rifle."

"Teach you that in the infantry, did they?"

"You'd better believe it. We learned how to take apart and reassemble these things blindfolded."

"Shoot straight?"

"I don't know yet. I put it together about a week after I got out, and I've been too busy since then. I need to do a bit of target practice to get the sights aligned properly."

"What are you so busy with? You brought me way out here with some other news ... didn't you?"

With a smug smile, Will proudly announces, "Well, Miss Clarinda Thompson has agreed to be my wife! What d'ya' think?"

"What do I think? Hmm." He suppresses a laugh. "I guess pickings for the women must be pretty thin with the war going on."

Will gives him a slight push. "You too, with that wing of yours, you'll be a great catch. Ha!"

"Thanks for the reminder," Robert concedes.

Will thinks he may have gone too far. "I'm sorry, but what *will* you be left with once you're out of that contraption?"

"Not sure. The doc has some names for it, but wants to wait and see when I get back."

"Any guesses?"

"Nope. Think I'd rather wait than try to second-guess the possibilities. I envy you, Will. You're out already, and about to be married, and on to a new life."

"You're the one who wanted to jump in early. Five years," he says with disgust. "How you gonna handle that?"

"Don't remind me. I didn't know what I committed myself to. Sure sounded exciting at first."

"Aside from your arm, just how bad was it?"

Robert's poise starts to unravel. "You've been under fire. You know what it's like. The noise, the chaos … the blood."

"Easy, brother. I just want to hear about it from your standpoint, you know, as an artillerist."

Still tense, he replies, "Yeah, well, don't go there. Please."

"Listen. I know guys who came out of battle affected by it … affected bad. Hell, over fifty of our men died at Cedar Mountain, sixty more wounded, and another ninety-some captured. I get it."

Robert tries to reign in his emotions. "How'd you like to see them ripped apart and laid out right in front of you?"

In a soft voice, Will asks, "You share this with anyone else?"

"Not here. The guys I fought with know. They've seen it first-hand. They learned how to cope with it. I mean Sergeant Welker, he'd seen it, lots. Seemed like any other day in battle to him. Now he's dead, too."

"You've always been sensitive. Hope you can find a way to deal with it, and let it go. Think it's best not to tell the folks about it."

"I agree. Let's talk about another topic."

"Okay. Speaking of other topics, what's with you and the Harmer girl?"

"Susan? She's nice, and she sure grew up while I was gone, but we haven't spent any time together. Never talked about much except weather and family. And look at me. I've got this arm, no money, and have to finish the war first. Won't be pondering much about marriage until then."

"Just remember what you said, 'Slim pickins'."

Robert looks straight at him. "You never said——"

"Never said what?"

"When you're getting hitched."

"Wanted to see if you'd be here for it. We plan on Sunday the nineteenth."

"Where?"

"At her folks place on Lake Ontario. Real pretty there. Want you to be my best man. You up for it?"

Robert puts his arm around his brother's neck. "Be an honor, Will. You got yourself a good woman there."

Will picks up the gun, and they head deeper into the forest. They come upon a clearing bordered by fallen trees.

"Think I'm gonna feed this a few rounds to test it out. He loads, then with his face flush against the gunstock, tells Robert, "I'm aiming for the split point on that y-shaped limb."

"Okay. I see it."

He lines the rear sight with the front, then pulls the trigger. The discharge causes the brothers to flinch. Will looks at Robert wide-eyed, and with a nervous laugh says, "Guess I'm just a little bit on edge here."

"Got me, too, brother. I watched you fire, but still jumped at the report."

"How close did I come to the target?"

"Hell if I know. You're never much of a shot. Safest thing ever happened to the Rebs was when you signed up."

Will laughs, then offers the gun to Robert. "Let's see if you can do any better."

"Maybe next time, brother. Next time."

They spend the rest of the afternoon together. Will does more target practice, and they reminisce about their times in camp, and how army life differed for the two of them. The thought of hunting passes by the wayside.

"I'm sorry that you weren't here for the parade Medina put on for the return of the Twenty-eighth. Seems the entire town turned out for the celebration."

"That's great they honored your service. I imagine they'll throw a rip snorter of a parade after the Confederates are finally beaten."

"You honestly think we're gonna win this thing?"

"Of course, I do. I wouldn't be in it if I didn't."

"With all that Bobby Lee has pulled on us, how can you think that? We've yet to put up a general who knows what he's doing."

"That's odd. Sergeant Welker and I shared this same conversation after Chancellorsville." He hesitates again, then adds, "I don't think the South has a chance."

"How do you figure?"

"As the sarge pointed out, we have an endless supply of equipment. You know a lot of their soldiers are still barefooted?"

"Imagine going through the winter like that," Will adds.

"The South's economy relies upon their agriculture, the North on its industry. We've suffered terrible losses in this war, and the Rebs too, despite their victories."

"What's your point?"

"It's a matter of numbers. We have more men available to replace our losses than they do. I heard that Stonewall Jackson died on the tenth … Lee's right-hand man … irreplaceable."

"Go on."

"Someday, somewhere, we'll find that general, the one who knows how to use our armies and equipment, and has the guts to take the fight to them."

Like most political discussions that rarely resolve anything, theirs comes to an inconclusive end.

goin' to meetin'

It's Robert's first Sunday back home, and promises (or threatens) to be a big day. There will be many people at the church service, which means many well-wishers and many more questions. With dread, he decides he has to face them sometime. Might as well get it over with.

He heads downstairs for some coffee. To his surprise, both his mother and Hannah are already up. "Can't sleep, son?"

"I slept alright. Just thinking about the day ahead."

She hands him a mug of coffee. "Yer father's already up 'n workin' with William. Soon as breakfast is over we can get ready for meetin'."

The coffee clears Robert's head. He enlists Hannah's help with his bandages, and reconfigures the splint to enable him use of his thumb and forefinger. He's now able to fully dress on his own.

Wagons populate the grounds around the Methodist church. Just off Shelby Street, and up and down the avenue, the overflow competes for parking with the nearby Baptists and Presbyterians.

As they enter the sanctuary, Robert removes his forage cap and imagines every eye turned his way, but his suspicions are baseless. The Harmers arrived first and saved them places, six pews from the front. Done on the sly, the mothers, try to position Robert and Susan together, but Hannah picks up on the ruse and discreetly moves in between them. Robert squeezes Hannah's hand in appreciation when they sit down.

The church grew substantially during the great revivals of 1857 and

'58, but has settled back to a steady attendance of one hundred thirty to one hundred fifty each Sunday. Its walls are white-washed and the floor is unfinished wood planking with a narrow carpet that runs the length of the center aisle. A beautifully ornate reed organ, crafted by Mason and Hamlin, seems a bit lavish for a church this size, but the membership felt the instrument worth the price. When the organist starts to play, the congregation stands in unison. The first hymn is #471 - *All Hail The Pow'r of Jesus' Name!* They begin singing:

> *"All hail the pow'r of Jesus' Name!*
> *Let angels prostrate fall;*
> *Bring forth the royal diadem,*
> *And crown Him Lord of all!"*

As the congregation continues to sing, the processional of choir members works its way forward, followed by the pastor in a long black robe, singing from memory in his sonorous baritone voice. Pastor Elias Foye has been the minister at this church for over eight years. His wife, three daughters, and son have woven seamlessly into the fabric of the community. Clean-shaven with black hair, which he wears slicked back, Pastor Foye's demeanor is open and friendly.

The church's elder stands and welcomes the congregation. He invites them to pray——for families in the community whose loved ones are away, and for those who've suffered loss. He asks wisdom for the President and his advisors, blessings on their families, and for a quick end to the terrible conflict.

He then asks anyone who has or currently serves in the war to stand. About forty men rise, including Robert and William. Most of them were with the regiment that formed in Medina——the Twenty-eighth New York——and mustered out at the start of the month. Some are still in their uniforms, either from patriotism or necessity, most are not. The congregation gives them enthusiastic applause.

The pastor rises and signals it's time to quiet down. The men sit in unison. "Well-deserved, indeed. Thank you for your sacrifice. We are happy you are here and able to join us this morning." He pauses, clears his throat, and adds, "We need to remember, too, those who won't be coming back." He then starts to read the names from the prepared list of local men who paid the ultimate price. When the names are read, their families try to contain their emotions, a few unsuccessfully. The names are already known, but the announcement of some bring about murmurs from congregants who hadn't heard of their loss.

"With us this morning," he continues, "is one young man recovering from wounds he received at Chancellorsville last May." He looks over at Robert and motions for him to stand up. Another loud round of applause as an embarrassed Robert stands half way up and sits back down immediately. It's the last thing he expected or wanted.

The pastor uses his introduction to start his message on sacrifice, those made by the country, the communities, the families, and gesturing toward Robert, the individual men. He gives a patriotic sermon filled with support for the President and the Union, and tied to the morning's Scripture reading in One John, about the sacrifice that God made through His Son, Jesus Christ, for our sins. Then he speaks fervently of the sins for which our country must atone——slavery, pride, vanity, disunity, unforgiveness, and the devastating consequences it has burdened our country with.

He closes the service in prayer and the organist plays as the congregants file out. The pastor makes a point to visit with Robert's family at their pew, greets each of them and pats Robert on the back. He thanks him for his sacrifice, tells him he prays for him daily, and asks if there is anything he needs. Robert humbly nods and waits for the rest of his family as they speak with the pastor.

When they leave the building, the congregation, with few exceptions, waits for him. He gets a number of back-slaps and jostling from people who try to get close. Of course the questions follow, and Robert does his best to deflect them. William and Hannah run interference for him, and he gets away, shaken, but unscathed.

Quiet for the better portion of the ride back, Robert eventually speaks with Hannah, and thanks her for the help. Then to Will he says, "I thought he was going to call me up for an interview, and ask me about my arm and being in battle."

Will tilts his head to the side, and raises his eyebrows. "You're lucky he didn't. Maybe I'll suggest it to him before the service next week."

news from the front

At the beginning of the week, Robert and Will are tasked with taking the wagon into town to pick up supplies from the mercantile. Robert's clothes are getting threadbare and his mother insists he wear his uniform. Tying off the wagon, they notice an unusual amount of activity centered around the office of the *Medina Tribune*. Long streamers of news are posted and people jockey for position to get a better look. As the crowd sees Robert approach, they part, and give him a clear view of the board——Gettysburg.

One reads,

> *"Waterloo Eclipsed!!*
> *The Desperate Battles Near Gettysburg!*
> *Repulse of the Rebels At All Points!!"*

Another,

> *"Severe Battle Near Gettysburg,*
> *Maj. Gen. Reynolds Killed."*

Yet another,

> *"Gettysburg. A Great Victory Won!,*
> *The Second Battle on Thursday, July 2.*
> *Official Dispatches from Gen. Meade.*
> *Heroic Conduct of the Third and Fifth Corps.*
> *The Rebel General Advance Repulsed at All Points."*

Finally,

> *"Splendid Triumph of the Army of the Potomac,*

Rout of Lee's Forces on Friday,
The Most Terrible Struggle of the War,
Tremendous Artillery Duel,
Every Charge Repulsed with Great Slaughter."

The people cheer and clap with each dispatch they read. Robert gets slaps on the back and congratulations. *His thoughts are focused on his battery mates. How did they fare ... tremendous artillery duel ... great slaughter. Don't they understand ... I need to see the casualty lists.*

Will catches up with his brother. "What's going on over here?"

Robert struggles to speak, "Big battle at Gettysburg. News claims a huge Union victory, tremendous artillery duel, great slaughter. Another claimed III Corps heroic ... great slaughter."

Will sees how the news affects his brother. "Let's get you to the wagon." Will takes Robert by the arm and settles him in. "Will you be okay?" Robert nods. Will pulls out his list, and adds, "I still need to pick these things up. Then we can go take a look at the news together."

"Okay, sure." Will double-checks Robert, then leaves him for the mercantile.

A couple minutes later, Robert wanders back. "Are there any casualty lists?" he asks no one in particular.

"Too soon to tell, son. Those lists don't usually get posted 'til days, sometimes weeks, later," a familiar voice answers.

"I need to see the lists," Robert says as he tries to jostle his way closer to the bulletin boards.

The man turns around and puts his hand on the front of his chest. "Robert, the postings won't be here for a couple more days at the earliest." It's Pastor Foye.

"But I need to find out," he repeats as he tries to look past his shoulder. He physically resists, but the pastor strengthens his hold on him. Pastor Foye's large hands reflect the power behind them, growing up on a farm and working hard until he received his "calling". Finally Robert breaks down. The tears stream down his cheeks. The pastor folds him into his arms and leads him away from the crowd. He helps him to the wagon and stays with him until Will returns.

"Pastor Foye? That's some news about Gettysburg, huh?" Will says as he throws the crate from the store into the back of the wagon, then looks to Robert. The pastor doesn't respond. "Everything okay here?"

"No, William. Robert's having a bit of a struggle with all the excitement. If you wait here, I'll get my horse, tie it to the back of your wagon, and ride home with you."

"Yeah. Okay. Sure."

"Keep an eye on him while I'm gone."

Twenty minutes later, he returns with his saddled horse. He ties it to the back of the wagon and climbs aboard next to Robert, who still seems to be in shock, silently staring toward the back. Will looks over at the pastor, then glances at his brother with a look of concern. He snaps the reins and they head back home. Robert continues to focus on the crowd until they are out of sight.

* * *

Sitting on their front porch, Elizabeth sees the wagon with the three men and the trailing horse. Something isn't right, and she runs into the house to get her husband and daughter. James rushes over as Will pulls the wagon around the back. "What's wrong, Will?"

"News of a big battle in Pennsylvania. Supposed to be a big victory for the Union boys," the pastor answers. "Robert's a bit overwhelmed by it all. I think he needs to lie down for a while."

Hannah takes Robert by the arm. "Gimme a hand, Will, and we'll get 'im inside."

Robert's awake and responsive, and accepts their help. Hannah asks, "Mother can we put 'im on yer bed for awhile?"

"Heavens yes, dear … just be careful with 'im."

As the three siblings work their way inside, James says to the Pastor, "What do you think is going on with him? His arm seems like it's healing okay."

"It isn't his arm. Well, maybe, but I think there's more he's holding inside. News dispatches are being posted of an over-whelming Union victory at a town called Gettysburg. The casualty numbers look to be bigger than any battle yet. He may be having trouble with that."

Through her tears Elizabeth asks, "Can I bring ya' some cold tea, Pastor? Gedda chance to sit 'n talk?"

"That's nice of you, Elizabeth. Thank you."

As Will and Hannah enter the porch, she leads her daughter back into the house to help with the refreshments.

James starts the conversation. "I appreciate you lookin' after our son, Pastor."

"It's the least I can do, James. Your family has sacrificed much to this effort, and it's a blessing for us to be able to support you in any way possible."

"That means a lot."

After a few more minutes of small talk, Hannah and Elizabeth walk out with three glasses of ice tea and a small plate of biscuits.

"With your permission, I'd like to come over and spend some time alone with Robert. Hope to get at the root of what bothers him."

"Think you'll be able to help 'im?" asks Hannah.

"I don't know, but I think he needs to talk about it."

William looks away. In his mind, it's not the right approach. Hannah scans the faces of her parents and Will, then addresses the pastor. "I don't know how much he's shared with the rest of ya', but I know he's holdin' things in, and has no desire to talk about it."

William confirms, "She's right. I tried to discuss the subject with him close on to two weeks ago, and he seemed to be struggling then. Trying to get him to open up about it may be more painful for him than we imagine. He may not be as cooperative as you think."

Looking to their father, the pastor asks, "Has he said anything to you about this, James?"

"He seems to be dealin' with it in his own——"

Hannah jumps in. "But he isn't, father. He's hurtin' right now."

Elizabeth, visibly upset, stands and stares at James. "Seems he's been tellin' y'all more'n me. Tryin' to protect me I 'spect … it'd been better ya'd been more honest 'bout my son with me." She realizes her emotions are getting the best of her, and leaves the porch. Hannah follows.

"Think it's time I get back to the parsonage." Pastor Foye asks, "With your permission I'd like to come visit Robert?"

"You are always welcome here, Pastor."

"Thank you, James. I'll offer special prayers for you. I'll have the latest news when I come out on Wednesday. The Lord's blessing on you and this household."

William brings the horse around and hands the pastor the reins. He easily mounts the animal, acknowledges the family with a nod, and heads south.

When they return to the porch, the men are surprised to find Robert standing in the doorway.

"How are you doing, son?"

"I heard what you said."

"Are you gonna be willing to see him?"

"Doesn't seem like I have any choice."

"He just wants to help. Think it'd be better if you'd try," says James.

Watching the pastor and his horse disappear into the distance, Robert softly adds, "Think I'll go up and get that nap you set me down for."

the pastor

Anticipating the impending visit, Robert has difficulty sleeping through the night. True to his promise, Pastor Foye arrives at their front door by 8:30 a.m. Robert answers, shadowed by his mother. The pastor removes his wide-brimmed, black hat when he enters and greets Elizabeth first, then gently places his hand on Robert's shoulder. "How are you doing today?"

"Okay, I guess. Hard time with sleep, but otherwise——"

Elizabeth interrupts, "Can I get ya' some coffee, Pastor."

"Thank you Elizabeth." The two men take seats at the kitchen table and Elizabeth pours both of them a mug.

Despite his reluctance, Robert asks, "Do you have any news updates?"

"I do. It's pretty consistent from the other day. It sounds like the initial reports are accurate. Lee was utterly routed, and headed back toward the Potomac."

"Any casualty reports yet?" Robert persists.

"Not yet. It sounds like they're guessing. I did read that General Sickles lost a leg. He's your general isn't he?"

Robert shakes his head, "Indirectly." He then asks with a little edge in his voice, "How many?"

"Well, for what it's worth, initial numbers are fifteen thousand Union and anywhere from twenty- to forty thousand Rebels, with six- to ten thousand prisoners taken. Wouldn't put much stock in it, though."

Both Robert and Elizabeth gasp.

Elizabeth sits down, and rubs her hands. "Do ya' think this might be over now?"

"I can't say. Those Rebels are a resourceful bunch. Look how they countered after Antietam where Lee left the field—Fredericksburg then Chancellorsville. No, I don't think it's over by a long shot."

"Dear Lord," Elizabeth exclaims.

"You keep praying, sister." The pastor motions to Robert and the two of them stand. "Going to take your son for a stroll if it's okay with you." She looks up and nods her head.

Robert leads the two of them out the back door.

"Where's a good place to talk?" asks the pastor.

"You up for a walk?"

"Lead the way … where's the rest of your family?"

"Father's in the barn. William took the wagon over to the Harmers' to help them out for the day."

As they make their way to the back property, the pastor says, "Your families seem pretty close."

"We've known them for as long as I can remember … back to our time in England."

"I'm not too familiar with that country."

They reach the fallen tree at end of the property line and take a seat together. The pastor tries to break the ice and get Robert to open up about his war experience. "Tell me about your injury."

"I honestly don't remember a whole lot about it. We got hit pretty hard. A shell exploded near us at the same time I got hit. Next thing I remember I'm being moved to safety."

"Are you worried about your arm?"

"A little. The not-knowing's the hardest part, and I won't for a while. I might get everything back, or maybe not. Guess it's in the Lord's hands at this point."

"Do you want to talk about the other day?"

Robert starts to tense up. "I worry about my friends and battery mates. Sounds like it was a nightmare for everyone, in either uniform."

"It's admirable that you're concerned about the welfare of others."

"Doesn't much matter, does it?" he says bitterly. "Can't make any difference my sitting here."

"Are you more frustrated that you weren't with them, or that they beat Lee without you?"

Robert lets out a derisive laugh. "Hadn't thought about it that way. It's just the cost seems so high … all those men … boys most of them." His eyes start to well up. "Billings, Welker …"

"Who are they? Men you fought with? Friends?"

Robert stares into the distance, struggling with his emotions. "It's over for them now … won't get to see their families … won't see another sunrise. It's my fault."

The pastor is confused about Robert's quandary. "How are their deaths your fault?"

"Lew's is!" He snaps. "If I'd kept my big mouth shut."

"You think you played a role in his destiny? Our paths are preordained by the Lord."

Robert stands up, takes a couple of steps and turns back to the pastor. "Well, He did a right fine job with that, didn't He!"

"I know you feel guilty, but you weren't to blame."

He points directly at the pastor's face, "You don't know!" he yells. "You don't know about the men I've killed. The part I played in it. Handfuls at a time. Men mutilated …" His voice cracks then drops to a murmur, "ripped apart in unimaginable ways."

Pastor Foye stays silent. He realizes he isn't equipped to deal with the issues Robert struggles with. "How about we pray together, son?"

Robert shakes his head. "You go ahead, if you like."

Robert stays standing while the pastor drops to his knees in front of the log and spends time in silent prayer. He realizes Robert's in no mood to hear any words of consolation. He prays for his soul, and the desire for God to make His presence known to him. He prays that Robert comes to the realization that he can cast his worries at the feet of the Lord, and be free of his burdens. It comes to him in his meditation that he'll write these words in a letter for him to read when he's alone and in the right frame of mind. He thanks God for the revelation and stands. He sees that Robert has already started back toward the farmhouse. It doesn't take long for him to catch up.

"Thank you for your honesty with me, son. I know it's difficult to face these things. You've given me good direction in how to pray for you."

Robert doesn't acknowledge or look at the pastor the rest of the way back. James greets them as they near. "You two get things talked out?"

Robert doesn't say anything and continues inside. Pastor Foye stops, and follows Robert's departure with his eyes. He shakes his head. "No, but I better understand what your son struggles with. I'll pray for your family."

"There anything we can do for him?"

He turns back to face James. "Be patient and keep him in your prayers. I think it's best you wait for him to come to you. You can't force the issue." He shields his eyes as he locates the sun. "It's best that I start back." He rides off, feeling like he wasn't able to help, frustrated that he felt out of his element. He resigns himself to the knowledge that it's up to God to do the healing in Robert's heart.

The days pass uneventfully. The news of the great victory at Gettysburg is tempered with the reports that the Union does not pursue Lee's army. The pastor is right. The war is not over. Not by a long shot.

will & clarinda

Will and Clarinda's wedding, in four days, keeps everyone busy. Hannah helps with her mother's dress, her own has long since been finished. Will has gone into town on a "secret mission". Once he returns, he asks Robert to follow him out back. When they get out of sight of the house, Will reaches into his pocket and brings out a small velvet pouch. He pulls out a gold ring, and hands it to Robert. "How do you like it?"

Robert inspects the ring closely and notes the engraving inside, "'WC & CT 7-19-63'. It's beautiful, Will." He hands the ring back to him, who tucks it into the pouch and returns it.

"Now don't you go losin' that."

He smiles, "I'll try my best."

Sunday, 19 July 1863

Everybody's up early at the Thompson household. To save the four hour ride in the morning, Will and his family arrived the evening before. Clara's grandfather has lived in the area since the turn of the nineteenth century. Her father, James, built their place on the adjoining property. It's a beautiful home with an unobstructed view of Lake Ontario. The vast expanse of the lake serves as the ideal backdrop for the gazebo, festively decorated with seasonal wild flowers.

Robert's in the backyard with Will, their father, and Clara's dad.

Her brother, Elias, keeps to himself. The Thompson's son, Abner, six years older than Elias, signed up with the Eighteenth Independent New York Artillery, and at last report has been hospitalized with a serious illness. Elias resents William and Robert, visual reminders of the empty chair the family keeps reserved for his brother.

After everyone is seated, the ceremony begins, "Friends and relatives, we are gathered here today …"

At the start, Robert looks at the pastor, but his eyes soon drift past him to the blue expanse of Lake Ontario. *It's so beautiful here. Will has done it. He has found a way to get through the war. Found a way to break free of his life on the farm.*

"William do you take Clarinda …"

He retreats back into his thoughts. *Now he has someone to share his new life with. I am still bound to my choices. It's my own fault, but there is nothing I can do about it.*

Robert nearly misses his cue to hand Will the ring. Much to his relief, he does so without fumbling it. The pastor shares a brief homily before the benediction. Robert thinks, *I should be ashamed of myself. I'm jealous, jealous of my own brother. I'll miss him. We've been so close, and now our lives can't help but be different.*

"By the powers vested in me …", the benediction is prayerfully offered concluding the ceremony.

The women have laid out a large assortment of finger foods for the wedding guests to celebrate the couple.

It's a two and a half hour ride to Albion, and as Robert needs help to handle both the wagon and transport the luggage for the newlyweds, he asks Hannah to go with him. When it's time, William and Clara work their way, through the throng of well-wishers, to the carriage driven by Elias.

* * *

Will and Robert say their good-byes at the station. "You realize we won't see each other for a while. Who knows how long."

"Just be careful, little brother. You come back wearing anymore lead and you might be totally useless around the farm. Not that you aren't already."

"I love you, too, Will. Now let me go hug my sister-in-law. I need to let her know I'll be available whenever she gets tired of you."

"Careful, brother. The Rebs may not be the only ones using you for target practice."

"As if you'd ever hit me with that eagle eye of yours." The brothers hug and work their way over to the women.

Hannah grabs Will and gives him a kiss and a long hug. "Either ya' take care of my new sister or you'll answer to me."

Robert takes Clara's hand. "Welcome to the family, sis. You do realize he doesn't deserve you."

Clara laughs and swats his arm lightly. "When are you going to join the ranks of the respectable?"

Robert shrugs. "I'm working on it."

"Work harder, brother. She's worth it."

"I'll see you before you know it. This war won't last forever, especially since your husband isn't out there wasting anymore of our precious ammo."

Clara laughs. "You two are gonna miss each other ... but then, you already know that."

expiring furlough

∞

Wednesday, 22 July 1863

Elizabeth wakes up before sunrise, stokes up the stove, and puts the pot on to boil. She didn't sleep well. Robert's return to duty weighs heavily on her——the unresolved issues he has to deal with, the new dangers he'll encounter, the uncertainty of his arm——he's leaving today. She has tried her best to overcome her fears and not burden others with them, but they constantly nag at her. He's her youngest and vulnerable. Elizabeth can no longer rest in the fact that he's home and out of harm's way. She can no longer protect him. The only thing she can do is pray for him, and that she will do daily. In a short while, he'll be up and finishing his packing, then …

"You couldn't sleep either, dear?" James is up to start his daily routine of running the farm. He pours a mug of coffee for Elizabeth and one for himself, and has a seat across from her.

As he reaches for his coffee, Elizabeth intercepts his hand and holds it tightly. "Been dreadin' this day, hopin' it wouldn't get here, but here we are."

James weaves their fingers together. Through all the challenges they faced in their forty-three years together, they know they can still draw strength from one another. "I couldn't sleep much myself. You know we can't let him see how worried we are. With everything else he holds onto, he doesn't need to carry that burden with him. I expect once he talks to the doctor and gets back with his friends there will be a lot less for him to worry about."

"Do ya' think they'll put 'im back in battle? Or maybe let 'im come home instead?"

"I doubt he'll be back anytime soon. He still has an obligation to fulfill. I'm sure they'll find something for him. I can't imagine that he'll be put on the front lines with his arm."

Elizabeth drops her head to their hands and says in a low voice, "Best be hopin' yer right."

Hannah makes her entrance shortly. "Mornin'. Guess ya' didn't sleep much neither." Elizabeth and James unclasp their hands and drink their coffee, which has started to cool. "Don't stop whatever yer doin' on account'a me. Think I hear 'im rustlin' 'bout. Imagine he'll be down soon. What time's he goin'?"

"Later this morning."

"Got room for us to go along, too?" asks Hannah.

"Your mother figures it'd be best for her to say her good-byes here. Be glad to have your company on the return, and I'm sure Robert appreciates you seeing him off ... call me in for breakfast."

Hannah sits next to her mother. "I heard ya' up 'fore sunrise. Figured with him leavin'——"

"Better start the breakfast fixin's." Elizabeth interrupts as she stands. "How 'bout ya' gettin' the table set."

"Yes, ma'am." She goes over to her mother and gives her a long hug from behind. Elizabeth pats Hannah's forearm.

Robert appears in the doorway of the kitchen in full uniform.

"Little early to be gettin' gussied up, isn't it?" asks Hannah.

"I'm gonna make a quick trip over to the Harmer's to say 'bye' after breakfast."

"The Harmers', huh? Guess ya' must wanna be sayin' bye to George. Ya know, with his health 'n all," Hannah says with a glint in her eye.

"Gonna miss this, sister," he says as he pokes her rib cage. She laughs as she flinches.

"No room for you two to be foolin' in here. 'Sides, I need your sister to help with the meal. Best ya' go talk with your father a bit."

Robert dutifully leaves the house for the barn. "Morning, father."

"Looks like you're fixing to be leaving sooner than we planned."

"Wanna take a run over to the Harmers' after breakfast, say my good-byes."

"Think you can handle the wagon?"

"I've been feeling stronger lately, and I'd like to give it a try." Within the hour, Robert's on the road to call on Susan.

* * *

Little George steps off the porch as the wagon pulls in. "Morning, Robert."

"Headed back down south today. I wanted to say good-bye."

"Yeah, right. Susan's in the kitchen. Just go on in."

He knocks on the doorframe as he opens the screen. "Hello? Anyone home?"

Ann walks out from the kitchen. "Robert, what a surprise." She wipes her hands on her apron and clasps his left with both hers in a warm greeting. "I'm glad you came to see us before you leave." She looks up at him with a wink and adds, "I'm sure someone else will be happy to know you're here." She points him to the kitchen and escorts him in. "Susan, look who's come to see you."

Susan turns toward the two of them and her face lights up. "Robert. Glad to see you before you go. Can I get you some coffee?"

"I'm good, but pressed for time." He points to the door. "Think we could take a walk?"

Susan looks to her mother who nods her assent. She doffs her apron, and leads the way out the door and around to the back of the house. A narrow lane winds through their apple orchard that's a favorite walk of the family's.

"Anxious to get back?" Susan asks.

"About some things I am. Anxious to find out about my arm. Looking forward to seeing the men in my outfit, to see how they fared at Gettysburg. It's been hard not knowing."

She asks, "What's it like?"

"What's what like?" he counters, and dreads what's coming next.

"You know ... being in battle?"

He tries not to sound elusive, but has no desire to wallow in that abyss. "It's difficult, but we focus on our jobs, and it's over before we know it."

"Did it scare you much?"

Robert nods, "You bet. Everyone, no matter how brave a face they put on it, is scared at least a little. Some more than others, I guess. Do you mind if we talk about something else?"

"Okaaay. What would *you* like to talk about?"

"Well, I'm glad we got to spend some time together, and that pie ... I sure do appreciate you doing that special for me."

"Hannah told me it's your all-time favorite."

"She has thoughts about us ... seems like a lot of people do."

She looks down, and paws at the path with her shoe. "Well, what about you?"

"What? You, too?"

Susan blushes. "Well, I *do* care for you. And I think you're kinda sweet on me, too." She catches herself, and looks for a reaction. "Am I wrong?"

"No," he confesses. "I wanted to see you again before I head back."

"You don't need to be afraid of me."

"I'm not. It's just, well, I got this two and a half year commitment left to do, and then there's my arm. What if it's crippled? You wouldn't be put off by that?"

Susan stops and gently takes his right arm, wraps her small hand around his two good fingers and strokes his forearm tenderly. "When I think about you, and I do, a lot, I don't think about this arm. I think about other things, mostly about us and a life together. Haven't you ever thought about that?"

"I guess ..." He paces a bit then adds, "More lately, but what about my obligation to the army? I can't get out of that."

"It won't be forever. I'll still be here when you get back." He lifts up her face to his. Their lips meet for the first time, softly. She gasps. He pulls her closer, the next kiss is tender, full of longing. When they break, he notices her eyes probing his. "We'd be so good together. I've cared about you for a long time, Rob."

Reluctantly, he looks at the sky, then at the horizon and realizes their time is rapidly drawing to a close. "Will you write?"

"Of course I will. I hope that you'll write me, too. Tell me what the doctor says. Tell me how you get along. Tell me you miss me."

They pause in front of the wagon. "I'll miss you ... more than you can imagine," she says. He boards the vehicle and leaves her with nothing more than a smile.

As she steps onto the porch, her mother greets her at the door. "You two able to work some things out?"

She blushes as she nods.

With a knowing eye, Ann says, "You're a little flush, dear. I suggest you wash your face, drink a cool glass of tea, and get back to work."

* * *

Robert throws his bag into the back of the wagon and goes over to the front porch where Elizabeth stands. "Well, mother, it's time."

She throws her arms around him in a warm embrace. "May God be with ya', my son. Please stay safe."

"Try not to worry, mother. I'll be back. I'll write as soon as I can."

James waits in the wagon with Hannah. "Ready, son?"

He turns to wave to his mother, but she's already left the porch.

* * *

Robert shows his pass at the ticket booth; there's still time before the train is scheduled to leave. James gives him the few good words fathers give their sons at times such as these. They hug, then he surprises Robert with a kiss on his cheek, something he hasn't done since Robert was much younger.

Hannah smiles as she watches the two of them. "Come on, it's my turn." She gives him a long hug and a peck on the cheek. "I'll miss you, too. Don't worry. I'll keep my eye on her for ya'."

return to carver

Friday, 24 July 1863

Compared with his trip home, the return to Washington is incident-free. Union troops put down the draft riots in New York City by the sixteenth, and the downed telegraph lines are now repaired. There are no further Confederate troop movements up north, and no rerouted or cancelled runs.

The train pulls into Washington's Union Station early in the day. Robert grabs his bag and steps onto the platform. It feels good to be outside. He's been holed up in the train the last couple of days, and he wants to put off reporting back for as long as possible. He decides to take the time to walk the three plus miles to the hospital. As much as he wants to hear about his arm and see his friends, he also dreads it. He stops at a restaurant for cold tea and a sandwich before he resumes his trek over an hour later.

As he walks, his mind wanders, first to Susan, then inevitably to Pauline. His pace quickens. As much as he does not want to report in, he looks forward to seeing her again. When he enters the hospital, he bypasses the usual reception area and makes his way straight to her desk.

"Reporting for duty as ordered, ma'am."

Pauline gets up to give him a quick hug, then thinks twice about it. She doesn't want a lapse in decorum to compromise her position. "I hoped we'd see you today. How did your furlough go? How are your mother and sister?"

"I loved being back home again, but it is good to be back. Hannah has her hands full with the kids, and my mother worries about me constantly."

"Well, you've missed a lot here. In the aftermath of Gettysburg, Benjamin has been transferred to a hospital in Baltimore and Dr. Cross to Philadelphia, both on temporary assignment. Dr. Rucker's still here, but you won't be reassigned to my, I mean, this ward."

He does nothing to mask his disappointment. "Why not?"

"Well, it's full, and you're on your way to rejoin your old unit. Most likely nothing will happen for a few days. You'll get a physical, and they'll decide what to do with you then. Are you free to come over for dinner tomorrow? I know Nicholas and the girls, especially Addie, will be happy to see you again. It won't be your mother's home cooking, but you won't go hungry."

"That'd be great ... thank you."

She gestures toward the duty officer's desk. "You'd better check back in before they list you as a deserter."

Robert heads back out to the corporal at the desk, and presents his pass.

"Welcome back, Private. We'll place you in the transit ward for the night. After the doctor sees you in the morning, he'll tell you what to expect from there." The corporal hands him a replacement identification tag and starts to give him directions to the ward.

Robert holds up the card, "I remember where to go." The fatigue from the day's travel catches up with him. When he gets to the cot, he takes off his shoes and jacket, lies down, and loses himself in thought.

* * *

Robert has a surprisingly restful night. The steward places his chart at the foot of the bed, then serves him a full breakfast. He cleans up, gets dressed, and within the hour, morning rounds begin.

Dr. Rucker reads through his chart. "Glad to see you've rejoined us, Private. Hope your furlough helped."

"Grateful for the break, sir. Thank you."

"Let me unwrap all this and see what we've got." As he begins to cut away the bandages, he asks, "Any problems with this while home? Notice any changes?"

"No problems, but I did start having some prickly sensations a couple of weeks ago. The tingling moved to my other fingers and from there along the right side of my palm. It's been a little painful, but not bad."

The doctor leaves the bandages and splint on the bed, then examines the entry point on his forearm. "This looks like it's healed well." He starts to gently squeeze then manipulate his wrist area. "Let me know if any of this hurts. Did you try anything that might stress the injury?"

"No, sir. The family didn't allow me to do much."

"How's the wrist feel now?"

"Well, it's stiff and sore as you move it."

"That's not unusual. Go ahead and turn your hand palm-side up."

His last three fingers are still curled down toward the palm. "Are you doing that?"

"No, sir."

"Try moving them." Robert makes the effort, without response. He rubs his fingers along the scar on his palm, then says, "Well, your incision has healed perfectly." The doctor tries moving the fingers, but they resist any kind of manipulation.

"What am I going to be left with?"

The doctor senses the alarm in Robert's voice. "This may be as good as you can hope for. But, look, it won't impede most of your functions, and you'll learn how to adapt to it. Everything else has healed up nicely, and though it may seem like a disappointment now, you'll be able to lead a relatively normal life."

"Will I be able to stay in the army?"

"I don't see any reason why you can't. We've reassigned amputees back to their outfits. In fact, we will give back to your command within the week."

"What happens in the meantime?"

He points to the splint and bandages. "For starters, you won't need these anymore." Robert silently bids the paraphernalia, *good riddance,* and starts to gingerly rubs his newly freed hand and arm. "Take some time to relearn some basic skills——how to dress, your toiletries, feeding yourself, and writing. Try not to depend upon others. There will be an adjustment period, some fumbling and frustrations. Don't be too hard on yourself. Those skills will come back." He grabs the tops of his arms and gives him a little shake. "Attitude. Keep a positive attitude, young man." He releases his grip and walks to the next patient.

Robert isn't surprised, but the stunning reality of it settles in——he won't be whole anymore. He starts to exit the ward and sees the silhouette of someone standing in the doorway. When he adjusts to the light, he recognizes Pauline.

"I thought you might need a little moral support today."

He's relieved it's her, and a bit puzzled.

"Don't worry. I've made arrangements for you to spend some time at our place for a couple of days. Things quieted down at work for Nick, and he's home for the time being. Thought you might like a couple of friends to talk things over with. Make yourself presentable, then let's take a walk."

Robert holds out his shirt-sleeve for Pauline to button up. "Don't you think you better do that yourself?"

"I'm on my own now, huh?"

"Get used to it."

After he fumbles a bit, he finishes the buttons and grabs his jacket and forage cap. "Where to?"

They start the walk back to her house. "Tell me what you're feeling."

"Give me a minute." He thinks about her question for a long time. "I thought this might be one of the results, you know, and now it's a reality. How'd anyone want to be with me like this?"

"You mean a woman?"

He nods and starts to tell her all about Susan. He goes into their family ties, his furlough, the visits, and Susan's declaration to him.

"You haven't said how you feel about her."

"I think I feel the same, but I'm obligated for two and a half more years, and then there's this," pointing to his arm.

"If she loves you, she'll wait, and the arm shouldn't matter to her."

"She pretty much said the same thing."

"Sounds like she's a special young lady. As far as the army and this war goes, just do what you can to survive, and then come home."

"That's it, huh? Think that's a bit out of my hands, don't you?"

"I do. So there's no reason for you to worry about it."

Robert spends the next couple of days with the Bakers. He enjoys the family environment, and finds out Pauline is a great cook. He spends a lot of time with Nick, helps him with the endless chores the house places on him, and has many heart-to-heart talks about life, love, and the military. He helps him as best he can, handles the tools, and assists with the repairs which helps Robert with his coordination. Their oldest daughter, Addie, coaches him as he learns to write with his thumb and forefinger. She's patient, nonjudgemental, and laughs easily, especially as she watches him fumble the silverware.

Monday, 27 July 1863

The Bakers share a final breakfast with Robert. Good-byes are exchanged with their daughters, then he and Pauline leave for the hospital.

"I appreciate you opening your home to me, and mine."

"I figure with the help you gave Nick, we got our money's worth. Listen, you'll be released back to your outfit this Friday, sent on the early morning train to Alexandria, then transferred to another that'll put you back with your unit by nighttime. Nick said he'd be happy to take you to the station that morning."

"How do you know all this?"

"I've worked here for over two years and am pretty well-connected. It's not too hard if you know who and what to ask."

There are no more obligations placed on Robert by the hospital staff for the remainder of the week. He finds it helpful to read, write home, visit, and play games with the other patients. The doctor gives him one more check-up on Thursday, asks him several questions about his progress, and releases him for duty effective the next day.

Friday, 31 July 1863

Nick waits at the turn-around with the carriage, and Pauline gives Robert a hug. Wiping the tears from her eyes, she says, "You be safe," then waits as he climbs on board. With her arms folded, Pauline lifts up her right hand in response, recrosses her arms, and returns to her duties in the foyer.

Once Robert settles in, Nick reaches down and lifts up a cloth sack. "It's from Addie … I think she has a crush on you." Robert gives him a sideways glance, but Nick looks straight ahead, and smiles. When he tries to open the sack, Nick adds, "Save it for the train. It's some snacks to tide you over."

"Tell Addie, 'Thanks'. She's been a great help."

"Don't be surprised if you find that life in camp is not the same. Gettysburg changed the expectations in Washington. People here are impatient with Meade's lack of follow-through after their remarkable victory. They want, and are expecting this war to be over … the sooner the better. Just watch your step. We'll pray for you. If you get the chance, drop us a note now and then."

"Thanks, Nick. I'll try." Robert holds out his hand, but Nick surprises him with a hug.

"Take care of yourself, son. Look forward to seeing you back here, safe and sound."

return to duty

The Army of the Potomac is encamped on the north bank of the Rappahannock River, around Warrenton, Virginia, a four-hour train ride from Washington. The heat and humidity hit Robert as he disembarks. When he enters the command tent, Corporal Wingate sits at a desk working through the endless paperwork.

"Robert! The last time I saw you was when, three months ago?"

"It's been about that," he says, shaking Wingate's hand.

"You look a lot better than the last time I saw you."

"Thank you, Thomas. Captain Turnbull on duty today?"

"You mean *Major* Turnbull."

"When did that happen?"

"After Gettysburg. He received another well-deserved brevet for actions on the field. He's currently on temporary assignment. We now answer to a Lieutenant Barstow."

"How *did* things go for the fellas at Gettysburg? I wasn't able to get much news back home."

"Just be thankful you weren't there." Robert gestures wanting to hear more. "On the second day of the battle, General Sickles ordered our unit forward, to the far right flank of the line, and lost his leg in the fight. Lieutenant Livingston was killed, and Captain Ransom was wounded. All totaled ten were killed, and fourteen wounded."

Robert shakes his head, but when Wingate doesn't offer, he has to ask, "Who didn't make it?"

The corporal tries to divert his question. "And the horses ... the Rebs purposefully took them down. They killed forty-five of them. Never seen a massacre like that. I guess they figured if they killed 'em, we wouldn't be able to get our guns off the field. Worked too."

Robert loses his patience. "I'm asking who died that day, Thomas, not what."

He fumbles through some paperwork, finds the list, and starts to read through the names. He sets down the paper. "Robert ... we lost Will Hickman too. I'm sorry. I know that you two were friends."

The news stuns him. "Will? I thought he'd been placed on light duty from his concussion?"

"He started to get better, and they needed him on line." Robert shakes his head in disbelief. Wingate continues. "You'll notice several replacement troops when you get settled in. They send us these young kids now with no training whatsoever. We have to nursemaid them from the ground up. Military indoctrination, field drills, stable duty, then on the cannon—everything from scratch. Word has come down that the army will be on the move as early as tomorrow. We are again assigned to General Tyler's Reserves, which means I don't know if we are going to strike tents or not."

After hearing about Will, nothing the corporal says registers with him. "Mind showing me my billet, Thomas? It's been a long day."

"No problem. I'll get you a bedroll then take you to your quarters."

Men are clustered together in groups, some playing cards, lots of laughter, and some singing. Robert thinks, *Church hymns! This is army life fresh off a victory—confident and secure. Despite the rumors around Washington, it looks like we finally got a leader.*

"These are only temporary quarters. Report back after breakfast to meet the lieutenant. You may want to take some time and think about what you'd like to do ... and what you *can* do."

"Thanks, Thomas. I'll sleep on it and see you then."

Robert's exhausted, physically and emotionally, but has one more task. He tosses his bag and bedroll into the tent, and goes off to find an old friend.

ramsey's story

He eventually finds Ramsey sitting on the ground alone, his back against a boulder, staring into the fire, as he nurses a mug.

"Jim. It's me. Robert."

Ramsey looks at him in disbelief. "I thought I'd lost you too." He strides over to his old friend and embraces him. He tries to speak, but starts to sob. "Will's gone, Robert."

"I'm so sorry."

Ramsey eventually settles down, and grabs a cloth from his pocket. As he wipes his eyes, he says, "Why don't you grab a mug by the kettle and take a seat."

Robert shakes the pot. "There's no coffee in here, Jim."

Ramsey leans down and produces a bottle of bourbon.

"Oh." He reaches out the mug and says, "To fallen friends?" as Jim pours.

Jim echoes his toast. They sit together silently for a long time. Staring into the fire, Jim lets the memories unfold before him like a vision replaying through the flames. "It was bad ... bad as any of us might imagine. On the second day our entire corps was in a line atop Cemetery Ridge ... far as we could see in either direction. We were facing the Rebs west of us. General Sickles decided we needed to be on higher ground, which was closer. He moved the entire corps forward. Our battery was in reserve, but he ordered us right alongside 'em." He stops to takes a long drink from his mug. "Once underway, a Lieutenant Chris ... ter ... something ... well, it doesn't matter, he intercepted Turnbull and directed us to follow him for placement."

Robert places his hand on Jim's shoulder to interrupt. "Who was he?"

"I don't know … some faceless general's idiot staff officer. He wanted to help, I guess, so follow him we did. The head of our regiment, Captain Ransom saw what was happening, intervened, and redirected us to our proper placement. We were out there, on the far end of the right flank, unprotected, and immediately under fire. Ransom and Turnbull set us up to return fire right away … pretty accurate too. Ransom left to check on another battery's placement. By then, we were fully engaged. Just before he returned, he'd been shot in the leg, right above his knee. Despite his protests, Turnbull summoned one of the men to escort him to the medical tent, then continued to direct our fire."

Robert holds his empty mug toward Jim. "Refill?"

Jim grabs the bottle and tops off both mugs. He nurses his drink for a while, then resumes. "Seems like we were dueling with the Rebs for hours. They kept gaining ground, and our ammo ran low, we ended up switching to 'rotten shot'."

"What's that?"

"Oh, they mentioned it once at Camp Berry——we removed the fuses from the case shot before firing them. They exploded as soon as they left the muzzle. It placed all of us in danger, shrapnel flying everywhere, but with it, we were able to keep the Rebs at bay until they replenished our ammo stores. The teamsters rode up to the line and dropped canister rounds on the ground between our guns to help us get to them faster. We started firing double-loads, careful not to hit our own boys. It was a mess … an effective, lethal mess."

"Where was Will in all of this?"

Jim stares at him, trying to organize his thoughts through the fog of bourbon. "That's right. You didn't return after Chancellorsville. Will was still pretty weak, and they placed him on light duty in the stables until he was fully recovered. With the loss of Welker, Billings, *and you*, he said he'd just as soon stay with the horses, but when he got better, they put him on the line, just not back with the gun crew. They used him as a teamster, but the Rebs picked off our horses so fast, it left Will as more of a runner ... anywhere they needed him. As the Confederate's kept gettin' closer, our lines kept moving back. General Carr ordered Turnbull to 'retire the line while firing'."

Jim senses Robert doesn't understand.

"The general thought that if we limbered up and left the area rapidly, it'd look more like we'd been overrun, and the troops might follow in panic. Turnbull cut the traces to the harness teams, and had the teamsters lead the remainder off the field." Ramsey pauses for a drink. "We lost so many horses that day ... more 'n forty of 'em. Can you believe it? Never seen anything like it. Turnbull directed Will and the new guy, a Virginia boy no less, to grab the prolonge ropes and tie them to the axles."

"Who was that?"

"Oh, I forget his name ... he filled your open billet. He and Will hit it off, and we started to hang out together. You'd have liked him ... 'bout your age, energetic, and funny." Jim chuckles to himself, remembering a humorous moment. "He and Will pulled the cannon back with the ropes as the gun recoiled. We retreated at a walking pace, the cannon firing as we continued. I was in the number four position. I replaced the firing pin between rounds, then pulled the lanyard when ordered. We were all doing our jobs ... all the while we continued backward, facing the oncoming Rebs. We crossed the Emmitsburg Road and worked our way toward Plum Run. We acted as the rearguard, when Lieutenant Livingston took off with two of our guns, moving forward and to the right to cover our retreat. The Rebs killed him soon after, his two gun crews overrun, and both his cannon lost to the Rebs."

"Couldn't Turnbull stop Livingston?"

"We we're fighting for our lives ... especially Turnbull. With so many of our men going down, we couldn't keep our four remaining guns going, so he ordered one of them spiked and abandoned. He constantly checked our movement to match the pace of the retreating line, firing his revolver in the process. Once he ran out of ammo, he looked for ways to get us safely off the field." He paused for another drink. "Do you remember how frightened Will got at the Peninsula?"

Robert nods.

Jim refills his mug, looks at the dregs in the bottle and finishes them off. He wipes his mouth with his sleeve, then continues. "What happened there, happened to us. The Rebels overran us ... left us fighting hand-to-hand. We grabbed anything we could get our hands on to fight them off. James ... that's his name, James ... same as me ... James tried to spike another cannon when a Reb came from behind, and crushed his skull with the stock of his musket. Will grabbed one of the handspikes to use as a club, and ran toward him, yelling, which alerted the Reb ... he spun his rifle around and shot poor Will through the chest." Jim starts to sob. "He crumpled and fell." He fumbles for words, his voice raspy, "Will! ... I kept screaming his name ... Will! ... fighting to get to him ... when Turnbull grabbed me by the collar and dragged me off the line to the rear. Even though we'd lost our guns, Turnbull got fifty of us back to safety ... just not Will." Robert remains quiet, and watches Jim wrestle with his emotions. "He was a sweet kid. He didn't want to be there ... but he didn't panic ... he didn't run ... he just died." Jim continues to sob.

Robert sits with him silently. Eventually Jim's mug falls to the ground as he passes out. Robert tosses the empty bottle, finds a blanket, and covers his friend.

in camp

Saturday, 1 August 1863

The aches and sounds of the early morning hours are a reminder to Robert that he's back in camp. The stale smells of men in close quarters, and the clatter of pots, pans, and cups are accompanied by a swell of coughs, groans, and chatter. He heads out of the tent and over to the fire pit where coffee is already on. Ramsey isn't there, and the other men are unfamiliar to Robert.

Once dressed, he makes his way to headquarters. Lieutenant Barstow sits at his desk when Robert appears.

"Good morning, sir. Reporting for duty."

The lieutenant looks up from his paperwork. "And you are?"

"Private Canham, sir. I reported back from hospital last night."

"Yes, the corporal mentioned you'd be in this morning. Welcome back, Private."

The lieutenant stands. He's as tall and lean as Robert. He wears a thick mustache that wraps around to full sideburns that General Burnside made fashionable. His eyes are dark, alert, and underlined with heavy bags. He transferred into the unit after Gettysburg, and is still trying to find his way with the men.

"The corporal mentioned that you are left with some physical limitations after Chancellorsville." Robert holds up his hand. "I see. He tells me you handled yourself well under fire and are respected by your battery mates. We can use good veterans to guide the replacements. Seems the army has deemed fit for us to get raw, untrained recruits. But before that, we'll need to assess what you are capable of. Are you up for it?"

"Yes, sir. Whatever I can do to be of use."

"Good attitude, Private. We are currently conducting training with some of the replacements until we move out. I'd like you to go through the paces with the men, practice each of the positions, and see where you can fit in. You will most likely be held in a reserve status when we go into the field."

"Any idea of when we may be moving out?"

"The way we hear it, General Meade wants a 'reconnaissance in force'. That usually means cavalry. I think we're okay for now."

Corporal Wingate returns from the mess tent when he runs into Robert. "I take it you got a chance to meet our new lieutenant."

"What's he like?"

"He seems okay, but he's new, and a bit disorganized. He treats the men well, but I think he still has to show himself under fire before they can accept him as one of us."

"Ready to show me around?" Robert asks.

"Let me check in with the lieutenant first to let him know I'll be gone." Robert wants to hear about the challenges they face, and the exhilaration of finally claiming a victory over Lee's vaunted Army of Northern Virginia.

After the tour, Robert breaks off to find the mail wagon. He passes neatly aligned rows of tents, and sees the wagons ahead—the sutlers's carts, the reporters' vacant assembly area, and the one marked U.S. Mail. Robert queries the sergeant in charge, and within minutes receives a small packet of envelopes. Two from the family, as well as a couple from Susan, and to his surprise, one from Pastor Foye. He tucks them into his jacket to read later.

He aimlessly strolls through the grounds and looks for a familiar face when he finds Ramsey tending a newly lit campfire. "Hey, Jim. How are you feeling?"

He squints to see who's addressing him, winces his eyes from the smoke, and says, "I'll live ... I guess."

"Where are the rest of the men?"

"They'll be back soon. Most are at the stables. The horses need a lot more attention. A bad run of hoof rot took most of them out of service. We break in replacements as fast as we get them. I think it's one of the reasons we're still in reserve. How are you now that you're operating with one good arm?"

Self-consciously covering his hand, he answers, "I can hold my own."

"As part of the crew?" Jim asks.

He shrugs his shoulders. "I don't know yet. I need to get to the range and go through the paces with the replacements."

As they continue to talk, more of the gun crews straggle into the tent area. Handshakes and back slaps come from old acquaintances, and introductions are made to some of the new men. They share dinner together and catch up late into the night. The newer troops pepper Robert with questions.

Jim smiles at him. "They hit all the veterans the same. We must'a been like that, too."

"That bad, huh?"

"Oh, yeah. You remember how Will was." Robert nods.

"Who's the Gunner, now? What's he like?"

"Sergeant Melnick. I think you'll like him. He's patient, but firm with the new men, likes a good time when we're off, and laughs easily. We often find him singing … great voice."

"I look forward to meeting him." Sensing his fatigue, he excuses himself, "I'm sorry, but I've got to turn in."

Saturday, 8 August 1863

Twelve men report to the artillery range for orientation, half a mile from the command post. The Gunners split up the teams, one manning the cannon fifty yards to the east, the other staying put.

"How many of you have experienced combat with one of these?" Sergeant Melnick asks while patting the bronze barrel of the Napoleon cannon. Robert and one other man raise their hands. The returning soldier is with Battery K, injured at Gettysburg, and just back for duty.

He has no apparent infirmities, and can fully participate in the training. The other four men in Robert's team are young, too young. Some are here against their parents' wishes, yet here they are, smart, and eager, but still boys, wanting the fun, the adventure, not to miss out on the action.

As they break off to begin their rotation, Robert discovers that he can easily man the numbers three and four positions efficiently, but the others present different challenges. He will be held in reserve, ready to be called upon for any reason——as a runner, teamster, messenger, or observer. The artificer will make use of his experience repairing the wagons, limbers, caissons, and cannon carriages.

That night, he finds a place where he can be alone and go through his mail, the oldest one first, written by his father a couple of days after he left. It's full of reassurances, but Robert can hear his mother feed him admonitions through his father's pen. He quickly scans the letter from Pastor Foye. It looks long and involved, and more than Robert wants to deal with. He repacks the envelope and makes a promise he will read it when he has the wherewithal. The letters are much as he expected from Susan, filled with news of her immediate family, her hopes for their future, and how much she misses him, and prays for his safe return. He answers the letters from his folks and Susan, then calls it a night.

Warmth and humidity bathe the troops with prickly heat, and partner with the endless profusion of mosquitos to rob them of sleep.

***

As the weeks progress, Robert's training continues. His responsibilities are juggled between artillery drills, and the stables. The Supply Corps has done a good job with replacements for the horses, and the men focus on getting them harness-trained, and how to assimilate them as part of a team of six.

One day passes to the next with no word of movement, no word of General Lee and his troops, no word of the war drawing any closer to an end.

Sunday, 30 August 1863

in camp

Six men are circled around the campfire sharing good-natured banter when one of the recruits rushes over, out of breath. "Hey fellas, I just heard about a mass execution of our troops. The padre mentioned it in his prayers at chapel this morning."

The men turn in unison to hear what the boy has to say. Ramsey asks, "Well, what did you hear?"

"That this Saturday past, 'bout three in the afternoon. Several of the men from the 148th Pennsylvania were marched out in front of the whole Fifth Corps ... then were shot ... right there in front of everybody!"

Lieutenant Barstow and Corporal Wingate join them, while the young lad shares his understanding of the rumor. The men stand, but the lieutenant asks that they relax and sit back down.

"Smoke, Lieutenant?" asks Price, holding out a freshly rolled cigarette.

"Thank you." He takes the offering, draws a small branch from the fire, and lights up. He takes a draw from the cigarette, and tosses back the branch. "Look, fellas, we've been asked to let you know what happened." He looks at the excited young news-bearer. "Before it gets blown totally out of proportion. Young Rodgers here is correct, in that an execution was carried out on Saturday, near Rappahannock Station. The Provost caught five men from the 118th, not the 148th, who had high-tailed it from their company once they got on their home turf in Pennsylvania. They brought 'em back in irons, tried and convicted 'em of desertion, and sentenced 'em to death."

Murmurs spread around the group as it digests what the lieutenant shares.

"Our young recruit's telling the truth?" asks Price.

"Pretty close. The entire Fifth Corps assembled and the men were marched out in manacles while the band played the 'Dead March'. Each followed his own coffin, carried by four others and stood before their prepared grave sites."

"Why so harsh, Lieutenant?" asks Robert.

"Desertions are on the rise, and General Meade hopes this will reduce the numbers of those that entertain notions about joining the exodus."

Ramsey shakes his head. "Imagine having to walk out in front of their own men, and to to see where they'll spend their eternity."

"I doubt *that's* where they'll spend their eternity," adds the young recruit, confidently.

The lieutenant looks over at him. "Right." He sighs and shakes his head slowly. "The chaplains said prayers, the charges read, the order given, and thirty six rifles sent them to their creator. They conducted a makeshift funeral service to encompass the three faiths——"

"Three faiths?" asks Robert.

"One a Catholic, one a Jew, and the other three Protestant."

"A real ecumenical execution," Sergeant Melnick says after he spits out a wad of tobacco juice. "Seems they'd have kept them in irons for the duration, rather than kill 'em."

To avoid fueling a contentious debate, the lieutenant and Wingate excuse themselves, and head over to the adjacent gathering to convey what command wants circulated throughout.

Robert looks at the others, deep within their own thoughts. "Think I'd rather get my final comeuppance in battle, than by a firing squad. You don't know when it'll happen, no humiliation, no shame in that."

"At least they didn't suffer," says the recruit.

"Didn't suffer!" yells the sergeant. "Can you imagine what they thought about as they waited for their day of reckoning? That long walk they took shuffling out to their *own open grave sites*, then to face the men, the people they knew, now an audience to their execution. Then look at the rifles facing them square on, knowing what's coming next. What about their families? The shame they will most likely bear until they make the trip to their own graves. Didn't suffer? Oh, they suffered, sure enough. They suffered."

* * *

Over the remainder of summer and into the early fall, Robert works hard at practicing the positions in the battery. Training the new men becomes more comfortable, and they find him open and affable. They know they can come to him with problems and questions and get straight answers without the judgement and criticisms they've gotten from others.

in camp

The Army of the Potomac - executions of five deserters in the fifth corps
Alfred R. Waud drawing
Harper's Weekly

Tuesday, 22 September 1863

After muster the men gather for breakfast. Sergeant Melnick says, "I talked with a couple on picket duty yesterday. They tell me Lee's forces are over the other side of the Rapidan river. That comes as no surprise, but they saw hundreds of them in the river. It looked to them like they're getting baptized."

"Sounds to me like they've gotten religion. They must be getting ready for maneuvers," Robert adds.

The sergeant continues. "I think you're right. Don't be surprised if we get orders to move out. Looks like General Lee's itchin' to do battle."

* * *

For the next couple of months, both armies see action in the region with battles and skirmishes at places named Bristol Station, Rappahannock Station, and Mine Run. Robert's unit remains held in reserve throughout the campaigns.

Despite the lack of a major battle or a clear-cut victory, the South leaves the field for the winter with the knowledge they delayed the campaign season until the following spring. Even after their devastating defeat at Gettysburg, Lee and his army are still a force to contend with, and Lincoln's re-election the following year is not assured. The Peace Democrats may yet impose their will in the coming election.

unexpected

Friday, 19 February 1864

"Private Canham, front and center!" Robert's in his tent, trying to keep warm, and wonders to himself, *what now?* It's Sergeant Major O'Connor, who never shows his face in this part of the camp unless someone has done something pretty serious. Like the time Watson missed the troop movement because he took off for an unauthorized night on the town. Or Compton, who decked Corporal Fanning from Battery K for trying to discipline him on a minor infraction when he wasn't in Compton's battery. Neither of those incidents turned out well for the privates. *What's he want with me?*

He throws on his jacket, makes his way out of the tent, and stands before O'Connor, who looks him over. Despite breezy, bitter cold temperatures, his jacket's unbuttoned, his forage cap is still on his bedroll, and he looks generally disheveled. "Sorry, Sergeant Major. I wasn't expecting you."

"I can see that. Lieutenant Barstow requests you report to him immediately. Take a few minutes, get yourself in order, dress warmly, and we'll go together."

"Am I in some kind of trouble?"

"You will be if you don't hurry up. It's cold out here."

"Kind of over-qualified to be a messenger, aren't you?"

"Astute observation," he says with a smile. "The usual runners are busy finding others. That left me to get you."

Robert wonders, *if others are on their way, it must be for some kind of work detail the lieutenant's put together. It figures that he'd pick a day like today, in these conditions, to work us outside.*

As the two make their way through the camp, some of his battery mates started to kibitz Robert when he passes by:

"Looks like you've gotten in deep this time, *Private*."

"Don't worry, they can't bust you any lower than you already are."

"Must be you haven't given the camp followers enough personal attention."

"Better you than me, Robert."

Finally, the company bugler, Private Karney, gets into the act playing "Taps" on his mouthpiece as they walk by. Even the normally stoic sergeant major breaks into laughter at that one.

Robert looks over at O'Connor. "Always good to know we've got each others' back."

It's a fairly long walk to company headquarters. By the time they reach the tent, Robert can't help but feel a little anxious. The sergeant major tells him to stand fast and enters the tent to find out when the lieutenant can see him. He returns right away. "Lieutenant Barstow's ready for you now."

Robert enters, comes to attention, and salutes.

He returns the salute, and says, "At ease, Private. I half expected you to be fully packed and dogging me for your papers."

"I don't understand, sir. Papers?"

"Your discharge, Private. You're out of the army."

Robert can't believe his ears. *There must be some kind of mistake. My enlistment isn't up for another two years. How can this be*? He keeps his mouth shut, and lets the lieutenant continue. "Orders came down from command last night that a number of you have expiring enlistments. Corporal Wingate and I spent the morning filling out discharge papers … yours included." He hands Robert the document. Robert's mind works around a myriad of scenarios, and lands on, *if it came down from command …*

The Army of the Potomac will soon be engaged in some of the bloodiest fighting of the war. But for Robert, he's on his way home.

home again

Monday, 22 February 1864

The knock at the front door interrupts Elizabeth's food prep for their evening meal. "Robert! Bless my soul. What a surprise."

"Got enough food here to feed a poor soldier?"

She gives her son a hug, then holds him at arm's length to look into his eyes. "Are ya' in some kinda trouble? Whatcha doin' here?"

"I'm out. They gave me my discharge last Friday, and I knew I'd make it home before I could get word to you."

Elizabeth has to sit down. The great relief of her youngest back home is a complete shock. "Better go to the barn. Yer father'd be glad to se ya', son."

James stands up and takes the pipe out of his mouth. "Well, I'll be! It's good to see you back home, son."

"Got work enough to keep a farmhand busy?"

"What are you doing here? Didn't expect to see you back for a couple more years. You're not in any trouble are you?"

Robert chuckles, "No, no, they gave me an early out. Where are Will and Clara now?"

"Guess your mail didn't catch up with you. They never returned from their honeymoon. Seems they went to Chicago, then got wind of cheap land and doubled back to Michigan."

"Doesn't land cost money?"

"Apparently not much," says James. "They're taking advantage of a program called homesteading. The President signed it into law a couple of years back. They're offering a hundred and sixty-acre tracts of land for twenty-five cents an acre. They need to work the land for five years, put up a small structure, grow crops, file the claim, and it's theirs. The other bit of news is Clara's pregnant, due sometime this spring."

"Will's gonna be a father. I go away for a couple of months …"

James goes into the workshop and comes out with a long burlap bag. "Will wanted me to give you this. It's the rifle he culled together from parts. You went out to shoot this with him didn't you?"

"Yeah, on furlough last year. He did the shooting, while I watched him miss. No sense him taking it with him I guess. Think you might like to go with me sometime to test it out?"

"There's plenty of ammo to go with it, sure, we can go out, but I'd like to wait for it to warm up a bit first."

"Hope you don't mind, father, but weather permitting, I'm going to call on Susan tomorrow. What do you think of her?"

"Listen, son, whatever I, or anyone else, thinks of her is of no consequence. You need to do what you believe is right for you. You know our families' histories. She comes from good people."

"It's kind of a premature conversation. There's much to work through, starting with making that commitment in the first place."

"I'll say."

Robert raises his eyebrows. "Say again?"

"Well, son, she's been right there in front of you your whole life, and you're just now getting around to thinking about her like that."

He thrusts his hands out to his side. "What can I say, I'm a slow learner."

Tuesday, 23 February 1864

"Susan, come here quick," cries her mother. She stands at the front window, and waves her oldest daughter over. All three of the older girls rush to take a look. A sleigh, driven by a man too bundled up to be recognized, pulls into their yard. They know the vehicle, but who is driving? Susan knows. She elbows past her younger sisters, and runs to grab her coat. Before Robert can finish tying up the horse, Susan has leapt off the porch and into his arms.

"I can't believe it's you!" she says giving him a kiss. "You're the last person I expected to see at our front door today. How is it you're home?"

"Can we get inside to talk? I'm cold."

Susan takes him by the hand, brings him into the house, and leads him into the front parlor. "Look who's home. It's Robert."

Her sisters stare up at him and giggle. Ann says, "I guessed as much as soon as you threw yourself at him. Welcome back, Robert. Your return must be a surprise to everyone."

Susan can't take her eyes off him as he removes his layers of clothing and walks over to the radiant warmth of the fireplace. "Yes, ma'am. Nobody's more surprised than me."

"Well, it's good you're back safe and sound." She gathers a daughter with each arm. "We'll finish up in the kitchen, and give you two a chance to catch-up."

Susan faces Robert and reaches up for a hug. "I'm delighted you're back. I don't understand, but I'm delighted."

He holds her close, "I couldn't wait to see you either. Before we get too involved, I wouldn't turn down something warm to drink."

She jumps up. "I'll be right back." She hurries into the kitchen. The women chatter away as cups are brought down and liquid poured. A few minutes later, Susan returns with a plate of cookies and two cups of coffee.

He tests the temperature with a sip, then takes a full drink before grabbing one of the treats. With his mouth half-full, he starts off the conversation. "First off, I didn't expect this. With two more years left to do, they let me out. I didn't ask for it, and it wasn't because of my arm. They called me to the lieutenant's tent last Friday and handed me my papers."

"I'm so filled with joy right now. I can't believe you're here."

Robert takes another sip of his coffee, then asks, "How do your folks feel about me courting you?"

"I doubt it'll come a surprise to anyone." She stares at him for a few moments, then says, "What are your plans for work?"

"For the immediate future, my folks need help at the farm, but there's nothing else lined up right now."

"I know that my dad needs a hand around here. Little George does what he can, but with his heart, Dad needs a grown man to help him."

"I can talk to my folks about it, but my father's alone right now. Will's moved to Michigan, and that leaves me."

"You've heard from Will and Clara?"

"My folks told me last night. Apparently Clara's due this spring——"

"They're pregnant! I haven't seen them since they got married. Now I know why."

"Yeah, five or six months along by now."

"Good for them. What took them out west?"

"That's where they honeymooned. Father tells me land's real cheap through homesteading."

"I read about that; didn't pay much attention to the details though."

"I think it'd be exciting to join them there." Robert looks at her over the edge of his cup as he takes another drink. "But that decision isn't only up to me."

Susan is upset and hesitates a long while before she speaks, processing what he just said. "Aren't you kind of getting ahead of things? You're already talking about *our* going west, when we aren't even officially a *we*."

"I just assumed——"

She repositions herself in the chair, then crosses her arms. "I care for you, Robert. No, that's not true. I do love you ... but I want to be courted properly." Her eyes narrow. "I don't want to be taken for granted. Seriously, we have a lot to work through first."

He notices she hasn't touched her coffee or anything from the plate. "I'm sorry. Guess I haven't taken the time to sort this out. I just thought this would be ..."

Susan doesn't say anything. She keeps glancing back at the kitchen, and feels like she's been backed into a corner. She hopes her mother will walk in to rescue her, but realizes she's on her own. She stands, and says, "I think it's best that you go home now."

Robert's taken aback. "Really. That's what you want?"

Without answering, Susan walks out to the kitchen in tears, leaving him standing there alone. When he realizes she's not coming back, he puts his things on and leaves without another word.

Tuesday, 15 March 1864

His new routine centers around the upkeep of the farmhouse and care of the livestock. Planting season will be upon them soon, and much needs to be readied before then. It's been weeks since his last visit to see Susan and he knows he can't keep putting off the inevitable.

James walks in the back door and notices Robert's not dressed in his work clothes. "Looks like you've made other plans for the day. What's going on?"

"I need to go straighten things out with Susan."

"Yeah, ya' do," says Elizabeth.

"I don't know how long I'll be. Guess it depends on how it goes."

"Just listen to her, son … you'll be fine," says James.

Elizabeth adds, "Remember she has feelin's too ya' know."

"Thanks you two. See you later." He walks out knowing he's alone.

* * *

"It's been a while, Robert," says Ann awkwardly. "How've you been keeping yourself?" She gestures for him to come in.

"Fine, ma'am. I'm here to see Susan?"

"I can imagine. She's out back with the young ones. I'll call her in."

"Hello, Robert." He stands as Susan walks in the front door several minutes later. She doesn't show the same amount of enthusiasm as his last visit. "I didn't expect to see you."

"We can't avoid each other forever. I needed some time to sort things out. Figured you did, too."

Ann leaves the room. Susan stands about four feet from him, arms folded together tightly, hesitant to draw any closer. She fights the urge to throw herself into his embrace, and she releases the tight grip on her arms. "I'm sorry the way things ended the last time. I've thought a lot about what you said … and what I said——"

"You're right." Robert interrupts. "I hadn't considered what may be on your heart."

"I honestly don't know who you are anymore. What's happened to you the last three years? I know you've changed, but I don't know how much. I don't know what kind of a man you are." She starts to well up, and struggles to maintain her composure. He takes a step toward her but she motions him to stop. "I want a godly man, Robert. A man whom I can trust. A man totally open and honest with me." Her tear-filled eyes are staring straight at his. Shaking her head, and wagging her finger for emphasis, she says, "There can be no secrets between us, and I feel you're holding onto things inside of you."

"I don't know what else you want from me." His voice more elevated. "I think I *am* dependable. I've done nothing to violate your trust. What more do you want?"

"When you can answer that question, then we can talk about whatever future we might have together."

Frustrated, Robert turns to walk out and lets the door slam shut in back of him. He knows what she wants. That's the dilemma he's fighting ... to let her in completely, to open that dark abyss within.

Before he mounts his horse, Susan's father comes from around the side of the house, and approaches him. "Robert, it's good to see you again, son. It's been a while. I've been meaning to come over for a talk with you."

"Yes, sir. I'm just been trying to readjust to civilian life."

"I'm sure you have. How's your arm doing?"

Still shaken, he answers, "Better, sir. I'm a little more used to what I can and can't do."

"I've been thinking I'd like a man around here for the upcoming season."

"My father needs help at his place, too."

"Well, keep it in mind. I'm sure Susan would like to see more of you around here."

Robert mounts his horse, looks at George and says, "I'm not so sure about that." He flicks the reins and leads the horse toward the road.

George stares at Robert as he heads out to the Ridge, then goes back in the house to find out what that's all about.

surrender

Thursday, 21 April 1864

Robert hears movement in the distance. It's vague, but sounds like marching, drawing closer. He can't make out who approaches, but the steady noise grows louder. The anxiety wells up from his gut ... a bright flash! Where's that coming from ... artillery? A loud boom rattles him to his core ... artillery ... but where are they, he must hold his position ... another bright flash ... another ripple, this time higher up ... the shells land closer ... the footsteps are sharper ... is that musket fire? ... another flash ... another explosive crash ... he can't make out their faces ... another flash, brighter, closer ... must hold this position ... another explosion ... where are they ... another crash, he starts to run ... the pain ... he starts to yell——

"Robert, wake-up!" His father squeezes his shoulder hard, and tries to shake him out of his nightmare.

He bolts upright, gasps for air, his nightshirt is soaked through.

Holding a lamp, James says, "Wake up, son. It's me, your father."

Robert looks at the lamp, then at him, then around his room, and starts to come back to reality. He's home. He's safe, but with another flash of lighting, and peal of thunder, he jumps to his feet. His head violently turns toward the window.

"It's just a storm. You're safe."

Robert sits back down on the bed. He gradually starts to breathe normally, and finds his bearings. "What time is it?"

"It's early, too early to get up. Think you can you go back to sleep?"

"I don't know if I even want to. Please, leave the lamp on. I'll try to read a bit."

James nods, closes the door behind him, and works his way downstairs to his own bedroom and startled wife.

The rainstorm, laced with hail, beats heavily on the window. The lightning is less frequent as it moves off, and thunder, though fading, still rattles the panes and sends shivers down his spine.

Eventually he starts to root around the top right-hand drawer of his dresser. He flips through the letters until he finds the one he wants, the one he received in camp last August. He also discovers the booklet the chaplain gave him, *Come to Jesus*. He opens Pastor Foye's letter first.

Monday, 27 July 1863
Dear Robert,

> *I pray this letter finds you safe and in good health. I spoke with your family last Sunday after service and mentioned I would send this. They seemed pleased that we are in contact, even though you are so far away in such perilous times.*
>
> *I've prayed for you daily since we spoke a couple of weeks ago. I rue the fact that I didn't extend to you the comfort of God's grace that is available to everyone, and can ease the burdens that you carry.*
>
> *Though I cannot fully understand your experiences, nor can I relate to what you are harboring, I am firmly convinced that the Lord knows your heaviness and understands your pain.*
>
> *The Holy Scriptures clearly tell us that it is God's desire we cast our burdens on Him. I hope you can derive some sense of relief in His Word. He only wants His best for you. Saint Peter tells us:*
>
>> *'Humble yourselves therefore under the mighty hand of God, that he may exalt you in due time: <u>Casting all your care upon him; for he careth for you</u>.'*
>
> *I know, Robert, that if you submit your burdens to the Lord, He will lighten your load, and give you the peace you desperately seek. May God's abundant blessings be upon you.*

We love you, son,
Pastor Foye

Robert reads through the letter several times, taking in the scripture and the counsel, allowing it to make its way into his innermost being. He also starts to read through the booklet, but realizes he's too tired to give it its proper due. This time it's his turn to drop down to his knees.

He closes his eyes and meditates a long time on the pastor's words. With tears, he starts to talk to God, asking His forgiveness for his hand in the deaths of so many, for the anger he has harbored toward Him, for turning his back on the church, and His message, and finally for how poorly he has dealt with the concerns that Susan has expressed. His tears flow more freely as he asks God to help him, to remove the guilt and the pain, and to give him the wisdom for the decisions he has to face. He gradually succumbs to the draw of sleep on his body, from both the lack of a good night's rest and the relief that comes with having a great burden lifted from his soul.

The chill from the bare wooden floor and the glow of the early morning sun nudge him. He awakens with a stiff neck, sore back, dry throat, and the need to clear the congestion that has settled in his lungs. He also notices something different—a lightness he hasn't felt in a long time, and a realization he has to make things right with a couple of people.

Sunday, 24 April 1864

The ride to church is unusually arduous. The closer they get, the greater Robert's anxiety. It's the first time he's been back since last June, and hopes Pastor Foye will be available for a talk after the service.

Robert leads his parents down to the pew they usually share with the Harmers, but motions his mother and father to sit first while he takes a seat on the aisle-side of the pew. The Harmers arrive a short time later. Robert leans forward to look over at Susan, but she's bowed in prayer.

The church leaders take their seats after the procession. Pastor Foye catches Robert's eye and acknowledges his presence with a nod. After the service, Robert waits for the congregants in the pew behind him to vacate their seats, and quickly steps around to Susan. "Are you free to get together this afternoon?"

"Not today." Her expression remains stoic. "Tomorrow'd be better. Why don't you make it over for lunch with us. We can talk after that."

"That sounds good. See you then." She manages a slight smile and rejoins her family.

"Well, good morning, son." The pastor's hand rests on Robert's shoulder.

"Good to see you, Pastor."

"I'm delighted you're here today."

"Thank you, sir. Are you available for a chat? Maybe sometime soon? I need your counsel."

"Of course. How about you break bread with us today. We'll have that talk, then I'll take you home afterward."

Robert looks at his mother, who's been eavesdropping. "Are you okay with that, mother?"

"Of course, son."

* * *

The pastor invites Robert into his study after lunch, and slides the doors closed behind him. "If I don't do that, the children will never leave you alone."

"I don't mind them, sir."

"How are you getting along? There are many families praying for you."

He's embarrassed, but appreciative. "I have a confession to make. When I saw the letter you wrote me last year, I didn't want to read it. I wasn't ready, and I put it away until the time was right."

"When was that?"

Robert looks at him sheepishly. "Uh ... this last Thursday?"

The pastor's a little surprised, but responds, "It's in God's good time."

"The storm last Thursday night, maybe it was God talking to me ... at least getting my attention. I don't know, but it did lead me to find your letter and read it." He then pulls out the booklet the chaplain gave him. "I also found this beneath the letter."

"I haven't seen one of these in some time."

"The hospital chaplain gave it to me the day after I got the news one of my friends died. I think mother brought it back from Washington."

"This is an excellent resource on coming into a relationship with our Lord. Did you take the time to go through it?"

"Honestly, no. It seems pretty complicated."

"Are you willing to do that now, together?"

"I'd like that."

The two of them spend the next couple of hours talking through the booklet, and looking up the cited Scriptures. Pastor Foye then asks Robert if he believes in Jesus, and the atoning sacrifice Christ made for him personally.

"I never thought about Jesus doing that for *me*. The chaplain assured me that I needed that personal relationship with Him as well."

"Jesus died for all of us, *individually*. His grace is a free gift. We just need to be willing to believe in Him, and accept His gift. If you are, why don't we pray together."

This time Robert agrees, and when the pastor kneels on the floor to pray, he joins him. When they rise, Robert tells him how the scripture he cited spoke to him personally, how he *did* help him with his counsel. He tells him of his prayer after the storm, surrendering his burdens, the release, and his acceptance. He confesses everything that he withheld when they first met at the farm—his experiences in battle, his guilt, anger, the loss, and the horror. The pastor sheds tears with him, now knowing the degree of pain he has harbored.

Robert talks in detail about his relationship with Susan, and asks for prayers and wisdom for their upcoming meeting. The pastor invites him again to pray with him, then suggests he share his new-found commitment with others.

Their ride back is animated with conversation, laughter, and sage advice. When they reach the farm, Robert feels good that he has gotten back on better footing with him, and encouraged about the meeting with Susan tomorrow. Pastor Foye is gratified knowing the Lord enabled him to help.

grace

⚜

Robert is more than a little anxious about seeing Susan today. Her entire family shares in the sit-down meal. Most of the attention centers around him. George tries to feel him out about his availability. The children are giddy, playful and curious, and Susan tries to keep the younger ones in order, which helps keep her mind off their post-meal get-together.

Too nervous to eat a heavy meal, Robert makes an attempt to help clear the dishes, but Susan's two younger sisters take over the chores and push him in her direction. He laughs, looks at Susan, and shrugs his shoulders. She nods her head toward the outside, and he follows her lead.

They take the path through the apple orchard, this time without the distraction of imminent departure hanging over them. Susan's wary of how this will go. Her arms are crossed, their conversation superficial, and measured. Robert does not want to make the same mistakes he made weeks earlier.

Out of sight of the house, he reaches out for her hand, but she pulls away. He stops in his tracks to work up his nerve before speaking. "Susan, I'm sorry! I'm sorry for everything. I'm sorry that I've taken you for granted ... that I haven't been completely honest with you. I'm sorry that I've withheld, and haven't let you in."

She stands silent for a long time, then buries her head in his chest and holds him, afraid he'll vanish in the moment if she doesn't. "I just didn't know how to reach you."

"If you're ready to hear, I'm willing to tell you ... all of it."

"I want that more than anything ... but I'm afraid."

"I am, too," he says softly.

They find a place to sit under a tree and he opens up. He starts with his breakdown after he heard about the news from Gettysburg, the aborted initial counseling with Pastor Foye, and the letter he subsequently received from him, and how he led him to prayerful confessions and acceptance of Christ's leading.

Calmer now, he talks about his experiences in battle, and the depth of the horror he participated in, the guilt he carries. The loss of Lew Billings, Sergeant Welker, and Will Hickman, and how he's internalized it, keeping it from everyone, and the way it's been tearing him apart inside. He tells her about the freedom in Christ he now has in trying to put it into perspective, and his desire to move on, with her.

Susan pulls a handkerchief from her dress pocket and wipes off her cheeks. "For what it's worth, I forgive you, and I think I understand where you're coming from. You were trying to protect me."

He wears a faint smile. "Actually, I've been trying to protect myself." After a pause, he adds, "I'm just sorry it's taken me this long to realize it."

She puts her face up to his, and kisses him tenderly.

He pulls back slightly to say, "I don't want to go another day without you in my life." Then fervently returns her kiss.

"I want that, too," she says. "But how are we going to manage this?"

"Your father has mentioned needing help around here——"

Susan lets out a delighted yelp. "Perfect!"

"Let me talk with him when we get back to the house. I'll try to work something out with my father, maybe split time between the two farms."

They walk hand-in-hand back to the farmhouse. George is asleep in the parlor.

"He gets tired this time of day and tries to rest," says Ann apologetically.

Robert nods to Ann then looks at Susan, who's still holding on to his arm. "I best be getting back. I'll speak to the folks and come back to see your father soon."

Ann hugs her daughter after he leaves. "Oh Mommy," she starts crying. "He said everything I've been praying to hear." Ann says nothing, but draws Susan's head back to her shoulder.

* * *

After dinner that evening, Robert asks his folks for some time to talk with them together. James senses the chill in the room, stokes up the fire, then settles in his chair. When Elizabeth and Robert enter, he asks, "What's on your mind, son?"

Before he begins, Robert takes a sip of his coffee. "I want to know what you think about my splitting time between here and the Harmer's."

"George needs ya' right now," Elizabeth says. "And you need her."

Robert looks to his father quizzically.

"George came over for a frank discussion with me earlier this month. Guess his heart issues are more serious than we thought. He needs a man to do the heavy lifting around there. I think he'd appreciate anything you can do at this point."

Elizabeth asks, "Did ya' get yer problems with Susan settled?"

"I think so. We talked through a lot, and made some decisions."

"What's that mean?" She starts to mutter under her breath. "Can't keep up with you young folks nowadays."

Feeling his temper rise, Robert stands to faces her. "It means I love her. It means I want a life with her. It means I need to start thinking and making plans for a future ... *with her!*"

James puts his hand on Robert's forearm to calm him down. "Take it easy, son. That's the first time you've ever mentioned being in love with Susan. Sounds serious enough. Any plans we need to know about?"

Robert steps back, looks down at his father's hand, retakes his seat, then lowers his voice. "I'm sorry, mother. It's been tense, but we got things out in the open today, made some declarations and a commitment, but no dates."

"We're happy fer the both of ya'. She's been frettin' over it. I'm happy to hear ya' worked things out."

Robert then looks at James. "Are you sure you're alright with this?"

"She's a fine girl, son."

Still a little testy, he snaps, "I mean with my working for George."

Still holding onto his son's arm, James tightens his grip and just stares at his youngest before calmly answering. "You talk to George, and find out what he needs. You got any time left, we can find something for you here."

Robert rubs his arm after James releases his grip.

decision

～

Friday, 12 August 1864

James flicks Robert's thigh with his finger at the kitchen table after breakfast.

"You still up for that hunt you mentioned a few months back? Maybe late this afternoon?"

"Great. Soon as I get back from George's place we can hitch up the wagon."

* * *

The ride to the field, west of the woods, takes a little over an hour, but it's the perfect time for woodchucks. They can usually be found in abundance in the early evening hours. When they get within fifty yards of their destination, they find natural cover behind a downed tree. James taps Robert's shoulder and points to the edge of the grassy field to the left where they easily count over a dozen rooting around near their burrows.

He has some difficulty working the hammer on the rifle, but once set, it takes him a couple of tries to load the percussion cap successfully. He's not used to the rifle's heft, and he uses the tree for support. This time Robert doesn't jump from the report, and the woodchuck doesn't move. However, the remainder in the field take cover in their holes.

"Guess your eyes are still working well enough. Clean through the head … stew meat tonight."

James then notices Robert's arm draped over the stock of the rifle and his chin resting on it.

"You seem to be distracted. What's on your mind, son?"

Robert straightens up to look at his father directly, then sighs. "I've been thinking about going back to finish out the war."

"What's going on in that head of yours, son? You've done your share, more if you ask me."

"It's mostly to do with Susan."

"What's she got to do with this?"

Robert shakes his head. "That's misleading. I haven't even mentioned it to her. The government's recruiting for volunteers again. They want to get this over with, and I'd kinda like to see it through."

He repeats Robert's words back to him slowly. "'I'd kinda like to see it through' ... I don't understand."

He tries to work out in his head what he wants to say. "I'm here, right back where I started three plus years ago, now the town of Medina is offering five hundred and eighty-five dollars as a bounty to help fill its quota. It'd be with a volunteer infantry regiment from the state. It's my chance to put together a grubstake to start a life with Susan. I don't know how else to raise that kind of money."

"That *is* a powerful incentive, but in their push to end this, wouldn't you just end up as cannon fodder?"

"I doubt it. With his siege on Petersburg, Grant has Lee hemmed in, and the rumors of Rebel desertions are widespread. I don't see how they can hold out much longer."

"Keep in mind, son, that when a dangerous animal gets cornered, it lashes out most desperately. If you're in their path when that happens, it only takes one bullet or one shell to end you. Have you thought about that, or that just maybe the army doesn't want you back with your hand?"

"They kept me in after I returned from furlough. I think they'll take me back now. I know there are risks, but I'm willing to take them ... and well ... we need the money."

"How do you think Susan will take this?"

"Not well, I'm sure. I hope that I can convince her to see it my way."

James places his hand on his son's shoulder as they walk over to collect the woodchuck. "I guess that we'll both have our work cut out for us. Your mother isn't going to take too kindly to this, either."

* * *

Hannah's family shares this evening's dinner with the folks. "How come no one's said a thing this whole meal? Me and mother put on a pretty good stew here, and not a peep outta either of ya'." Her eyes dart back-and-forth between James and Robert.

"Best get used to it, dear." Elizabeth glances at the two of them. "They got somethin' to talk 'bout with us."

Robert stands up, excuses himself, and goes out to saddle up the horse.

Elizabeth looks over to James. "Well, husband, what is it you're not sayin'?"

James waits until he hears Robert's horse gallop off, then looks over to Hannah and back to his wife. "He's on his way to tell Susan that he's going back into the army."

"No!" exclaims Hannah.

"Oh dear," says Elizabeth. "Whatever is he thinkin'?"

* * *

As Robert ties up the horse, George senior greets him from the porch. "Didn't expect to see you 'til the morning."

"Yes, sir. I'm hoping we might talk."

"Sure. Lemme go get Susan."

Robert grabs his elbow to stop him. "No, sir … uh, just the two of us … I don't want to be interrupted before talking this out with you."

"Sure, sure." George points the way to the barn.

As Robert closes the door behind him, George asks, "Well?"

"I'm going back into the army."

George is astonished. "Why? When?"

"As soon as they'll take me. We need the money, and the town is offering a healthy bounty to sign up. Five hundred and eighty-five dollars to be exact."

"That is healthy, but what about Susan?"

"That's why I wanted to talk with you first." Robert looks over to the door, expecting her to burst in at any moment. "I want to marry her, but I can't provide for her any other way. It's a chance to start a life together."

George thinks on what Robert has shared with him. "I understand. I just don't know that *she* will."

"I'd appreciate any suggestions you——"

George lifts his hands in front of him and with both, starts to wave-off that idea. "Oh, no, no you don't. I'm not getting in the middle of this. You two need to work this out together ... just the two of you."

"Do I at least have your blessing?"

George puts his hands on his shoulders. "As far as I'm concerned, you're already part of our family, Robert. You've been a great help to me this year, and we figured that it's only a matter of time before the two of you get married. Any thoughts on when?"

"I plan to ask her as soon as we get back to the house."

"That's good. That's good. The sooner the better."

As they walk out of the barn, they see Susan on the porch looking their way. George pats him on the back. "Good luck, son. Hope it goes the way you want." He turns around and goes back to the barn.

Susan wonders what the two of them are up to. "I saw your horse. What bring's you over this time of the evening? What're you and daddy talking about?"

He holds out his hand. "Let's go for a walk."

The two of them takes hands, and head down the path through the orchard. After a spell, Susan can't take the wait any longer, and pulls him to a stop. "What's going on, Rob?"

"I've made a decision that affects the both of us," he responds hesitantly. "I already talked to my dad and yours, and I do want to know what you think, but I've already made up my mind. I'm going to reenlist. They'll pay five hundred and eighty-five dollars to sign up for the duration of the war. We'll finally have the money we need to get married."

Stunned, Susan hesitates before she speaks, but doesn't feel she has any say in it. "How long do you think you'll be gone?"

"The way things are going now, the war shouldn't last much

longer."

Susan thinks through everything he said for a long time.

Robert faces her, "Well?"

She hesitates, then answers, "I want one thing from you." He raises his eyebrows. "I want to get married before you go back in."

"No other objections?"

"You're doing what you want. This is what I want."

"Anything else?"

"When, Rob? When can we plan the wedding?"

"I guess as soon as I can get a date from the army."

robert & susan

Tuesday, 20 September 1864

The Harmers' house is adorned with fragrant wild flowers for the afternoon's festivities. Chairs are set up in the shaded yard for forty guests, but are not nearly enough for the numbers that will attend this day. Ann and Elizabeth, along with several of the women from their church, are in the kitchen busy at work on food preparation for the guests. Susan is with Hannah, putting the finishing touches on her gown——a light purple silk and cotton dress, with an attached jacket and full, pleated skirt, that has been meticulously recut and assembled.

Robert negotiates the throng of well-wishers as he makes his way to the front of the assembly. He looks handsome, and a little nervous, in his full-dress uniform. Everyone stands as Susan starts her way down the grassy path, arm-in-arm with her father. Her bouquet is a compliment of wild red and pink roses accented with white yarrow and purple alfalfa flowers. Her hair is oiled and parted in the center, worn back in a low bun at the base of her neck. A row of soft ringlet curls cascade along the side of her face and extend to her shoulders. A light dusting of powder, with a hint of rouge on her cheeks and lips, does nothing to conceal her joy.

As Robert watches them proceed down the aisle, his thoughts start to wander to the life he hopes they can share. *I want to be a good husband and a good provider, but can I be? I wish Will was here.* A last minute of panic tries to take hold, *how will I handle the ring?*

A nudge snaps him out of his thoughts. "Here is my daughter, son." Robert looks at him, smiles at her, then turns to face the minister.

Pastor Foye presides over the ceremony. Enthusiastic in his invocation, he knows the trials the couple has gone through, and has been a witness to the work that God has done in Robert's heart. He asks for prayers for the couple, and especially for Robert as he returns to duty. After their vows, Robert ably manages the ring, not telling anyone how many times he practiced with Hannah to build up his dexterity and confidence.

As they are introduced as man and wife, they turn to face an enthusiastic crowd who lets out whoops and cheers for their local soldier and his bride.

* * *

At the passenger's platform of the train depot, Susan holds Robert's arm close to her chest. Hannah and James stand off to the rear next to Ann and George, to give the newlyweds a modicum of privacy. As before, Elizabeth does not want to see her youngest off to war, and she stays at the Harmers' to help the family put their house back in order.

"Not much of a wedding night or a honeymoon," Robert apologizes to Susan. "I promise we'll have one when I get back."

"You just make sure you get back to me in one piece. We'll worry about the rest of it later."

He breaks her grip and goes over to say his good-byes to his family and new in-laws. A few tears are intermixed with well-wishes. Hannah gives him a big hug and promises to keep Susan company.

"Tell mother, well, you know what to say to her."

"I will. You take care of yourself. Don't go doin' nothin' foolish."

With the final call for boarding, Robert wraps Susan in his arms.

"I'll be back before you know it." She gives him a tear-soaked kiss and walks over to Ann, and puts her arms around her mother.

Robert boards the train, finds a place to sit, and pulls down the window. He leaves his cap on the bench, reaches out the window, and waves. The five of them return the gesture as his train pulls away from the station. They visually track the train until it carries him out of sight.

first sergeant grover

Wednesday, 21 September 1864

    First Sergeant William C. Grover is alone at the front of the first passenger car, sound asleep. His dark blue, high-collared frock is carefully folded on the seat next to him, his forage cap sits atop and centered on his coat. He made an arrangement with the conductor to awaken him five miles from the depot at Elmira, at the southernmost border of central New York.

    It's close to 6:00 a.m., and Grover stretches as he stands, then straightens and aligns the black seams on the sides of his light blue pants. He puts on his hat and takes more than a glimpse of his reflection in the passenger's window. He carefully dons his coat. The nine brass buttons are polished to a high gloss. Each sleeve is adorned with three pale blue stripes topped by a diamond, which signifies he holds a high enlisted rank in the army. He catches another glimpse of himself in the window, then sets off to awaken the other fifty-seven recruits on the train. At twenty-seven years old, First Sergeant Grover has been in the army for three days.

* * *

    Grover works his way through the two passenger cars, and unceremoniously kicks the facing bench seats where the recruits sleep in groups of four. "Get your gear together men, we're pulling into the station."

The morning sun has barely cleared the horizon.

"What time is it, Sergeant?" asks the youngest of the four between yawns.

"It's after 6:00 a.m., get to it, Private." The first sergeant moves along to the next set of seats in the car, and follows the same routine until the entire group is up. Robert's the oldest in his group, and still in his artillery uniform. They share a glance, Grover looks at him suspiciously, then moves on without a word spoken between them.

The youngest in Robert's foursome is seventeen year-old Edward Pruitt who signed on the same day as Robert, with the same recruiter in Medina. He says to no one in particular, "That took us over twelve hours to get here."

"First time on a train?" asks Robert.

"Yes, sir. I just thought the ride'd be faster."

Robert quickly pinches a fold of the young man's jacket, looks around the train car, then says in hushed tones, "Whatever you do, do not call me 'sir'. That's reserved for officers only. You'll get us both yelled at."

"Oh … okay. Thanks for the warning."

* * *

Three-stripe Sergeant John Henry McLaughlin awaits the arrival of the train. Grover reaches the train's rear platform first, and looks out over the waiting crowd before he steps off, quickly followed by the company of new recruits. Other than the soldiers, there are not a lot of passengers disembarking. One of the recruits starts to light up, but is quickly chastised by Sergeant McLaughlin. "No smoking without permission, recruit!" He then directs the entire group to the street, out of the way of the other people trying to board the train.

Grover eyes McLaughlin, and quietly asks, "Sergeant, can you give us directions to the camp?"

McLaughlin looks the nattily attired senior NCO up and down before he loudly answers, "I have orders to gather you men and march you to the camp *myself*." He drops off the depot platform and addresses the group. "Form up by height in one straight line facing me. The tallest man to my right on down to the shortest at my left." The men immediately start to see where they fit into the line. Robert finds his place. "Good. Now," pointing to John Blume, easily a head taller than the other recruits, "count off by twos, starting with you."

Once done, the sergeant continues, "Left face." The men turn. *Good to see they know their left from their right.* First Sergeant Grover defers to the junior NCO, and assumes a position in back of the sergeant. The company turns west on Water Street for the two mile march to to the front gate of the camp.

The scenic trek to the base follows the north shoreline of the Chemung river, lined with hemlock, ash, poplar, and pine trees. The deciduous trees have yet to turn. The men know that when the time comes, it will be a spectacle of colors, not that they'll get a chance to enjoy it from camp. The sergeant clears access from the sentry at the main gatehouse and continues a short distance to the administration building. He orders the men to stay in place while he enters to turn in their orders. First Sergeant Grover follows him into the office, uninvited.

The men are left to themselves for close to an hour. They drop their bags, and several use their luggage for seats. Some pull out tobacco pouches. Many of the recruits ask Robert what they can expect while they're in camp.

"I don't know what to tell you. I was in the artillery, and can only assume that training is different from the infantry's. We'll be learning together."

McLaughlin walks out the door alone. Robert stands as the sergeant faces off in front of him. "You must be the artillerist. I'll speak with you later. For now, get in line with the others."

"My name is Sergeant McLaughlin. I will be your best friend for the next several weeks. I hope that you experienced a nice comfortable trip." He walks back and forth along the line, sizes up the recruits. "I can assure you that will be the last bit of comfort that you can expect for the duration. Come to attention …"

* * *

The men are led to their quarters, a former barrel factory

repurposed as temporarily housing for new recruits. The accommodations are spacious but spartan. Robert takes the lower bunk by a window which overlooks Foster's Pond and forms the rear border of the compound. Three hundred feet beyond that runs the Chemung river.

The men are mustered in, fed, and given new uniforms. Whatever they brought with them needs to be shipped back, at their expense, or tossed out. Robert is extended the courtesy of keeping his artillery uniform. He procures an extra blanket, neatly folds his old uniform into it and stows it under his mattress. As he holds his replacement forage cap with the infantry insignia, it starts to sink in that he's no longer in the artillery.

He sits on the edge of his cot and stares out at the scenery. He closes off the clamor the recruits are creating, and lets his mind drift back to home and the bride he left behind. *Was this a big mistake, or fair to her? I couldn't even give her a honeymoon. Is the money worth what I left behind? I guess this isn't exactly the best time to be thinking about it.* He slides his legs up on the bed, lays back, and falls fast asleep.

* * *

At 6:00 a.m., Sergeant McLaughlin wakes the men by beating a large tin pot with a huge serving ladle. *CLANG ... CLANG ... CLANG*. It reverberates throughout the building. "Up and at 'em, boys." *CLANG ... CLANG ... CLANG*. "Outside in fifteen minutes, dressed and in formation. Move it." *CLANG ... CLANG ... CLANG*.

The next fifteen minutes are filled with panicked men scrambling to put on their new uniforms and boots, rinse their faces off, and drink anything to clear their throats of the night before. There's fretting, mass confusion, and loud complaints. Robert smiles, gets himself prepared, and is calmly the first one out the door. The sergeant looks at his pocket watch and waits for the the rest of the men to show. He lets Robert know that he wants to see him in his quarters after the day's drills are done.

the request

Robert knocks on the closed door of the sergeant's quarters. McLaughlin, cigar in hand, opens the door, and invites him in. The room's decor is bare-bones——a small cot, a smaller table, with a well-worn deck of cards, two stools, and a footlocker. The sergeant points to one of the stools. "Take a seat, Private. Try to make yourself comfortable."

He's solidly built, and stands eye-level with Robert. Before sitting he extends his hand. Robert skeptically shakes it with his left. The sergeant doesn't release the grip, but rather holds up his left hand. "What's with this? Your other one not work?" Robert holds up his folded right hand. "Where did you get hit?"

He points to the back of his forearm, and explains his experience during and after Chancellorsville.

"Will you be able to function in the infantry with that?"

"The doctors seem to think——"

"Hell, the doctors will take anyone warm and breathing right now. I've already gone through your records." The sergeant shifts a box of cigars from the windowsill to the table and opens it. "Can I interest you——"

Robert's caught by surprise, but the opportunity for a smoke, especially a cigar, is rare. "Sure. Thank you." He smells it, rolls it, bites off a nip from the cigar, and takes advantage of the light offered by the sergeant. He inhales a long first pull, coughs a little, looks at the cigar, then back to the sergeant. "This tastes good, but I don't imagine you asked me here to share a smoke."

The sergeant stands and starts to pace, trying to find the right approach. "Let me tell you a little bit about this place. Along with Albany and New York City, Elmira was originally designated as one of the three hubs to process and train new recruits from New York state. Two months ago, they reclassified and converted it to a Union prison for captured Rebels. Initially, our colonel, a good man by the way, figures we'd take in five- maybe six thousand men. By the end of August, the count swelled to ninety-three hundred prisoners! There are not enough quarters, mess facilities, or even a hospital to take care of them. The prisoners are undernourished, many of them are desperately ill. Close to eight hundred of them arrived with scurvy from the prison compound at Point Lookout, Maryland. Our medical facilities are stretched thin to begin with … more so now …" The sergeant beats his fist into his open palm. "I'll tell you the grave diggers will have their hands full this winter. It has all the makings of a disaster, and Washington turns a deaf ear to us." The sergeant continues to pace and tries to calm down.

Robert wonders where this is leading. McLaughlin stops and looks him in the eyes. "I'd like you to help with these recruits. I need someone with experience to give me a hand."

"I'm only a private, and there are several NCOs already in the company."

"They're all raw recruits, with no experience. I need a veteran."

"What are your expectations?"

"Get the men into formation in the morning. Take roll call. Help the NCOs march them to and from the various exercises they need to complete … the parade ground, rifle range, the chapel, etc." He finally sits back down. "If things work out, I can put in a good word with the colonel, maybe get you some stripes, and keep you here for the duration."

"Please don't take this wrong, Sergeant, but when it's time, I want to join my regular command. No offense, but a prison camp is not how I envisioned finishing out my tour."

"Disappointing, but understandable. Are you willing to help out *the request*

while you're here?" Robert nods. "I'll talk you up with the other NCOs and ensure they leave you be. Thank you, Robert. Do you mind if I call you that?"

He says, "I don't mind. What should I call you?"

"Sergeant," McLaughlin answers without hesitation.

* * *

The next several days are devoted to marching in formation, drills, and protocol. The recruits are issued Springfield rifles and trained in how to clean and care for them, and learn the "Manual of Arms" drills. The sergeant keeps his promise and places Robert into a position of influence. The men seem to accept him in his enhanced role, and Robert does his best to look out for their well-being. Those who recruited in as NCOs take to his instruction, eventually assuming the leadership rolls in the company.

sergeant kempf

Wednesday, 28 September 1864
Elmira, New York

Robert assists one of the recruit NCOs, with a squad of ten men, to march to the rifle range. The area's a wide-open grassy field with soil embankments built up in the distance for target placement. Beyond that is a vast, unused pasture land safe from any bullets that might stray from the confines of the range. A corporal awaits the newcomers at the east end of the firing stations. When the recruit sergeant brings the men to a halt, the corporal pulls open the flap of the tent to alert the range sergeant that the next squad has arrived. He walks over to the corporal with a profound limp he acquired on Grant's Overland Campaign. He hates his assignment as a training non-com, but understands there's no longer a place for him on the front lines.

He takes the rifle from the corporal, and holds it up for them to get a good view. In a clear and commanding voice, he says, "Good morning, men. I am Sergeant Kempf, responsible for the training and safety on this range. Today you will learn to use these implements you've shouldered for the last couple of weeks." He looks over to the recruit NCO, and asks, "Are your men's rifles fieldstripped and cleaned?"

"Yes, Sergeant."

"You personally inspect them?"

"I did."

Kempf checks out the rifle of the first man in line. He does an external inspection of the weapon wiped clean of oil from storage, then examines the inside of the barrel. He hands it back to the private, steps over to the next man in line, and repeats the process. Once he checks through the third gun, he's satisfied the recruit NCO is on the level.

"We're here to teach you how to learn the 'Load in Nine Times' technique. First a demonstration, then you will go through the drill step-by-step. Pay attention. Corporal, front and center." The guard walks over to the front of the squad, "Step number one ... withdraw the cartridge." The corporal reaches into his cartridge belt and draws out a .58 calibre Minié bullet with gunpowder held together in a thin white paper wrap. "Step number two ... place cartridge between teeth ..." At the command of the sergeant, the corporal follows the nine steps proficiently and ends with shoulder arms, his rifle is now ready to fire. The sergeant continues, "Thank you, Corporal. Please distribute the ammunition and percussion caps."

Each man assumes one of the stations. The sergeant stands by Robert who is at the station closest to the tent. "I'll walk you through the nine steps slowly. Please follow along as I give you the commands." At the first step the men retrieve their round of ammunition. Once everyone has loaded and shouldered their weapons, the sergeant points out the target for Robert, seventy-five yards downfield. At the command, he assumes a stance, feet spread apart far enough for stability, raises the rifle, takes a bead on the target, exhales, then squeezes the trigger. Some of the men flinch at the report.

The sergeant lifts his field glasses to see the results. He looks over at Robert. "Think you can do that again?" Robert follows the reload process, takes his stance, aims and fires. Kempf refocuses on the target with the same results. "Where'd you learn to shoot like that?"

"My older brother was in the Twenty-eighth New York Infantry. I had several opportunities to practice with his rifle."

"He *was* in the Twenty-eighth?"

"They mustered out in June of 'sixty-three after their two-year enlistment expired."

"Lucky him," mutters the sergeant. He turns back to the other men and says, "You've seen how it can be done. Take your time, and try your best. Once you've taken your shot, stand back and I'll evaluate your results." Most of the men fire high, a common problem with new men and often seasoned riflemen under fire. A couple of the recruits show early promise. The sergeant tells them to resume their stations and has them reload, slowly, in step with his commands. By their fifth round, the sergeant steps up the pace of their loading. Robert does his best to keep up, but struggles with the percussion caps in time with the drill.

Kempf has the men fire the remainder of their ammunition under the guidance of the corporal while he walks over and pulls Robert aside. He looks him straight in the eye and speaks with him confidentially. "I see you struggle to keep up with the pace."

He responds, "I have some issues with my right hand."

"If you don't mind——"

He interrupts, "Chancellorsville."

The sergeant hesitates. "I heard that you've faced battle." He holds up a finger to give Robert pause, bends over, and rolls up the cuff of his own left pant leg. It becomes clearly visible why the sergeant has a limp. "Spotsylvania Courthouse. They stuck me with new recruits after I got out of Carver Hospital."

"When were you there?"

"Close on to two months ago."

Robert asks about some of the people he knew and befriended, but none of the names are recognized by the sergeant.

"I got transferred here a month and a half ago."

"Do you want to get back to field duty?" asks Robert.

"No. I've given enough. Regardless, why are you here ... weren't you already out?"

"About eight months ago, but I wanted to see it through. Everyone along the way figures I can be of some use."

"Any chance you'll regain full use of it?"

"They weren't as positive about that. Been told I need to learn to work with it."

"Can I help before you receive orders to move out?"

"I'd appreciate some extra time on the range."

"I'll see what I can do."

"Thanks, Sergeant. What's your first name?"

"When we're anywhere on base, it's Sergeant Kempf. Off-base it's James. My friends call me Jim."

"Same as my father and oldest brother. Good to meet you." They shake hands, and he turns his attention back to the troops.

The sergeant can't help but chuckle. The men have tell-tale streaks of black gun-powder down the sides of their mouths from tearing open the cartridges. "Resume your practice, men. Make your shots count."

Elmira Prison, Elmira, New York

Moulton & Larkin photograph
Library of Congress
Prints and Photographs Division
LC-DIG-ppmsca-33993

sentry duty

Thursday, 29 September 1864

Robert uses whatever free time he has to familiarize himself with the layout of the base and the region. Built on part of the old State Fairgrounds west of the city, the thirty-two acre camp sits in a geographic basin surrounded by hills rising several hundred feet. The prison yard is encompassed by a twelve-foot tall fence. A narrow walkway runs the entire distance on the outside of the fence, four feet from its top. Ladders from the ground to the walkway are at varied intervals. There are forty sentry boxes with a hundred to a hundred and fifty feet of space between them. The guards command a clear field of view from the high vantage point, over a frightfully pitiful sight. The men, who aimlessly wanders around inside the pen, are shells of the once robust soldiers who faced-off against the Union blue.

Now that Robert and his squad have trained at the rifle range, they are scheduled to stand sentry duty along the elevated walkway that surrounds the prison compound. Forty men gather outside the Provost's office for muster and instructions. Their primary duty is to look for suspicious activity inside the compound. The enclosures are there to protect the sentries from inclement weather. They aren't allowed to congregate with adjacent guards, and are cautioned against interactions with the prisoners which may cause provocation. It's a caution only a few of the men take to heart.

The compound has three hundred and fifty-six buildings. Most of them are hundred foot-long, white-washed barracks running north to south and parallel to each other. Some of the buildings are not in the best of condition. Their main roof joists sag badly and threaten imminent collapse. Heavy snows that usually accompany the New York winters may be enough to finish the job. Nevertheless, the sheer volume of prisoners completely fills the buildings, each sixteen foot-wide with two rows of bunks. The unlucky late arrivals to the camp are relegated to the pup tents that fill in the balance of the grounds. Close to two thousand men are forced to stay in the flimsy shelters. The coming winter months promise harsh conditions for the prisoners, and life-threatening for those who are tent-bound.

With the exception of a lucky few, the prisoners are unoccupied. A few dabble in crafts with whatever material they can scavenge. The guards then try to sell the crafts to the townsfolk to procure extra rations for the prisoners. A few of them, talented with woodworking skills, are brought out of the compound to complete projects around the facility, and are given token pay and food as a reward.

Built in August and September, two observation stands are set up outside the compound for the locals to come gawk at the prisoners, which they deeply resent.

The gaunt prisoners are undernourished, ill-dressed, and disease-ridden. It's not uncommon in the evenings to see a small group of men leave a tent with a shroud-covered body on a stretcher. Their destination, the dead house where the bodies are prepared for burial. Ex-slave, John W. Jones is by trade a 'sexton'——a grave digger. He has made it his mission to serve the men by giving them a dignified burial at a designated ground about a mile and a half north of the camp. He keeps meticulous records of their placement for future markers. Despite his color, the men, Southerners included, gratefully give him free reign to carry out his duties. The bodies are placed in a pine coffin by assigned prisoners. A piece of paper with name, rank, company, regiment, grave number, and date is sealed in a bottle and deposited with the body. The same information appears on the lid of the coffin, which are loaded six at a time into the dead wagon, four inside and two on top for transport to the cemetery.

* * *

The morning after their first night on the wall, the men that come off duty confront Robert. "What's going on in there?" says one.

"This is unChristian-like," murmurs another.

"It's inhumane."

"That's not a prison camp. It's a death camp."

"Why do we let the townsfolk come and gawk? People pay to come get a look. What do they think this is? A circus?"

Robert tries to calm the men down, but their emotions build higher the more they complain. From his desk in the administration building, Sergeant McLaughlin hears the commotion, and confronts the group. "Get into ranks. Now! Stand at attention, and shut your faces." The men scramble to get into place, but the grumbling doesn't stop. The sergeant glares at Robert, then faces the men. "Let me say a few words about what you've witnessed. *None* of the men on this side of the fence approve of what goes on here. Not one of us ... and that includes the commanding officer."

"I'll bet," mutters one of the recruits. The sergeant breaks through the ranks, and pushes men aside to confront the malcontent face-to-face. The man looks back at the sergeant defiantly.

"You got anything else you wish to add? *Private.*"

"I do, *Sergeant.*" He starts to speak louder, "Do you know what the prisoners call this place? ... 'Hellmira', that's what." He looks around for support, but fear has shut the others up.

The sergeant says, "I'm aware! Everyone based here hates it. You wanna know why?" His voice softens, "Because it's true. It's true, and there isn't a damn thing we can do about it. We lack the proper facilities to support this. Prisoners are transferred here from other facilities in terrible condition, under-nourished, and disease-ridden. The most our men at the hospital can do is make them comfortable, and watch them die." The sergeant returns to his place in front of the formation. The chastised trooper refrains from any further carping.

"The commanding officer, lead surgeon, and several local politicians made their voices heard in the capital, but to no avail. The most important point that you need to take to heart is this, you are recruit privates. You've been in the army now, what? A month? You have no standing to tell anyone how to run this army." He points to the malcontent, and adds, "That can be interpreted as insurrection." The men are stone silent.

McLaughlin looks to the NCO who leads the group. "Now, get these *boys* out of here and run them through their drills, and don't return before noon rations."

As they march to the parade grounds, Robert says, "We got off lucky. For a minute there, I thought we'd be facing court-martial."

"Are you joking?" asks another.

Robert recounts the news from August of 'sixty-three about the five men from the 118th Pennsylvania executed by firing squad in front of their corps.

"For complaining?" asks one of the youths.

"No. For desertion. Understand that the army takes discipline seriously. We're in a state of war, and for the sergeant to speak the word 'insurrection', well, that should shake you to your core."

"Killing our own men?" the youth asks.

"That's right," speaks another. "I remember my dad read it to us when it happened."

"Our own men. Imagine that." The conversation dies out, and the men resume their drills with renewed vigor.

Monday, 10 October 1864

As the assigned guards gather for their postings, Sergeant McLaughlin conducts the brief. "I assume that you've heard by now some of our 'guests' took the opportunity to tunnel their way out."

"Where 'bouts, Sergeant?" asks the recruit NCO.

He points to a nearby area of the fence. "Looks like they started the dig in their tent the other side of the wall there."

"How many got away?"

"We initially thought seven, but once we compared the rolls, it's more like ten. The cavalry is sweeping the countryside. I expect they'll be rounded up soon enough. Just keep on your toes. Anyone else gets away from us, there'll be hell to pay."

The ten escapees are never recaptured.

mrs. kempf

Wednesday, 9 November 1864

Several of the men gather around a dispatch posted in front of the command headquarters. It reminds him of the crowds back home when they receive news from the battlefronts. His friend, John Blume, has a clear view of the posts. "Lincoln Re-elected." He turns to Robert and says, "Looks like Little Mac didn't fare as well."

"Surprised?" asks Robert.

"Not really. With the successes that Generals Grant and Sherman are having, I guess the country isn't ready for a 'Peace Democrat' in office."

"How badly was he beaten?"

"It looks like the general won three states," he chuckles. "His home state of New Jersey, Delaware, and Kentucky."

"Sounds like a landslide. I voted for Lincoln. Back in 'sixty as well."

"Seems like the whole army did. Everyone I spoke with who did vote seemed keen on keeping President Lincoln in office."

* * *

Sergeant Kempf approaches Robert, as he finishes his range work for the day. "Is it going any better for you?"

"I'm making progress with the reloads, but I need to keep at it."

"Can't hope for more than that I guess. By the way, I got you a pass.

My wife and I'd like to invite you over for dinner."

"Your wife's here?"

"I'm on permanent assignment, and we found board with a woman whose husband is fighting with General Sherman's forces. I got her approval, and my wife looks forward to meeting you."

"That'd be nice, Jim. Thank you."

"I'll be outside the main gate around 6:00 p.m. That work for you?"

"Whatever you say, Sergeant."

* * *

The sergeant waits at the agreed-upon time. Robert, dressed in his artillery uniform, climbs aboard. "I didn't expect this," says Kempf. "Your current uniform is——"

"In bad need of a wash. Thought I'd be a bit more tolerable in an enclosed space with cleaner clothes."

"That's thoughtful. Guess I didn't know you were in the artillery earlier."

"Battery F, Third U.S."

"Regular Army, huh? When did you originally enlist?"

"February of 'sixty-one."

"Even before Sumter?"

"Wanted to get a better choice of duty, rather than … well … this."

Kempf laughs. They spend the remainder of the ride in small talk. Once there, Robert hops down, takes the reins from Kempf, and ties off the wagon. He pats the horse's cheek before he catches up with him on the porch.

"You two seem comfortable together."

"I learned the hard way. Cost me close to a month in the hospital a few years back."

"That's a story I'd like to hear sometime," Jim smiles.

His wife opens the door. "Come in, come in, please." She addresses their guest warmly, "Hello, Robert. My name's Catherine."

He nods and says, "Pleased to meet you, Catherine." She appears to be close to the same age as her husband, with brown hair, and a welcoming smile that reminds him of Susan. "Thank you for the invitation." A waist-high dog runs over to greet the visitor.

Catherine grabs the nape of the dog's neck to keep him from jumping up. "Sorry, but he doesn't get to see many new faces. In fact, Jim never has anyone over from the camp. It's a pleasure to finally meet one of the men he works with." She reopens the front door and nudges the dog outside. " Jim tells me you've been in battle, too?"

Robert removes his forage cap and hands it to her.

"Yes, ma'am." He looks around. The rooms are bigger than his family's place upstate, and nicely decorated. "What a lovely home."

"It belongs to Mrs. Britton. Her husband's away on his duty, and she has opened her home to us."

"Will she be joining us?"

"Oh, no. When we asked you over, she excused herself to spend the night with her sister on the other side of the city."

Pointing to the dining table, Jim says, "Take a seat, Robert. Hope you enjoy home-cooked fare. My wife's an artist in the kitchen."

Catherine grabs his arm. "Come give me a hand ... an artist," she mutters.

"Can I help in any way?" asks Robert.

"Just stay put. That's what I'm here for," he responds, as she yanks him into the kitchen.

Within minutes he reappears with a platter of roast ham, gravy, and yams. His wife follows with a basket of rolls covered by a napkin.

"Where are you two from? I never asked Jim."

"Ohio. Not too far from General Grant's hometown of Galena," she responds. "Is there someone special in your life, Robert?"

"Yes, ma'am. We're newlyweds. Her name's Susan. Just got married the twentieth of September; the day I left for Elmira."

"Have you known each other very long?"

"Long as I can remember. Our families' ties go back to England."

Catherine looks over to her husband. "You didn't tell me Robert's from Great Britain."

With a sheepish expression, he shrugs his shoulders. "That's 'cause I didn't know."

She turns her attention back to Robert, and asks, "And where's she right now?"

"At home with her folks in Ridgeway, between Rochester and

Buffalo."

"I have family in Batavia, and I'm fairly familiar with the area." Then to her husband, she says, "Oh Jim, wouldn't it be wonderful if we could have her here for a visit?"

The sergeant's pained facial expression reflects his discomfort. "It would …" He stops and looks directly at their guest. "Catherine doesn't know, Robert … none of you know yet, but your movement orders came through and you are heading to Virginia in a couple of days."

"When did they arrive?"

"This morning. They'll announce it to the troops at roll-call tomorrow."

"Oh, Robert. I'm sorry. I didn't know," adds Catherine.

"That's okay. Bound to happen sooner or later. No offense, ma'am, and to you, Jim, but I won't be unhappy about leaving here."

"I completely understand," replies the sergeant. "I don't think any of us knew what we were in for."

"I thought we were exchanging prisoners?"

"Grant figures the South can't replace their losses. It's a matter of attrition. We can. Unfortunately, we aren't equipped to deal with this many prisoners."

"What's it like under his command?" Robert asks. Catherine leaves the table to clear the dishes and let the men talk.

Jim watches his wife leave the room before he leans over to talk to him in hushed tones. "There's no finer man or more capable commander than General Grant, and now that he's in charge, we'll win this. But the cost in lives … in Union blood, will be immeasurable. Mark my words. I'm just glad I was wounded before Cold Harbor, or I probably wouldn't be here right now."

Robert's lost in thought about what's to come, when Catherine re-enters the room. "Either of you care for some fresh-baked apple pie? The apples are in season and especially tasty."

Robert nods his head, as does her husband.

"Coffee, too?" Robert agrees and offers to help serve.

"Stay put, Private. I'll go."

While he enjoys a second cup, Robert forgets conversations past and asks James, "Any desire to see this through to——"

"No!" shouts his wife unexpectedly jumping up. She glares at Robert, and after a pause, sits back down and quietly adds, "Jim has done his time. Besides he *is* seeing it through to the end, right here is all."

Robert apologizes and looks over to Jim, who reassures both Catherine and their guest that his time on the line is through. She tries to change the tone of the evening and asks him if she can play some music for them.

"I'd love to hear you play." An upright piano sits in the front parlor, and the men take their coffee, and follow her in.

As she looks through the sheet music for an appropriate piece, Catherine says, "Mrs. Britton has been kind enough to give me lessons, and I never have an opportunity to play for others."

"Have you been at this long?" asks Robert.

"I took lessons as a young girl, but after we got married, and Jim left for the army, I stopped. Now that we're here, there's plenty of time."

James adds, "She's surprisingly good."

She blushes as her fingers start to caress the keys; the music lightly sets a more contemplative mood. She plays several selections, and Robert unconsciously hums along with the familiar tunes. "You are in fine voice, Robert," she says to him.

He hadn't been aware and self-consciously stops. Jim has started a fire in the parlor stove. The warmth, music, and camaraderie are a civilized respite from the austere life of the military.

At the end of a most enjoyable evening, Robert again extends his apologies and asks Catherine's forgiveness for his *faux pas*.

"It was our pleasure. It's been great to finally meet one of Jim's friends. I hope you stay safe, and our paths cross again."

"Thank you for your kindness, and the wonderful home-cooked meal. This has been a most pleasant evening."

As they open the door to leave, the dog runs in, takes a quick sniff of Robert, and curls up on the rug by the parlor stove.

On the ride back, Robert says, "Thank you, Jim. That was special. You are a lucky man."

"I'm glad you enjoyed yourself. I guess we need to do that more often. Catherine loves to have company."

"I'm sorry about——"

"Don't worry about it. It's not the first time it's come up in conversation. It's a touchy subject with her." He pulls the wagon to a halt and Robert climbs out.

"See you tomorrow, Sergeant."

"'Til then, Private." With a smile, he turns toward home.

* * *

Seventy-six men are mustered outside the headquarters. Sunrise isn't for another hour, but the company has a train to catch. They are on their way to Virginia to join their regular outfit.

Sergeants McLaughlin and Kempf attend muster.

McLaughlin takes out a cigar and bites off the tip. Then he draws another from his pocket, and hands it to Robert. "We're sorry to see you go. You've been a great help."

"Best of luck to you," adds Kempf. "Keep your head down."

Robert stows the gift, shakes the hands of the two NCOs, and falls into rank.

"You've got a long trek ahead of you to get to Virginia. Sure we can't change your mind about staying with us?" asks McLaughlin.

"No offense, but not on your life."

"You sure you won't miss this?" quips Kempf.

He looks back at them and smiles. "I just might regret leaving here before this war's over, but I doubt it. Thanks fellas, for everything." He waves as they walk away, then turns to catch the train.

infantry command

Monday, 28 November 1864

Robert steps off the train at Cedar Creek, Virginia. The trek from Elmira to Washington City takes close to three days, and sleep was a challenge. The seventy-five men who made the voyage, rendezvous just off the depot's platform. Lieutenant Geary has First Sergeant Grover gather the men into formation and take a roll call. It's a short march to the two forts that comprise the camp, and dark by the time they arrive.

The duty officer emerges from headquarters and addresses the men. "Welcome to the Ninetieth New York. The hour is late, so we only have time to get you into quarters. I'll personally show your officers to their billets. Corporal Gaylen will take the rest of you to your temporary quarters. Report back here first thing tomorrow."

Grover asks, "How far is this place, Corporal?"

Gaylen looks weary as he takes off his spectacles, spits on the lenses, and wipes them with a rag from his pocket. "Don't worry, Sergeant, they're close by."

As the men walk to the tents, Robert asks the corporal, "How long have you been with this outfit?"

"Since it was formed in New York back in November of 'sixty-one. We spent our first year in Key West, Florida."

"What was Florida like?" asks Robert.

The corporal doesn't break stride as he glances at him. "Hellish …

hot, muggy, and countless insects. Then the yellow fever hit ... that took a hard toll on our outfit."

"Seen much action with the Rebs?" asks Blume.

"We just fought in a helluva battle a few weeks back. Right here at Cedar Creek. Rebels put us on the run, but General Sheridan rallied the troops and we turned them Rebs back. Lost a lot of good men in that fight."

"What's the commanding officer like?" asks Sergeant Grover.

"Colonel Nelson Shaurman has been with us since we first formed. He mustered in as a captain. As his superiors resigned, one after the other, he worked his way up and assumed command of the regiment last May. He was wounded in battle a couple of weeks ago, but not too seriously. We've seen a lot of action and lost a number of good men, but there's a heap of pride in this unit. The men respect the leadership."

They arrive at the NCO transient tents. Corporal Gaylen looks at Sergeant Grover.

"You and your fellow NCOs can take shelter here until you're assigned more permanent quarters." He points to the group of Sibley tents immediately to the west and says, "The rest of your men will be quartered there." There are ten Sibleys set up in a straight line.

"Split yourselves into groups of eight and find a place to bed down. I'll be on duty at HQ in the morning and will take care of you then."

The men do their best to get comfortable for the night. Sleep comes easily after their exhausting journey.

Tuesday, 29 November 1864
Cedar Creek, Virginia

It's a cool morning as the men make their way to roll call. They are greeted outside headquarters by Corporal Gaylen, who directs them to their place near the rear of the formation. After muster, the Command Sergeant Major walks over to welcome the new arrivals.

"Mornin', men. I am Sergeant Major Lydstrom. Welcome to the Ninetieth New York. I understand from the corporal that he gave you somewhat of an introduction to the regiment last night. As you're new here, and from the same vicinity in New York, we'll try our best to keep

infantry command

you together. For now, you're assigned to Company I. It's a temporary holding company until we can find more permanent assignments for you. For now, you'll stay in the transit quarters. No need to move you around just yet. I want you to break for chow before it's gone. After breakfast, the commanding officer will meet with your NCOs. I'll contact the rest of you individually over the next couple of days." The two senior sergeants shake hands. Lydstrom gives them directions to Colonel Shaurman's quarters, then directs them to the mess.

it's not personal

～

The twelve men stand at attention as Colonel Shaurman enters the tent. "At ease, men. Please take your seats." The recruit NCOs comply as the colonel walks over by his desk. The men's service records are stacked on his small table. "I'd like to personally welcome you to the Ninetieth New York. We've been together since the start of the war in a variety of engagements from Florida to Louisiana, up to our last battle right here little over a month ago. We've said good-bye to many fine men from disease, debilitating wounds, capture, to death in combat." His voice drops off for a second.

He looks down at the pile of paperwork, and drums the records with his fingertips. "The men in this command have proven themselves in battle. We are close, and rely upon one another, and they depend upon me to be open and honest with them." He hesitates for a long time before he continues. "Therefore, I do not believe that it's fair to them to be subordinate to new recruits."

The men collectively hold their breath, then look to each other with the realization the hammer's about to come down.

"As such, you will be returned to the ranks and no longer hold the titles, pay, or privileges promised you by your recruiters." He anticipates the inevitable pushback, and quickly continues. "This is in no way reflective of you. It's standard policy at this command that the men earn their stripes here. You do a good job, and you will be reconsidered for promotion in the future."

Sergeant Lydstrom stands, and calls the men to attention. As he holds open the flap to the tent, he says, "This way, men." Except for Grover, the group files out. They are angry, and carp to each other the entire way back to their tents.

Grover stands and faces the colonel. "That's tough on the men, Colonel. I'll do what I can to calm them down."

Sharman looks directly at Grover. "You *do* understand that this includes *you*, too."

Grover's eyes widen in disbelief. "Is this some kind of a joke? From first sergeant back to *private!*" His eyes start to well up with emotion. "That's half my salary. What's my wife supposed to think?" He drops his head and looks around to collect his thoughts before he starts to yell at the colonel. "How do you expect me to go out there, and face those men?"

The colonel has experienced similar responses from other new arrivals. "How do *you* think the men would take to receiving orders from someone who wears the stripes of a first sergeant earned by signing a piece of paper. A man who hasn't heard a shot under duress, who hasn't faced the enemy, who hasn't been in the army three months yet."

Grover fumbles for words. "You ... you treat the new officers this way?" No response from the colonel. "I didn't think so, this just isn't right."

Sergeant Lydstrom slips his hand under Grover's arm. "I believe the colonel has other things to attend to. Let me walk you back to your quarters."

"Get your hands off me!" Grover yanks his arm away from Lydstrom's grip. He faces the colonel and salutes, "Requesting permission to leave, *sir*."

"Permission granted," says Shaurman. As soon as Lydstrom escorts Grover out of the tent, the colonel lets out a big sigh. Looking down at the stack of files he says to himself, "That went about as good as I expected."

* * *

Corporal Gaylen intercepts Robert on his way to headquarters.

"Good morning, Robert."

He turns, "Good morning, Corporal."

Gaylen addresses the duty officer, a young second lieutenant, and says, "Sir, I'll take the new man here for an indoctrination. That way we won't disturb you."

The officer answers him without looking up. "Carry on, Corporal."

The two walk out of earshot of the tent.

"Carry on," the corporal mutters. "Got here shortly before you did and already thinks he's king of the roost."

"I don't know about him, but the lieutenant in my last outfit checked-in when he was seventeen. Turned out to be the best officer I served under. He's been breveted a number of times for his conduct in battle, and is now a major. The men love him."

"Yeah, I need to give this kid a chance. At least you'd think he'd have peach fuzz or something."

They hear two men yell as they walk past the colonel's tent.

"What's that all about?" asks Robert.

"Sounds like the 'indoctrination' of our new NCOs."

"What do you mean?"

"Every recruit NCO get reduced in grade back to private."

"Why?"

"The colonel feels it isn't fair to the rest of the command for brand new men to order veterans around. It isn't deferential. Unless an enlisted man makes rank with a line command, everyone starts out here as a private."

"And the noise?"

"Usually from the ranking recruit."

Within a minute Gaylen's prediction comes true as Grover storms out of the colonel's tent. He kicks hard at a rock on the ground, misses, spins, and nearly loses his balance. Sergeant Lydstrom grabs his arm to break his fall. "Here ya' go. How 'bout I walk you back to your quarters now."

Yanking his arm away, Grover glares at him for several seconds, then says, "I told you to keep your hands off me. I can find my own way back. I'm not stupid … a helluva lot smarter than you." He pushes aside men who have gathered to view the spectacle, and clears a path directly back to the transient tents.

Gaylen smiles at the scene then sets out to walk around the inside perimeter with Robert. It's a two-mile long encampment of earthworks and trenches that run along the east side of Valley Pike, south of Winchester.

"How do things work around here? I mean in an infantry unit, as opposed to what I came from," asks Robert.

"Our daily routine, I imagine is much like any other camp: breakfast is immediately followed by Police call at 6:45, Surgeon's call at 7:00, then we drill around 7:45 or 8:00 until 9:30. After that it's Guard Mounting at 10:00, then First Sergeant's call at 12:00. Dinner at 12:30, then we get to take a break. Drills resume at 3:30. Finally, dress parade half an hour before sundown, tattoo at 9:00, and Taps sounds at 9:30. I thought you'd been indoctrinated on all of this at boot camp."

"Things are a bit different at Elmira," he answers. "Barracks Number Three has been converted to a prison camp, responsible for around ten thousand detainees and climbing. Besides the drills, we were tasked with guard duty once we qualified on the range."

"We've heard rumors, but ten thousand! That's staggering to think about. How do they handle that?"

"They have a good commanding officer who's does his best, but is sadly under-resourced when it comes to housing, food, and medical support."

As they approach the battery emplacement, Gaylen says, "I have a question for you. Any interest in rejoining an artillery unit?"

"You can make happen?"

"Not me, no, but I did notice a request that came in yesterday ... Company C mans the Carysbrooke Redoubt right up ahead here. They have Napoleon cannon and the powers that be thought you might be of better service with the heavier guns."

"I didn't expect this. When?"

"Right after muster tomorrow."

* * *

The men quartered in the NCO tents have a fire going, and share their coffee, smokes, and discontent. A few of the older men who recruited with them ask permission to join their get together.

"Where's Grover?" asks Blume. "I understand he took this pretty hard."

Wilkinson points over to the tent. "He wants to be left alone. I think he's too embarrassed to be seen right now."

"He'll get over it." says Blume.

"I don't know. He took a lot of pride as a 'First Sergeant'. His entire world has been turned upside down. This isn't the army life that he signed up for," says Snyder.

"How do you guys handle it?" asks Blume.

Wilkinson shakes his head slightly. "Sergeant, private, doesn't matter that much. I wonder if we can we be sure of anything the army says?"

Robert walks past the group on his way to his tent.

"Robert," yells Blume. "Come on over and join us."

Snyder points to him and says, "Yeah, you talked with the corporal. What'd you hear?"

"About what?"

"About us getting busted back down to private," says Wilkinson.

"Not much, Gaylen says you weren't busted. You were 'returned to ranks'."

"What the hell's the difference?" asks Snyder.

"One's disciplinary, the other's administrative."

"Po-tay-to, po-tah-to."

Robert does a double-take and smiles. "Not necessarily. The way he explained it, if you got busted, you probably wouldn't be reconsidered for promotion. This way, you will."

"I wonder how the officers took the news."

"That won't happen to the officers. You can't demote them. They screw up, they're cashiered ... returned to civilian life."

"Yeah, well, who needs it? Think I'll just stay a private," proclaims Wilkinson with false bravado.

"You show 'em, George," says Blume with a chuckle.

Everyone starts to laugh, then grows suddenly silent as Grover makes an appearance. He looks completely disheveled. Impatience, frustration, and his foul temper led to tearing the right sleeve of the jacket when he ripped off his old rank. The left shows the outlined reminder of his other set. He holds up his chevrons, and says, "This, gentlemen, is what I think the colonel can do with this outfit." He casts the stripes into the fire then spits on them as they quickly catch fire and disintegrate.

"That a boy," says Blume.

"What did you say? Speak up!" Grover rages. As he clenches his fists, Wilkinson and two others jump up and escort Grover away from the fire. They understand his anger, but know he'd be seriously mismatched in a fight with Blume, who stands six foot four and can handle himself. Rumors followed him from basic that he made short work of a couple of roughs who tried to scam him in Rochester.

Robert walks over to Blume, who's facing the men as they escort Grover to the safety of his tent. "Come on, John. Let's head back." Despite their age difference, the two are close. A native of Ridgeway, Blume has known his family for years.

"Lead the way."

Wednesday, 30 November 1864

Grover receives his allotment of breakfast and finds a place by himself to eat. His field jacket shows the scars of his demotion. His plate of food is untouched, and he nurses his mug.

"May we join you, William?" It's Blume and Robert balancing their rations with their coffee.

Grover doesn't look up before he says, "My proper address ..." then stops himself short, and sighs. "Sure. Take a seat." Then he realizes who's joined him. He addresses Blume, "Here to have your fun with me again?"

"I've got no issues with you."

Grover has no appetite and lets his plate drop to the ground. He takes a draw from his mug. It holds a bit more than coffee. He offers it to Blume. "Here ... take a nip ... consider it a peace offering."

Blume takes his mug and says, "Sure. Thanks, William." He grimaces after he samples it, and hands it back. "You aren't planning to make a steady diet of this are you? That'd be a fast track to the guard house."

"I just need some help to face the day today."

"I understand," says Blume. They remain silent while they finish their meal.

"I don't know how I'll handle this," says Grover.

Robert says, "Gaylen tells me they've done that with each recruit NCO that's reported for duty. It isn't personal."

"I made it personal. I got into it with the colonel. Said some things I shouldn't. Said them louder than I should."

"Will you apologize to him?" asks Blume.

"Thought about it."

Robert adds, "It's none of my business, but from the tone of your conversation with the master sergeant, you may think about apologizing to him too."

Grover looks at the two of them. "As much as I hate to admit it, you're right. Guess I best be getting to it." He picks up his belongings and heads to the command post.

Blume looks at Robert, "Glad I'm not in his shoes." Robert nods.

acceptance

Friday, 2 December 1864

Most of the Elmira recruits, who mustered in with Robert, are directed outside the command sergeant's tent.

Sergeant Lydstrom addresses the gathering. "Men, you've been reassigned to Company C. Sergeant Butram here is one of their NCOs, and will march you over to the company's redoubt."

Located at the eastern end of the camp, the main body of the redoubt is on high ground, in position to protect any threats from the south. Robert noticed the cannon in the embrasures earlier. He tried to speak to some of their men, but was treated dismissively.

The men are led to the front of the sergeant's cabin where two corporals stand to greet the new arrivals. Sergeant Butram looks over the group and says, "Corporals Easton and Pegg will divide you into two squads and show you to your quarters. You will be briefed on your duties and given time to settle in. Our company cook is ole Charley. You'll usually find him by the mess tent. He's a contraband, but don't you let that bother you." He pats his own stomach and says, "He's a fine cook, and you are to treat him proper. You're dismissed." The sergeant disappears into his cabin.

The two corporals read off a list of squad assignments. Once Corporal Pegg identifies Robert he says, "Give me your pack. I'll drop it off in your cabin. The sergeant wishes to meet with you now."

Robert slips the shoulder strap off his arm, hands the pack to the corporal, and raps on the sergeant's door casing. "Enter." The space is minimal and efficient. A central stove has the place warmed up nicely. "I understand you come to us from the artillery."

"Third U.S.," he answers.

"There are six twelve-pounder Napoleons allocated to this redoubt. The battery has need for a replacement, and you're slated to fill the billet." When Robert doesn't respond, he looks up from his paperwork, and raises his eyebrows. "You're dismissed."

Outside the cabin, Robert waits for Corporal Pegg to show him the grounds. "I'd like to get to know the layout. Can we talk as we walk?" Robert questions the corporal about the redoubt and the company, until their conversation eventually drifts to the sergeant. "Is he always so warm and sociable?"

"He's okay. He's been here since we formed, and it's no secret that he wants more than a squad. He applied for a commission, and since that fell through, he's tried to get more stripes. He lost a close friend in the last battle and was slightly wounded. He's a tough bird, though. Reported back for duty the next day."

* * *

At first, the gun crew is stand-offish to Robert. They do not acknowledge his arrival, and when they start their drills, Robert's assigned the number three position. He handles whatever they challenge him with without missing a beat. When the men take their mid-day break from drilling, they invite him to sit with them. He does not offer up any conversation until the ammunition runner asks, "Where did you learn the drills? We thought we would have to start from scratch with you."

The Gunner speaks up before Robert can. "I knew. I just wanted to see for myself, and how you'd receive him. Word around camp is you're not the most welcoming bunch in the army." The entire crew looks to their sergeant. "Our private here's a veteran of the Third U.S. Artillery for three years and fought at Malvern Hill, Fredericksburg, and Chancellorsville."

The number one man looks at Robert and asks, "Why didn't you

acceptance

say anything?"

Robert, who looked away the whole time the sergeant spoke, looks back and says, "I figured it wasn't my place."

"You'll do well here, Private," says the Gunner.

chevrons

Friday, 10 February 1865

Colonel Shaurman is present for muster, flanked by Sergeant Major Lydstrom, who hands the colonel a small piece of paper with a list of seven names. "Corporals Peat and Pine, and Privates Gillett, Blume, Kearney, Pilchard, and Canham, front and center." The seven men step out from the ranks, and make their way to the front of the assembly.

The colonel addresses them as a whole. "It's my privilege today to promote the men who stand before you. They've proven themselves to be leaders and earned the new stripes they will be wearing." Lydstrom accompanies Colonel Shaurman down the line as he congratulates the men individually, hands them their chevrons of rank and certificates of promotion, then shakes their hand.

After they are dismissed, several gather around the new appointees, congratulate them with handshakes, pats on the shoulders, and plenty of ribbing. Lydstrom stands back, then greets them collectively once the others leave.

"Congratulations, men. Your promotions are well deserved. I'd like to meet with you in my quarters in two hours." With a smile he adds, "That'll give you enough time to get into your *proper* uniforms. Oh, and make sure you have a mug for coffee while we talk."

Snows from last Tuesday's storm still blanket the ground, and left the well-worn footpaths a slick, muddy mess. Robert and Blume have a lengthy, slippery trek back to the redoubt. Once inside, they peel off their jackets and each break out their sewing kit, known as a "housewife".

"You've worked around headquarters. Did you know about this?" asks John.

"Nope. Don't necessarily know if I want this either," replies Robert.

"I don't think we have a choice. And if it doesn't work out ... well, they can always return you to the ranks. We've seen that's not uncommon around here."

After a bit of fumbling the implements, Robert holds up the needle and thread to John. "I never was much good threading these things, even with two good hands."

"You want me to sew it for you, too? We're *both* corporals now. Don't try to pull rank on me."

"*Please* just thread it for me," he laughs. "I wonder what our new duties will be."

"I think we've been doing them right along, now with a bit more authority and pay," answers Blume.

"I hadn't thought about the money. My wife will like that. How much of a raise do we get?"

"I don't know. Guess that's a good question for Sergeant Lydstrom."

"We've got about thirty minutes and a long walk ahead of us. You ready?" asks Robert.

* * *

The seven new NCOs are warmly greeted by the Sergeant Major as they enter his quarters. They are given the choice of where to sit from a hodgepodge of small chairs, stools, and wooden crates.

"Make yourselves as comfortable as possible; we're informal here." The men do the best they can, given the diversity of choices. Robert takes a place atop a cut log that has been flipped on its end.

Corporal Sheppard, comes in with a big pot of coffee. He makes his way around the group, fills the mugs that are held out to him. Then he pours one for himself and leaves with the promise of brewing a new batch.

Smiles appear on the men's faces as Lydstrom breaks out a bottle of Kentucky bourbon from his foot locker. "Can I interest any of you in a nip to warm you up?"

Everyone enthusiastically takes him up on the rare offer. Lydstrom works his way around the room, and tops off everyone's mug. Some who anticipate his offer, drink as much of the hot coffee they can tolerate before he tops them off.

Once the sergeant takes his seat, he takes a long drink from his cup. "Okay, let's get started. Again, congratulations. Your promotions are well-deserved. This is the time to answer your questions."

Blume speaks up first. "What will our duties be?"

"You've been at them for some time already. When you were asked to take on a new responsibility, we evaluated how well you handled it and how well the men respond to you in the process."

"Will there be any changes in the future?" asks Pine.

"For you two sergeants there will be. You will oversee more men and be held responsible for assigned tasks … same as you have been as corporals, just on a broader scale. For you new corporals, you can expect to add some clerical functions to your duties, and you will direct more drills with your squads. Otherwise, you won't see a radical change unless other opportunities or openings present themselves."

"How do we know the men will take to our promotions?" asks Robert.

"That's a good question without a pat answer. There's one thing that has worked for me, and I wanted to give you an illustration of that when you got here. The corporal served you coffee. In turn, I served you the bourbon. Get the picture?"

"You want us to serve the men coffee and bourbon then?" Pilchard jokes. Everyone laughs heartily.

"That's close, but not exactly what I was going for," he chuckles. "The men want to know you care for them and are available to help them. That means you listen to and support them. I'll caution you that you will meet resistance from a few, but be fair, open, and honest with the men and they'll come around. If you do run into issues, the stripes give you the authority to do something about it."

"What about the pay, Sergeant? What kind of raise comes with this?" asks Blume.

Lydstrom looks over at the new sergeants, Peat and Pine. "How 'bout one of you enlighten these gentlemen?"

Pine speaks up. "There's no pay difference between a private and a corporal. You still make thirteen dollars a month."

That generates a few murmurs among those who did not know, and it's immediately addressed by Lydstrom.

"Listen up. None of us, and I mean none of us, are here for the money. There's a slight bump when you get your third stripe, but for enlisted men, well ... we're here to serve, myself included. Along that line, when my aide returns with a fresh pot, can I top anyone else off?" The men spend the better part of another hour hearing of the regiment's experiences. In turn, he asks Robert to tell the others what it's like to serve in the artillery. By the time they break up the gathering, the participants know each other a little better.

Both Blume and Robert are a bit light-headed as they make their way back to the redoubt. Blume returns to the cabin and Robert searches out the gun crew. When he makes his appearance, the crew enthusiastically greets their new NCO with handshakes and pats on the back. The Gunner gets a whiff of his breath and says, "I guess the Sergeant Major broke out his special brew of coffee. Can you handle your duties today?"

"Yes, Sergeant," replies the embarrassed corporal.

"Good, then let's begin. Ready. Load."

the best news

Monday, 3 April 1865

The weather gets appreciably warmer as the weeks pass, and the men wonder if this is the last spring they will be away from home. They are called to assembly at the main parade grounds. The colonel addresses the men. "I want to share two pieces of news with you from this morning's dispatches." He pauses, then produces a broad smile. "Richmond has been evacuated."

The men respond with unbridled joy. Hats are thrown into the air, the men cheer loudly, and more than a few shed tears of joy and anticipation—home. Shaurman holds up his arms, and waits a moment for order to be restored. "The second ... the lines around Petersburg have finally collapsed."

Lieutenant Wollpert attempts to restore order, but the colonel holds him back. "Let the men have this, Lieutenant."

With the successes of Generals Sherman, Sheridan, and Grant, it's apparent the days of the Confederacy are drawing to a close.

They are dismissed with the warning to stay alert; they are still at war. Talks around the campfires are filled with anticipation, speculation, and rumor.

Robert's gun crew calls off drills for the day. The Gunner believes they'd be too distracted.

Monday, 10 April 1865

The colonel is in his full regalia; it fuels the anticipation for this morning's announcement. "Yesterday afternoon, at Appomattox Court House, Confederate General Robert E. Lee surrendered his Army of Northern Virginia to General Grant. We will pass along more news when we receive it."

Men return to their quarters, break out their hidden stores, and start the celebration with gusto. The Gunner from Robert's crew gathers his team around the nearby campfire.

"Well, Sergeant, time to break into the good stuff?" asks Alexander.

"We've been given permission to. I just don't know if it's the wisest thing to do right now. Johnston hasn't surrendered to Sherman, and there is always that possibility ..." He looks over at Robert. "What do you think, Corporal? Time to give the sutler some business?"

"Last time I gave one of those purveyors my business, it didn't end well. I'll take a pass on this one." The men laugh as they break up and head to where the sutlers normally park their wagons. It's a boisterous, jubilant evening, and the men celebrate late into the night.

Thursday, 13 April 1865

Lieutenant Wollpert reads this morning's dispatch. *"Yesterday, the formal rite of surrender took place. The Army of Northern Virginia was required to stack their arms. Their men are allowed to keep their horses, and the officers their sidearms.* The colonel wants you to keep in mind that these people are, once again, our countrymen. You may run into some of them, as they make their way back to their homes. There are to be *no* reprisals." There's no reaction from any of the men. They are weary of war, and just want to go home. "A word of caution, General Sherman's forces are still in conflict with Confederate General Johnston's. Don't be surprised if we are ordered to head south to support his army."

The men *do* react to that with groans of disbelief. Wollpert realizes he has said enough, maybe too much.

the worst news

Saturday, 15 April 1865

The special assembly gathers with dreaded anticipation of orders to make preparations to join Sherman's forces. Colonel Shaurman's eyes are red and his demeanor troubled. The usually gregarious commander is silent, preoccupied with the dispatch that shakes in his hand as he starts to speak. His voice cracks when he says the words, "Our President is dead." He pauses for a long time to collect himself. "He was shot at Ford's Theater in Washington City last night by a Southern sympathizer, and passed at 7:22 this morning." Tears unabashedly stream down his face. The regiment is in shock. The colonel steps down from the dais, neither speaks to nor salutes anyone, but returns to headquarters.

Within the ranks, the gamut of emotions range from utter shock, profound sadness, to rage. Sergeant Major Lydstrom assumes the colonel's station in front of the men and raises his arms. "Quiet down, please. This most horrible of news is a terrible shock for all of us. I suggest you return to your quarters. We'll keep you apprised of any further developments."

Robert makes his way to his tent followed by his mates. He sits on his bedding quietly weeping. The others are in shock and disbelief.

"Do you think there's any chance that the reports are false?" says Parrish.

"I doubt it," responds Blume. "That doesn't make any sense."

Robert looks up with tear-stained cheeks. "I met him."

"What, at the review at Falmouth? You saw him as you paraded by?" says Parrish.

He shakes his head and answers him in a soft voice.

"No, I met him in person, when he visited Carver hospital in Washington City. He greeted each man in our ward, one-to-one, including me for a couple of minutes."

"What could the two of *you* possibly discuss?" asks Parrish.

"My injury." Then he smiles. "About how upstaters from New York like to differentiate themselves from the New York City folk ... about unmet expectations when people actually get to meet Lincoln." With the mention of home, the skepticism evaporates.

"What was he like?" asks Blume.

Robert looks at his friend, then directly at Parrish. "Kind. Soft-spoken. Humble. He appreciated what we soldiers sacrificed for the country. I ... I just can't believe he's gone." He quickly grabs his jacket and forage cap, and says to no one, "He didn't deserve this." He leaves the cabin, and sets off on a fast, hard walk, to nowhere in particular, just needing to find some solitude, a place to pray. Blume tries to follow him and yells ahead to ask if he wants company. Robert waves him off, puts his hands in his pockets, and continues on at a rapid pace. He doesn't return until nightfall.

* * *

Easter Sunday. The grounds for chapel service overflow this week, in part to celebrate the resurrection of the Savior, but mostly to mourn, in communion with others, the loss of their President. The men are quiet and subdued throughout the entire service. Not many participate in the hymns. The chaplain's prayers reflect the burden he shoulders—the collective sadness of the regiment. He keeps his message short.

"Today's passage is taken, in part, from the book of Isaiah, chapter fifty-five:

> *Seek ye the Lord while he may be found, call ye upon him while he is near:*

Let the wicked forsake his way, and the unrighteous man his thoughts:
and let him return unto the Lord, and he will have mercy upon him;
and to our God, for he will abundantly pardon.
For my thoughts are not your thoughts,
neither are your ways my ways, saith the Lord.
For as the heavens are higher than the earth,
so are my ways higher than your ways, and my thoughts than your thoughts …"

Chaplain Thurmond closes the service with a prayer for forgiveness and healing for our country, then gives the benediction. At the conclusion, the colonel stands and the men stand with him. He turns to look at them, nods, and leaves, still visibly shaken. He's closely followed by Lieutenant Wollpert and the chaplain.

Lydstrom stands to address the men. "I know that many of you have questions, and news comes across the wires sparingly. Let me tell you what we've heard thus far. The situation in Washington City is unsettled, to say the least. The known access points in and out are now sealed and Secretary of War Stanton has placed the city under martial law. Apparently, it was part of a conspiracy that also resulted in the serious wounding of Secretary of State Seward in his bed. A couple of the conspirators have been apprehended already. The President's assassin is believed to be John Wilkes Boothe, a well-known actor, who is still at large."

"What does this mean for us, Sergeant?" an anonymous voice shouts out from the gathering.

"Every unit, including ours, has been placed on alert. At present we are restricted to camp."

"Anything we can do to help?" shouts another.

"As far as I know, the Provost has not called for any assistance, at least not yet."

"Are we back at war with the South again?"

"War was never officially brought to a close."

"Will we be called to Washington?"

"Good question, but your guess is as good as mine."

"What's going to happen to the government? Who's in charge?"

"According to the Constitution, Vice-President Johnson took the oath yesterday as our seventeenth President." The sergeant pauses for a few minutes to collect his thoughts and composure. "Look men, this isn't the first time a President has died in office. As difficult as this may be, take solace in the knowledge that we will get through it."

Friday, 12 May 1865

It's been three weeks since their outfit was ordered to break camp for Washington City.

In a much brighter mood since the last time he stood before the troops, the colonel still wears his black mourning band, but shares some laughter with his adjutant and the Sergeant Major. The colonel invites Lydstrom to pass along the report to the men.

"This Tuesday past, in Irwinville, Georgia, men of the First Wisconsin and Fourth Michigan, captured Confederate President Jefferson Davis. He was covered in his wife's overcoat." Guffaws and derisive catcalls join the laughter that fills the ranks of the men. The leaders do their best to maintain their composure, and fail miserably. It's a long-overdue release from the previous month of mourning.

The colonel raises his arms to calm the men down, the ranks settle in short order. Lydstrom continues. "On Wednesday, the tenth, President Andrew Johnson declared a cessation of *all* hostilities. Men, the war is over!"

They hoot, holler, and hug each other as they jump up and down, throw their hats skyward, and abandon any sense of military decorum.

the package

Monday, 22 May 1865

Robert hopes to catch up with his old artillery unit, and sets out to locate them.

"Well, look at you, an *infantry corporal?*"

"Good to see you, too, Thomas. I've often wondered how you weathered the war since I left."

"Who are you with now?" asks Wingate.

"The Ninetieth New York. It's a volunteer infantry unit, recruited in part from my home town."

"Why infantry?"

"Honestly, Thomas, the bounty money to join up was too tempting. I stayed out for eight months, but when the opportunity arose to get back in, my wife——"

"Your wife!" Wingate interrupts. "I don't recall you were ever married."

"Last September. Signed up, got married, and left, after the ceremony."

"Great honeymoon, huh?"

"I figured that there'll be time once I get back."

"Tell me about her."

"She's from a family we've known since our childhood days in England. She suddenly grew up, came into her own, and showed an interest——"

"Well, congratulations," he interrupts again. "Better late than never."

"How's Lieut … I mean *Major* Turnbull and Lieutenant Barstow doing?"

"Yeah, them. Well, the officers are in town at Turnbull's place tonight. His folks are hosting a reception at their house for the officers in our unit. I'm sure they'll be sorry that they missed you."

"You sound disappointed that you weren't invited."

"I thought they'd at least include the NCOs. Hell, half of those guys wouldn't know where to find their bootstraps if it wasn't for us. You're a corporal. You know that."

"The way I look at it is they put their lives on the line just like us, and here we are, still alive, and soon to be going home, despite their supposed shortcomings. How are the rest of the men doing?"

"We've been ordered to stay in camp tonight to get ready for the big festivities tomorrow. They want us to look our best, but after the parade … hey, you feel like going around to see some of the guys?"

"That's why I'm here." The two of them make their way through the encampment until they reach a campfire surrounded by several men talking story. Robert's appearance, especially in an infantry uniform, surprises everyone. They share handshakes, hugs, laughter, and more than a few questions about his decision to get married and re-enlist. Conviviality sets the tone as the men renew acquaintances, and get caught up. He is as relaxed and open as if he'd never left. These are the men he has gone through the most upheaval and growth with, and who he feels the most comfortable around.

Tuesday, 23 May 1865

It's 5:00 a.m., and the encampment's already in full stir. Spread out along the banks of the Potomac, the Ninetieth New York makes preparations to march into the nation's capital.

They are part of the two hundred thousand soldiers bivouacked in and around the city to share in the celebration. People will turn out by the hundreds of thousands to pay homage to the soldiers who put down the rebellion and saved the Union.

Both the Army of the Potomac and the Armies under General Sherman are encamped in and around Washington City, but on opposite sides of the Potomac. Jealousy and fears of internecine rivalries have prompted the leaders to separate them accordingly.

Robert, still groggy from the activities of the previous evening, works to get ready. General Meade put out the edict for the day——spit and polish. The previous day they cleaned their uniforms, applied boot black to their leather, polished brass, disassembled and cleaned their rifles, and shined their bayonets. They've been issued fresh paper collars and new white gloves. The men are to look their best, act their best, and march better than ever.

"Corporal Canham." It's Sergeant Butram. "You're wanted back at command."

"Now? What's *this* about?"

"They didn't say. It sounded urgent, though."

Robert double-times it to Colonel Shaurman's tent.

Two officers are bent over the contents of a package, their backs turned to the tent flaps. Robert enters, comes to attention, and salutes the officers. When they turn around, he's shocked to see Major Turnbull with the colonel.

"Hello, Robert."

He can barely contain his surprise and delight.

"Major, I don't know what to say." He salutes then shakes Turnbull's hand.

The colonel tries to collect his thoughts, then clears his throat.

"The major here has made a most unusual request, and I've agreed to reassign you to the Regular Army for the next couple of days. Apparently there's a need for a qualified corporal and thought you may be able to fill the bill."

With a smile, Major Turnbull hands him the package and says, "You're out of uniform, Corporal. Get dressed and get back here double-time."

Robert looks at the contents of the package, then back to Turnbull——a new full-dress artillery uniform with the corporal stripes.

"Yes, sir, but my company?"

The colonel has a hard time suppressing his own smile and says, "Don't worry about your men. Sergeant Butram will look after them. You need to see to your other responsibilities now."

Try as he might, Robert can't hide his enthusiasm. He salutes the major, then the colonel, turns, and leaves. Within fifteen minutes he's back at command. Turnbull has a horse and mount ready for him, and they ride off together.

Major Turnbull speaks first. "It was Corporal Wingate's idea, and we ran it by the other men first. Lieutenant Barstow and I agree that it's appropriate you celebrate today with us. Everybody's happy with the gesture, and your colonel was gracious enough to grant the request."

"I don't know what to say," says Robert.

"You fought with us with honor for three years. You've earned a seat with us tomorrow."

"A seat?"

"You'll ride on one of the limbers and cannon along with Sergeant Ramsey."

"*Sergeant* Ramsey?"

"He's been promoted to Gunner, and I know he looks forward to seeing you."

They use the balance of the ride to share news of the last couple of years, especially Turnbull's account of Gettysburg. Before they realize it, they are in camp.

"You'll find Sergeant Ramsey waiting for you at the artillery park."

Within minutes Robert's ride pulls alongside. Ramsey's driving the wagon by himself. The bronze cannon has been cleaned and polished to the point it looks better than new.

"Hello, *Corporal*." His old friend smiles as he helps him aboard.

"Good Morning *Sergeant*, and congratulations."

The two quickly hug then Jim reaches down for his haversack. He pulls out an old, stained forage cap.

"I wanted a bit of Will with us today." He sets Hickman's cap between them.

Robert looks at the cap and nods.

"He'd have liked that."

"Better hold on." Jim flicks the reins.

* * *

The procession from the encampment ends at the staging area around the Capitol building. Even though it's been over a month since Lincoln's funeral on April nineteenth, the flag atop the building remains at half-mast; there are still vestiges of black bunting draped between the windows.

To mark today's occasion, a large banner hangs from one of them:

> "The PUBLIC SCHOOLS
> of Washington
> WELCOME
> The HEROES of the REPUBLIC
> HONOR to the BRAVE"

Another from the Treasury building reads:

> "The Only National Debt We Can Never Pay,
> Is The Debt We Owe To Our Victorious Soldiers"

The nation needs this tribute, not only to these men, but to the ones who are not marching——those left in the fields——a burden forever carried by the men in formation.

Tree-lined, cobblestoned Pennsylvania Avenue, the city's main thoroughfare, serves as the route for today's festivities. To keep the dust to a minimum, the four mile-long parade route has been swept and watered by the Washington City Fire Department. The double set of trolley tracks that run its length will be unused today. Arches of flowers and evergreen boughs span Pennsylvania Avenue, as does the banner:

> "All Hail Our Western Heroes"

Most flags no longer fly at half-mast. The black bunting on display earlier throughout the city, has been replaced with patriotic red, white, and blue.

Bars are closed to minimize the incidents of drunken mischief.

Prostitutes, pickpockets, and thieves are detained by the city's police. Cavalry patrols are posted along the intersections to prevent vehicles and spectators from blocking the marchers.

The parade will start at the Capitol building and proceed past the War department, the Treasury building, and by the large reviewing stands on the grounds of the Executive Mansion.

People from the surrounding regions join Washington's residents to jam the four mile-long parade route. Schools are closed and government offices are emptied of their employees to share the celebration.

Homes are festooned with the national flag and banners. Boarding houses, hotels, private homes, and any other available spaces are rented out at premium prices.

Several layers of spectators line the avenue, and compete for the best viewpoints to see the spectacle that will pass before them. Men in hats, some in long coats, women with parasols, and children are dressed in their Sunday best. Boys are perched in trees and on lampposts to see over the street-level crowds. Windows, balconies, rooftops and porches are filled with onlookers.

Grand Review of the Army. Artillery unit passing on Pennsylvania Avenue near the Treasury, Washington City

Matthew B. Brady photograph
Library of Congress
Prints and Photographs Division
LC-DIG-cwpb-02800

celebration

At 9:00 a.m., the *BAH-ROOM!* of a single cannon, firing a blank charge of gunpowder, signals the start of the parade. Commander of the Army of the Potomac, Major General George Meade, wearing his spectacles and astride his horse named Blackie, leads the procession with his saber out and held aloft. The crowds break out in spontaneous cheers, "Gettysburg, Gettysburg." His staff, followed by his infantry, march twelve to twenty abreast and span the avenue curb-to-curb. The division colors, tattered from their experiences in battle, are held proudly at the head of each unit they represent.

When General Meade's entourage reaches the reviewing stand, he dismounts and joins the other dignitaries. Those in the stands congratulate him for his part in the show. His edict of spit and polish has been taken to heart. His army looks spectacular—clean new uniforms, shined shoes, and white gloves holding rifles that are topped with gleaming bayonets. They march to the cadence of their drummers and the bands, their feet hit the pavement in unison. The crowds are stirred with pride and joy, unbridled in their enthusiasm—laugh, sing, shout, and cheer as they wave flags and their white handkerchiefs, and throw bouquets of flowers at the feet of the soldiers. Children run and skip alongside the troops. The men can't help but smile. In addition to the adulation and thanksgiving, foremost in their thoughts is the knowledge they are going home, soon.

After the seemingly endless lines of infantry, the light artillery prepares to roll out. Robert's wagon joins a long train of vehicles directed to proceed two abreast. The limbers and cannon, each driven by three men, are segregated by battery. Each battery is preceded by its respective officers astride their mounts that keep the pace marching six abreast. The procession wraps around the Capitol Building and continues down Pennsylvania Avenue toward the Executive Mansion.

As they make the gradual descent down Capitol Hill, a spectacular view unfolds in front of Robert's wagon. As far ahead as they can see, the avenue is filled with men marching, their bayonets sway in unison, and gleam in the sunlight, the horse artillery, two-by-two, and throngs of people curbside, celebrate their conquering heroes.

Robert flashes back to the stark contrast of jarring rides along corduroy roads, and mud-splattered trails they traveled in the open fields. The pace of the march is slow. There are no bugle calls to the ready, no battle lines to reach, no orders to advance, no "Slaughter Pen", no casualties—just reveling in the moment.

Built on the grounds of the Executive Mansion, the reviewing stand is an open-air structure with a covered roof for the President and his guests, and flanked by tiered bleacher seating ten rows high. The eaves of the structure are draped in red, white, and blue. Sewn into the material are the names of well-known battles, in which the Union armies emerged victorious—Savannah, Shiloh, Vicksburg, South Mountain, Gettysburg, Fort Donelson, Chattanooga, Resaca, Stone River, and Bentonville. At the peak of the roof, a huge national flag is flanked by three five-point evergreen stars. Flags unfurled at an angle from the main stanchions flap lazily in the breeze. Directly in front of the main gallery, the Veteran Honor Guard of fourteen soldiers wear their distinctive sky blue uniforms with dark blue piping.

The stand in Lafayette Park has members of Congress, the press, public officials, and other dignitaries.

As Robert's wagon passes the main stand, he sees many of the famous men he's heard so much about. President Johnson sits center stage surrounded by cabinet members, generals too numerous to count, and family members. General Meade stands in back of the President, swollen with pride at the sight of the mighty army he helped lead.

Once they reach the end of the route, the units start to disperse.

celebration

Major Turnbull doubles back to ride alongside Robert's carriage. "Did you men enjoy the festivities given in your honor today?"

"Mighty nice of them, going to all this trouble," says Jim.

Turnbull says, "Glad you spent your day with us, Robert."

"It's been my privilege, sir," he replies.

"Will you catch the parade tomorrow?"

"I hope to. I'll get the uniform back to you tomorrow night if you're okay with that."

"Forget it. You earned it. Keep it as a memento of your time with the Third U.S."

Rendering a salute, Robert says, "It's been an honor to serve under you, sir."

Turnbull smiles, returns his salute, and rides off to rejoin the other officers.

Robert points to Hickman's hat. "Glad a part of Will was with us today. What do you plan to do with it?"

"After I get home and settled in, I'll look up his folks and leave it with them."

He smiles then gives Jim a farewell embrace. "Will could not have hoped for a more loyal friend, and neither could I."

Once he steps down from the wagon, Jim stands as he snaps the reins. As Robert watches him ride off, another wagon pulls alongside with Corporal Wingate.

Robert points to his uniform, and says, "Thomas! Thank you for the gift and the gesture. It's more than thoughtful of you."

"It's right that you celebrate this with us. You needed the closure. Best of luck to you and your bride."

Robert says good-bye to the other two men on the wagon, then seeks the pre-arranged rendezvous with the men from Orleans County.

Grand Review of the Army. Presidential reviewing stand with guests and guards, Washington City

Library of Congress
Prints and Photographs Division
LC-DIG-cwpb-02792

celebration day two

Wednesday, 24 May 1865

The crowds are no fewer than the day before, and the enthusiasm hasn't tapered off a bit. Robert watches the parade with John Blume, and hopes beyond hope to see the Bakers in the crowd, to no avail.

Again, the signal cannon starts off the parade. This day celebrates the sixty-five thousand men of General Sherman's forces. Robert works his way out to the curb and looks east toward Capitol Hill to catch a first glimpse when the troops appear.

General Sherman, riding atop his favorite horse, a black bay, has asked one-armed Major General Oliver O. Howard to join him at his side as he leads the parade down Pennsylvania Avenue. Both of their horses wear the garlands thrown by the appreciative crowds. Robert can discern their proximity by the growing chants and yells of the crowds, "Sherman! Sherman!" A roar of approval rises as the troops come into view.

Accustomed to the Army of the Potomac in and around the city the last four years, the crowds are especially curious to get a view of Sherman's renowned forces. As the news of their conquests continued, their reputation has grown into legendary proportions. The crowds are not disappointed.

Sherman keeps his focus straight ahead, and plays the role of conquering hero to the hilt. When they reach Lafayette Square, he turns to acknowledge Secretary of State William Seward, at the window of his home, still recovering from the vicious stab wounds he received the night of Lincoln's assassination. Sherman honors him with a salute of his sword.

The dignitaries and guests in the reviewing stand rise to give General Sherman a boisterous ovation. He renders a salute, and dismounts followed by General Howard, the empty sleeve for his right arm pinned to his jacket. They join those in the main stand to watch his troops on parade.

In contrast to Meade's, Sherman's forces seem bigger, older, and stronger. The tallest of his men are positioned at the front of the lines. Despite their unkempt outward appearance of untrimmed hair and beards, they proudly wear their heavily worn, repaired, and, in some cases, tattered uniforms along with their array of slouched hats. Some march barefoot. A few of the troops received replacement uniforms, but opted to go along with the rest of the army and wear their old ones.

By the time they reach the stands, the warriors are festooned with flowers and bouquets thrown from the crowd. The men march in perfect stride and cadence. The intervals between the lines and the troops are flawless. Their determined faces are locked straight ahead, not wavering to gawk at the dignitaries in the stands. General Sherman stands for the entire six hours as his men pass in review. Any apprehension he harbored how his men may present themselves evaporates. He remembers this as the happiest day of his life.

They are followed by the massive train of supply wagons, fourteen artillery batteries, and ambulances that display the sober reminder of blood-stained stretchers. The unbridled display of power, shows the implements of war, and demonstrates the massive resources the North brought to the war effort.

Members of Sherman's "Pioneer Corps" follow the last of the wagons—escaped slaves who proudly carry their "weapons" on their shoulders—picks and shovels they used for heavy labor in support of Sherman's "March to the Sea".

The crowds move on to evening parties and celebrations, signaling the crews from the city and fire department to begin the herculean task of cleaning up the remnants of thousands of animals that traveled along the avenue.

* * *

Businesses start to reopen, and merchants take advantage of the swelled population in the city. The bars and restaurants are packed as the crowds disperse from the parade route. Several men from the Orleans County contingency of the Ninetieth New York are gathered at a restaurant/bar east of the city, a couple of miles from their camp. The men get a head start enjoying the food and drinks the establishment offers. It hasn't begun to get rowdy, but has the potential, considering the amount of alcohol they consume.

When Robert arrives in his artillery uniform, the men in his infantry regiment let out hoots and hollers, and pinch his red chevrons as he works his way through the crowd.

One of the men appoints himself the unofficial toastmaster and finds a sturdy chair to stand on. At his prompting, the crowd moves in to raise their glasses for everyone from their colonel, to General Meade, then Grant, and on up the line to the President. None of the officers are present of course, but they are paid homage nevertheless. The higher up the chain the toast goes, the louder and rowdier the men get.

One of the other men raises a glass to Lincoln. "He should have been here today."

"Here, here," the crowd responds.

The troops completely hush when a company of men from Sherman's Army of the Tennessee walk in. The proprietor makes ready with a club in case he needs to break up a melee. One of the troops says, "It sounds like you boys are having a good time. May we join you?"

A few men from the Ninetieth New York brace themselves, until the toastmaster, still standing on the chair, lifts his mug and yells out in a spirited fashion, "Here's to General Sherman."

A chorus of cheers lifts in unison from the rest of them. "To Sherman. To Sherman." The men from New York surround them, pat them on their backs and shoulders, and buy them a round. There will be no problem with the celebrations this night, not at this restaurant.

Eventually, Robert finds a place to sit with men in his company. They try talking above the clamor of the other celebrants, but surrender to the notion they'll do that around the campfires in the evenings to come.

By the time the men get up to leave, Robert has receded into his own memories, to recall the people he got to meet, know, love, and lose over the last four years——memories of men and women who might otherwise be forgotten, grateful they played a part in his life, an era that he will forever remember as his greatest adventure. Soon, this will come to an end. They will disperse to the cities, towns, and the farms they once considered home, to pick up their lives, and try to forget.

Blume beckons him to ride back with them, "Come on, Robert. Let's go. It's over! We're going home!"

glossary of terms

abatis - a line of felled trees, with the ends of the branches sharpened and turned to face outward as a defensive deterrent to advancing ground forces; the trees were often held together with wire.

abolition - in the Civil War era, the act of legally ending slavery.

ambulance - two or four wheeled wagons used to evacuate and transport wounded from the battlefield to either field hospitals or long-term facilities.

artificer - a skilled craftsman, or mechanic, in the army.

artillery crew stations - assigned positions for members of a gun crew. Referred to by their number:

- G - Gunner - sergeant of the gun, directs position of gun, and leads the troops during the firing sequence -

- 1 - seats the ammunition with the ramrod, swabs out the bore with the sponge after firing, and clear an obstruction with a worm when needed -

- 2 - ammunition runner from the limber to the muzzle -

3 - moves the trail of the cannon to aim the gun, covers the vent hole with a thumbstall to prevent premature firing, and breaks open the gunpowder packet with a pick inserted into the vent hole -

4 - connects the lanyard to friction primer, inserts the primer into the vent hole, then pulls the lanyard at the command of the Gunner, to fire the gun -

5 - carries the ammunition from the numbers six and seven men to the ammunition runner waiting at the limber -

6 & 7 - draws the ammunition from its case, at the behest of the Gunner, and affixes and cuts the proper fuse when applicable.

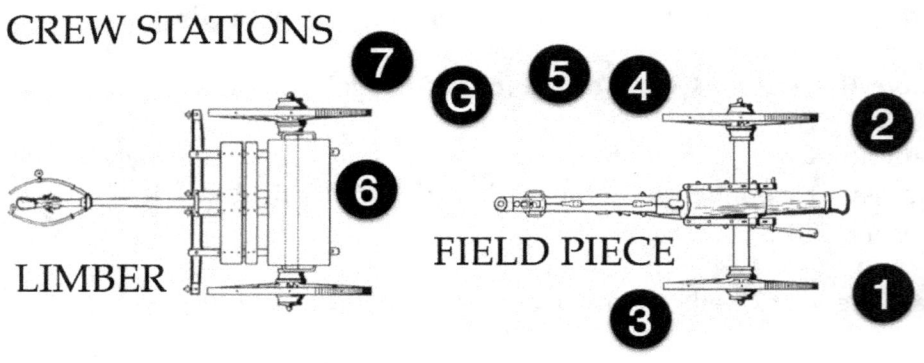

aurora borealis - (a.k.a. the northern lights) - the occasional luminescent glow in the sky at night in the Northern Hemisphere caused by meteoric activity.

battalion - a ground force of five companies of infantry.

battery wagon - a long-bodied cart with a round top, and hinged lid for the purpose of transporting forage for livestock, also used for tools, spare parts, harnesses and other equipment.

glossary of terms 339

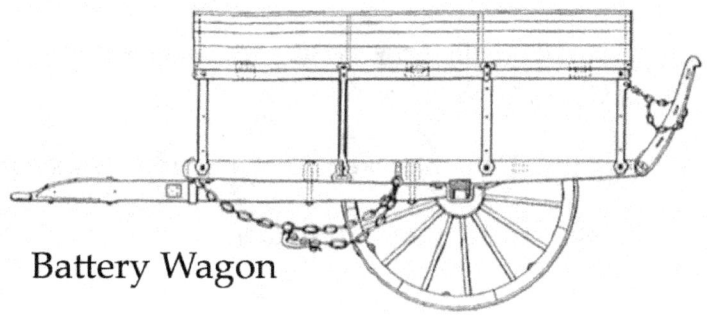

Battery Wagon

bore - the inside diameter of the tube of the cannon.

bounty - a sum of money paid to volunteer enlistees to serve.

bounty jumpers - men who collected a bounty, and either desert or attempt to repeat the process.

breastworks - a hastily constructed, temporary defensive fortification, built breast high, to protect infantry as they fire on opposing forces.

Breastworks

Edwin Forbes drawing
Library of Congress
Morgan collection of Civil War drawings
LC-DIG-ppmsca-20707

brevet - honorary title for gallant or meritorious action, with none of the authority, or pay of full or permanent rank.

brigade - consisting of 4,000 men, broken down into four regiments.

caisson - intended as an ammunition carrier along with a spare wheel.

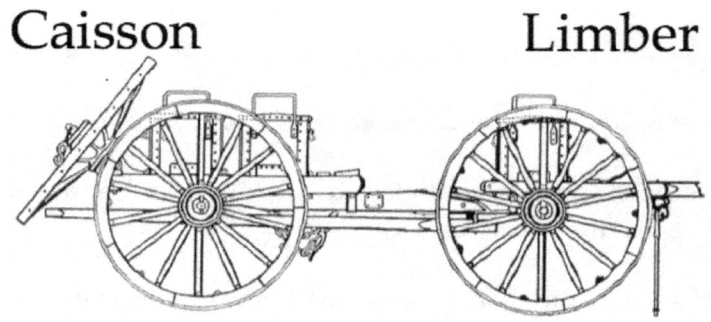

Caisson   Limber

canister - short range artillery ammunition; consists of tin cans containing iron or lead balls packed in sawdust.

case shot - thin-walled iron projectile, filled with lead balls and a small explosive charge, activated with a fuse.

contraband - a term used to describe runaway slaves who were not returned to their Southern owners.

copperhead - (a.k.a. Peace Democrat) Northerner who opposed the Civil War, and sought peace with the Southerners.

corps - consists of three divisions, commanded by a major general.

division - consisting of 12,000 men, commanded by either a brigadier or major general, broken down into three brigades.

dragoons - mounted infantry that served the role as cavalry.

earthworks - an excavation of earth used as a defensive fortification.

flank - the extreme left or right side, usually in terms of an army's line.

forage - to search for food or provisions.

friction primer - a two inch long brass tube filled with a combustible such as mercury fulminate.

fuse - made of wood or paper, ignited by the discharge of the gun and burned a predetermined amount of time (according to the size of the cut) before igniting explosive in the shell; unreliable and unfavored.

handspike - (a.k.a. trail handspike) - a bar used as a lever to aim a cannon, sometimes as a weapon (club).

hardtack - a quarter-inch-thick cracker made from unleavened flour, often infested, never loved by the men.

haversack - a foot-square canvas bag to carry daily rations and extra ammunition.

knapsack - poor-fitting bag of canvas with shoulder straps, eventually replaced by a more comfortable bedroll.

limber - the two wheeled, detachable front part of a gun carriage that supports one ammunition chest, tow either a cannon or caisson, and holds three riders when underway.

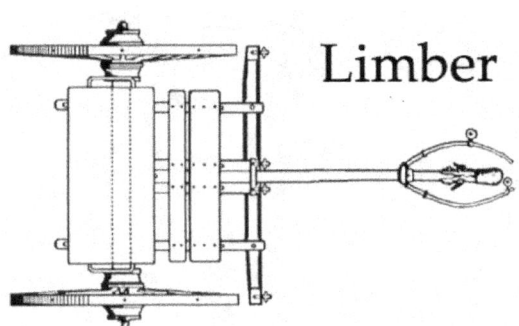

lunette - a ring at the end of a cannon's trail-stock, that drops over the pintle for towing.

Minié ball - .58 caliber conical lead bullet with a cylindrical body, the resultant wounds, if not fatal, usually lead to amputation.

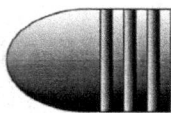

muster - a. an assembly of troops for roll call or dissemination of information.
b. enlist into, or discharge from the military.

muzzle - the business end of a cannon's barrel.

Napoleon cannon - 12-pounder bronze cannon able to fire a wide range of ammunition, muzzle-loaded, smooth-bored, with ranges up to 1,680 yards depending on the type of ammunition employed.

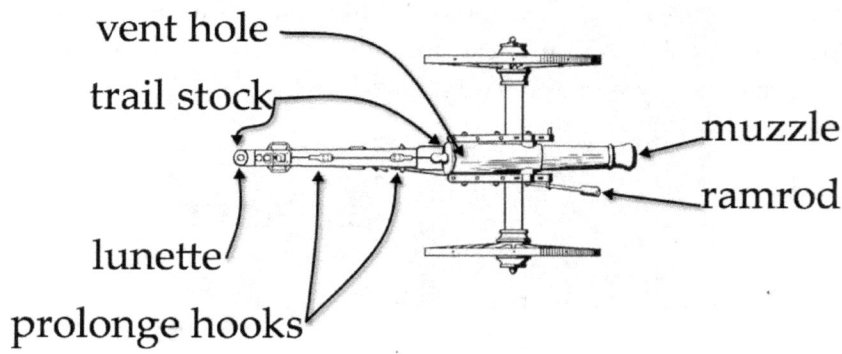

parapets - a more permanent version of a breastwork normally made of stone.

parrot gun - a cast iron, muzzle-loaded cannon that was developed in different sizes to accommodate a range of ammunition from ten to two hundred and fifty pound projectiles; has a telltale band of heat shrunk steel wrapped around the base of the tube to reinforce the cannon at the point of the greatest explosive force.

pick - used to tear open a gunpowder sack through the vent hole on a cannon.

picket - an advanced guard or an outpost for a large army or force. Considered the most dangerous of infantry assignments, picket duty was assigned on a rotational basis, and was comprised of a lieutenant, two sergeants, two corporals and forty privates from each regiment.

pintle - a pin, bolt, or hook by which a gun, or the like, is attached to the rear of a towing vehicle.

pontoon - flat bottom wood or canvas boat used as a support for temporary bridges.

Pontoon Bridge

Library of Congress
Prints and Photographs Division
LC-DIG-stereo-1s02791

prolonge - a large-bore rope used to tow a gun carriage.

rammer - for pushing and seating the ammunition packet down the bore of the cannon.

rampart - earthen mound built around defensive positions, most often topped with a parapet.

rearguard - detachment of troops and/or artillery to protect main body of army departing or retreating from a field.

redoubt - a complete enclosure to defend a prominent point, typically square or three or more sides as part of a fort system.

Redoubt near Ft. Brady, Virginia

Matthew Brady photograph
U.S. National Archives
111-B-787

regiment - consists of 1,000 men.

rifling - spiral grooves in bore of artillery (or rifles) to spin projectile for greater accuracy and distance.

sabot - a wooden disk attached to projectile and ammunition bag, to allow correct seating; falls away from the muzzle after discharge.

Sibley tent - a conical tent standing twelve feet tall, eighteen feet around, and holds twelve men comfortably.

solid shot - a solid iron projectile, usually a long-range weapon.

spike a gun - render a muzzle-loading cannon useless by driving a spike into the vent hole.

sponge - for swabbing out the bore between shots, to dampen sparks, often located on the opposite end of a ramrod.

strategy and tactics - Carl von Clausewitz wrote in his book, *On War*, "Tactics is the art of using troops in battle; strategy is the art of using battles to win the war."

Table of Fire - a reference sheet for artillerymen to determine range, elevation, and transit time for applicable ammunition and weapon, usually found on underside of lid of ammunition case.

TABLE OF FIRE. LIGHT 12-POUNDER GUN. MODEL 1857.

SHOT. Charge 2½ Pounds.		SPHERICAL CASE SHOT. Charge 2½ Pounds.			SHELL. Charge 2 Pounds.		
ELEVATION In Degrees	RANGE In Yards	ELEVATION In Degrees	TIME OF FLIGHT Seconds	RANGE In Yards	ELEVATION In Degrees	TIME OF FLIGHT Seconds	RANGE In Yards
0°	323	0°50'	1"	300	0°	0"75	300
1°	620	1°	1"75	575	0°30'	1"25	425
2°	875	1°30'	2"5	635	1°	1"75	615
3°	1200	2°	3"	730	1°30'	2"25	700
4°	1325	3°	4"	960	2°	2"75	785
5°	1680	3°30'	4"75	1080	2°30'	3"5	925
		3°40'	5"	1135	3°	4"	1080
					3°45'	5"	1300

Use SHOT at masses of troops, and to batter, from 600 up to 2,000 yards. Use SHELL for firing buildings, at troops posted in woods, in pursuit, and to produce a moral rather than a physical effect; greatest effective range 1,500 yards. Use SPHERICAL CASE SHOT at masses of troops, at not less than 500 yards; generally up to 1,500 yards. CANISTER is not effective at 600 yards; it should not be used beyond 500 yards, and but very seldom and over the most favorable ground at that distance; at short ranges, (less than 200 yards,) in emergency, use double canister, with single charge. Do not employ RICOCHET at less distance than 1,000 to 1,100 yards.

CARE OF AMMUNITION CHEST.

1st. Keep everything out that does not belong in them, except a bunch of cord or wire for breakage; beware of loose tacks, nails, bolts, or scraps.
2d. Keep friction primers in their papers, tied up. The pouch containing those for instant service must be closed, and so placed as to be secure. Take every precaution that primers do not get loose; a single one may cause an explosion. Use plenty of tow in packing.

(This sheet is to be glued on to the inside of Limber Chest Cover.)

thumbstall - heavy leather, padded sleeve to protect the thumb from the hot barrel while covering the vent as powder and shot are rammed down the bore.

traveling forge - portable bellows and a fireplace.

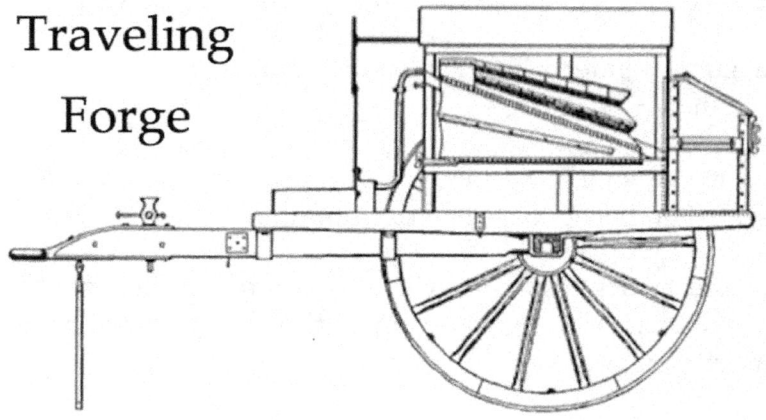

12-pounder cannon - (see Napoleon cannon) artillery piece which fires 12-pound shells.

typhoid fever - infectious bacterial disease that is characterized by extreme physical weakness, reddish spots on the body, and abdominal irritation; an often fatal disease during Civil War era.

U.S. Sanitary Commission - organization used to care for the wounded, send food and supplies to the soldiers, and provide a directory of the inpatients of the hospitals.

worm - device on long pole used to clear obstructions from the bore and to hold rags when cleaning it.

author's notes

The story of Robert Canham in the Civil War is a fictionalized account of a real person based on his: service records, pension files, units' involvements, and family lore.

Born 26 November 1837 in Tunstead, England, and immigrated to the United States in the early 1850's, "Big Grandpa" stayed involved in the Grand Army of the Republic (GAR) after the war. He spent his declining years at the home of his oldest son and daughter-in-law, George and Una (my paternal grandparents), on the Ridge Road in Gaines, New York. He broke his hip in a fall and died of complications a week later on 13 May 1938. He was one hundred years and six months old, and is interred next to his wife, Susan, in Mt. Albion Cemetery, Albion, New York.

There are numerous people involved in the production of this book. Words fail to convey my gratitude for their contributions.

Cindy Hiday is a working writer and editor who teaches Creative Writing through a local college. She has encouraged me to focus on completing the manuscript, taught us the rules of writing, and answered my countless questions. Cindy is the author of several works, including *Father, Son & Grace*. Her website is www.cindyhiday.com.

First readers include Loie Matthews and Jan Macdonald who fought their own battle with my rough first drafts, going to war with my punctuation, and educating me on appropriate behavior in the mid-nineteenth century.

Steve Wright read through the initial manuscript sharing his insights and suggestions, while serving as an adviser to his town's history museum, and successfully running for public office.

Pastor Jay Messenger reviewed the passages on the church service and pastoral counseling for accuracy and put me in touch with an agent, David Von Diest, who shared his time and expertise.

Dr. Karen Deveney corrected the German passages used in the text for the Battle of Chancellorsville. I learned that English to German translations on the web are not necessarily the best route to accuracy.

Dr. Richard Mullins gave of his time and expertise to help me work through the trauma, treatment, and long-term ramifications of Big Grandpa's wounding at Chancellorsville.

Tom Tabor has written two books on the Civil War period, *Hard Breathing Days* and *The Orleans Battery*, that provide a different, and more personal take on life both in the field and at home during that war. Tom also helped steer me through familysearch.com for genealogy searches.

Holly Ricci-Canham has written extensively on Orleans County. She gave me help with working with ancestry.com and answered my many questions.

It continually amazes me the amount of information now available on the internet compared to some thirty years ago when I first started looking into Big Grandpa's involvement in the conflict. To the faceless researchers that think you are doing a thankless job … "Thank you."

John Hennessy is the Chief Historian and Chief of Interpretation at the Fredericksburg and Spotsylvania National Military Park. He graciously supplied the graphic for Catharine Furnace.

Stephanie Loeb, Public Affairs Specialist with the National Park Service, granted me use of the map of Virginia at the beginning of the narrative.

Suzanne Isaacs, Community Manager, National Archives Catalog responded immediately to my inquiry and provided instructions for proper attribution.

Our country has access to a fabulous resource of period photographs and drawings in the Library of Congress. Several of the illustrations in this book were drawn from their online offerings.

Family played no small part in the production of the book. My brother and sister-in-law, Richard and Nancy Canham, and niece Leslie Allen did read-throughs of the rough initial drafts, served as a sympathetic sounding board, and gave great suggestions and encouragement.

Nephew Rick Canale shared his expertise of floral arrangements of the Civil War era.

Nephew Todd Shear patiently, and artistically, did the work-up of the book's cover. His website is at www.toddshear.com.

My cousin, Paul Canham, read through the manuscript, giving useful suggestions and support. His late father, Lester, was my father's identical twin brother. Uncle Lester preserved the original documents from Big Grandpa's military service, which were the keys to accessing his service records in the National Archives in Washington, D.C.

First, and foremost in my heart, my wife, Kathy, my best friend, and most ardent encourager, slogged through the initial reads, and served as one of the beta readers for the manuscript, and through the multitude of rewrites. This book would not have been the same without her. Her love, support and insights over the years, continue to be invaluable and cherished.

www.ingramcontent.com/pod-product-compliance
Lightning Source LLC
Chambersburg PA
CBHW052011070526
44584CB00016B/1701